T0143345

Artificial Intelligence & Blockchain in Cyber Physical Systems

This book explores the intersection of blockchain technology, artificial intelligence (AI) and cyber physical systems (CPS). It discusses how these technologies can be integrated to create secure and efficient CPS solutions.

The book covers various topics, including the basics of blockchain and AI, their applications in CPS and the challenges of integrating these technologies. It also explores real-world examples of how blockchain and AI are used in CPS, such as smart cities, transportation systems and healthcare.

The authors delve into the technical aspects of how blockchain and AI can be used together to enhance CPS security, data privacy and interoperability. They also discuss the potential benefits and limitations of these technologies and provide insights into the future of CPS.

Overall, this book provides a comprehensive overview of the use of blockchain and AI in CPS, making it a valuable resource for researchers, professionals and students in the fields of computer science, engineering and cybersecurity.

Artificial Intelligence & Blockchain in Cyber Physical Systems

Technologies & Applications

Edited by
Muhammad Arif
Valentina Emilia Balas
Tabrez Nafis
Nawab Muhammad Faseeh Qureshi
Samar Wazir
Ibrar Hussain

CRC Press
Taylor & Francis Group
Boca Raton London New York

CRC Press is an imprint of the
Taylor & Francis Group, an **informa** business

First edition published 2024
by CRC Press
2385 Executive Center Drive, Suite 320, Boca Raton, Florida 33431-8530

and by CRC Press
4 Park Square, Milton Park, Abingdon, Oxon, OX14 4RN

© 2024 selection and editorial matter, Muhammad Arif, Valentina Emilia Balas, Tabrez Nafis, Nawab Muhammad Faseeh Qureshi, Samar Wazir and Ibrar Hussain; individual chapters, the contributors

CRC Press is an imprint of Taylor & Francis Group, LLC

Reasonable efforts have been made to publish reliable data and information, but the author and publisher cannot assume responsibility for the validity of all materials or the consequences of their use. The authors and publishers have attempted to trace the copyright holders of all material reproduced in this publication and apologize to copyright holders if permission to publish in this form has not been obtained. If any copyright material has not been acknowledged please write and let us know so we may rectify in any future reprint.

Except as permitted under U.S. Copyright Law, no part of this book may be reprinted, reproduced, transmitted, or utilized in any form by any electronic, mechanical, or other means, now known or hereafter invented, including photocopying, microfilming, and recording, or in any information storage or retrieval system, without written permission from the publishers.

For permission to photocopy or use material electronically from this work, access www.copyright.com or contact the Copyright Clearance Center, Inc. (CCC), 222 Rosewood Drive, Danvers, MA 01923, 978-750-8400. For works that are not available on CCC please contact mpkbookspermissions@tandf.co.uk

Trademark notice: Product or corporate names may be trademarks or registered trademarks and are used only for identification and explanation without intent to infringe.

Library of Congress Cataloging-in-Publication Data
Names: Arif, Muhammad (Computer scientist), editor. | Balas, Valentina Emilia, editor. |
Nafis, Tabrez, editor. | Qureshi, Nawab Muhammad Faseeh, editor. |
Wazir, Samar, editor. | Hussain, Ibrar, editor.
Title: Artificial intelligence & blockchain in cyber physical systems :
technologies & applications / edited by Muhammad Arif, Valentina Emilia Balas,
Tabrez Nafis, Nawab Muhammad Faseeh Qureshi, Samar Wazir, Ibrar Hussain.
Description: First edition. | Boca Raton : CRC Press, 2024. |
Includes bibliographical references.
Identifiers: LCCN 2023019918 (print) | LCCN 2023019919 (ebook) |
ISBN 9781032040363 (hardback) | ISBN 9781032040370 (paperback) |
ISBN 9781003190301 (ebook)
Subjects: LCSH: Cooperating objects (Computer systems) |
Artificial intelligence. | Blockchains (Databases)
Classification: LCC TJ213 .A689 2024 (print) | LCC TJ213 (ebook) |
DDC 006.2/2–dc23/eng/20230523
LC record available at https://lccn.loc.gov/2023019918
LC ebook record available at https://lccn.loc.gov/2023019919

ISBN: 978-1-032-04036-3 (hbk)
ISBN: 978-1-032-04037-0 (pbk)
ISBN: 978-1-003-19030-1 (ebk)

DOI: 10.1201/9781003190301

Typeset in Times
by Newgen Publishing UK

Contents

Editors

Muhammad Arif, PhD, is an Associate Professor at Superior University, Lahore, Pakistan. His research interests include artificial intelligence, big data, cloud computing and cyberspace security, data mining, image processing, medical image processing, privacy, security and e-learning. Currently, he is working on the privacy and security of vehicular networks.

Valentina Emilia Balas, PhD, is currently a Full Professor in the Department of Automatics and Applied Software, Faculty of Engineering, Aurel Vlaicu University, Arad, Romania. She earned a PhD in applied electronics and telecommunications at the Polytechnic University of Timisoara. Dr. Balas is the author of more than 350 research papers in refereed journals and international conferences. Her research interests include intelligent systems, fuzzy control, soft computing, smart sensors, information fusion, modeling and simulation.

Tabrez Nafis, PhD, is an Assistant Professor in the Department of Computer Science Engineering, Jamia Hamdard (Deemed to be University), New Delhi, India. He has a rich experience of more than 12 years in the field of computer science and engineering. Dr. Nafis is an Associate Editor of the *International Journal of End-User Computing and Development* (IJEUCD), published by IGI Global, USA. His research interests include big data, machine learning, health informatics and the Internet of Things (IoT).

Nawab Muhammad Faseeh Qureshi, PhD, is an Assistant Professor at Sungkyunkwan University, Seoul, South Korea. His research interests include big data analytics, context-aware data processing of the Internet of Things (IoT) and cloud computing.

Samar Wazir, PhD, is an Assistant Professor in the Department of Computer Science and Engineering (Deemed to be University), New Delhi, India, and serves as a university National Cadet Corps (NCC) officer. His area of interest is association rule mining. He has published many papers on a wide range of topics in frequent itemset mining, probability, fuzzy theory and OWA.

Ibrar Hussain, PhD, is a Professor and Dean of the Faculty of Information Technology and Head of the Department of Software Engineering at the University of Lahore, where he has been since 2015. His research interests include artificial intelligence, human-computer interaction, machine learning, ubiquitous computing and accessibility. He has authored several papers published in SCI-indexed journals and premier international conferences. He is a Senior Member of IEEE and a Member of EAI and ICAD.

Contributors

Mohd Talib Akhtar
Department of Computer Science and
  Engineering
Jamia Hamdard
New Delhi, India

Shah Imran Alam
Department of Computer Science
  Engineering
School of Engineering Sciences and
  Technology (SEST)
Jamia Hamdard (Deemed to be
  University)
New Delhi, India

Muhammad Aqeel
Department of Computer Systems and
  Information Technology
Superior University
Lahore, Pakistan

Muhammad Arif
Department of Computer Science
Superior University
Lahore, Pakistan

Nazish Ashfaq
Department of Computer Science and
  Information Technology
University of Lahore
Lahore, Pakistan

Waqar Ashiq
Department of Computer Science and
  Information Technology
University of Lahore
Lahore, Pakistan

Muhammad Waseem Aslam
Department of Computer Science
Superior University
Lahore, Pakistan

Muhammad Khurram Zahur Bajwa
Department of Computer Science
University of Central Punjab
Lahore, Pakistan

Ajesh F
Department of Computer Science and
  Engineering
Sree Buddha College of Engineering
Alappuzha, Kerala, India

Ahona Ghosh
Department of Computer Science and
  Engineering
Maulana Abul Kalam Azad University
  of Technology
Kalyani, West Bengal, India

Praveetha Gobinathan
Faculty of Computer Science and
  Information Technology
Jazan University
Jazan, Saudi Arabia

Anjali Gupta
Department of Computer Science
  Engineering
School of Engineering Sciences and
  Technology (SEST)
Jamia Hamdard (Deemed to be
  University)
New Delhi, India

Honey Habib
Department of Computer Science and
  Engineering
School of Engineering Sciences and
  Technology (SEST)
Jamia Hamdard (Deemed to be
  University)
New Delhi, India

Naveed Habib
Department of Computer
   Science
Superior University
Lahore, Pakistan

Khalid Hamid
Department of Computer Science
Superior University
Lahore, Pakistan

Muhammad Waseem Iqbal
Department of Software
   Engineering
Superior University
Lahore, Pakistan

Adnan Kalid
Department of Computer Science and
   Information Technology
University of Lahore
Lahore, Pakistan

Gautam Siddharth Kashyap
Department of Computer Science and
   Engineering
School of Engineering Sciences and
   Technology (SEST)
Jamia Hamdard (Deemed to be
   University)
New Delhi, India

Khowla Khaliq
Department of Information
   Technology
Superior University
Lahore, Pakistan

Anil Kumar Mahto
Department of Computer Science
   Engineering
School of Engineering Sciences and
   Technology (SEST)
Jamia Hamdard (Deemed to be
   University)
New Delhi, India

Tabrez Nafis
Department of Computer Science
   Engineering
School of Engineering Sciences and
   Technology (SEST)
Jamia Hamdard (Deemed to be
   University)
New Delhi, India

Misbah Noor
Department of Computer Science
Superior University
Lahore, Pakistan

Muhammad Azeem Qureshi
Department of Computer Science and
   Information Technology
University of Lahore
Lahore, Pakistan

Toqir A. Rana
Department of Computer Science and
   Information Technology
University of Lahore
Lahore, Pakistan

Sriparna Saha
Department of Computer Science and
   Engineering
Maulana Abul Kalam Azad University
   of Technology
West Bengal, India

Syed Khuram Shahzad
Department of Informatics and
   Systems
University of Management and
   Technology
Lahore, Pakistan

Shermin Shamsudden
Faculty of Computer Science and
   Information Technology
Jazan University
Jazan, Saudi Arabia

Himanshi Sharma
Department of Computer Science
   Engineering
School of Engineering Sciences and
   Technology (SEST)
Jamia Hamdard (Deemed to be
   University)
New Delhi, India

Nazia Tabassum
Department of Computer Science and
   Engineering
School of Engineering Sciences and
   Technology (SEST)
Jamia Hamdard (Deemed to be
   University)
New Delhi, India

Samar Wazir
Department of Computer Science
   Engineering
School of Engineering Sciences and
   Technology (SEST)
Jamia Hamdard (Deemed to be
   University)
New Delhi, India

1 Facial Recognition Using Principal Component Analysis

Anjali Gupta, Samar Wazir, Anil Kumar Mahto and Shah Imran Alam
Jamia Hamdard, New Delhi

1.1 INTRODUCTION

Earlier facial recognition was done only when an exactly similar image was checked. Personal safety and security are an essential part of all industries. There are many techniques used for this purpose, one of them is facial recognition. Facial recognition is an effective way of reassuring a person. Therefore, face recognition can be used as an important factor in crime detection, especially the identification of criminals. There are several ways to deal with their recognition, Principal Component Analysis (PCA) is included in this chapter. The plan contains a website for a collection of individual facial patterns. Feature features, called "eigenfaces", are removed from stored images using a system trained for the subsequent recognition of new images.

Principal Component Analysis is a linear Dimensionality Reduction Technique. It is a mathematical process that converts the detection of parallel features into a set of unrelated elements with the help of orthogonal modification. These new modified features are called Principal Components. It is one of the most popular tools used to analyze predictive data and predictable modeling. It is a strategy to draw solid patterns from the data provided by minimizing variability.

The eigenface approach is one of the simplest and most effective Principal Component Analysis approaches used in facial recognition systems. This approach transforms faces into a set of essential characteristics, eigenfaces, into a training set which is the main component of the initial set of learning images. Recognition is done by projecting a new image in the eigenface subspace, after which the person is differentiated by comparing its position in the eigenface space with the position of known individuals. The advantage of this approach over other face recognition systems is in many components such as its simplicity, speed and insensitivity to small or gradual changes on the face. The problem is limited to files that can be used to recognize the face, but one other drawback is that the images must be vertical frontal views of human faces.

DOI: 10.1201/9781003190301-1

1.2 TRADITIONAL FACE RECOGNITION SYSTEMS

Facial identification biometrics is the science of computer programming to iden-tify a person's face. When a person is registered on the face recognition program, the video camera captures a series of facial images which stand for a completely unique code.

- When someone's face is verified by a computer, it captures their current look and compares it with face codes that are already stored in the system.
- If the face is identified, it receives authorization; otherwise, the person will not be identified. The existing face on the recognition system only identifies photos of still faces that are almost identical to one of the images stored on the database.
- If the current image is exactly the same as one of the saved images, then the person is identified and given access.
- If the current image of a person is very different, say, to the form of a face in the pictures of that person already stored on the system, the system does not identify them and access will be denied.

1.3 DISADVANTAGES OF TRADITIONAL FACIAL RECOGNITION SYSTEMS

Traditional face recognition systems have some limitations that can be overcome by using new techniques of facial recognition:

- The existing system cannot tolerate the variation of the new facial image. It requires a new image to be exactly the same as one of the images on the web-site, which will lead to denial of access to the individual.
- The level of performance of the existing system is not good.

1.4 FACIAL RECOGNITION USING PRINCIPAL COMPONENT ANALYSIS

The proposed face recognition system overcomes many disadvantages of face rec-ognition. It is based on extracting the dominant features of a human face stored on the database and performs mathematical operations on the corresponding numbers. Therefore, when a new image is added to the system to identify the main one, features are extracted and calculated electronically to determine the distance between the inserted image and the stored image. Some of the contrast in the image of a new face can be tolerated. When a new image of a person differs from photos of that person stored on the database, the system will be able to see the new face and identify who it is.

The proposed system is better because of the use of facial features over the whole face. Its benefits are:

- Accuracy of recognition and better discriminatory power.
- Computational costs due to small images (primary features) require minimal processing to train data for using PCA.
- The use of most effective principal features therefore can be used as an effective means of validation.

1.5 PRINCIPAL COMPONENT ANALYSIS

Principal Component Analysis (Figure 1.1) is one of the linear Dimensionality Reduction Techniques. It is used to reduce the dimensionality of large data sets by transforming the large variables into small ones and stores the maximum of its large set information. Working on these minimized variables is easy to explore and visualize as it can be used in machine learning algorithms, and also the runtime is less.

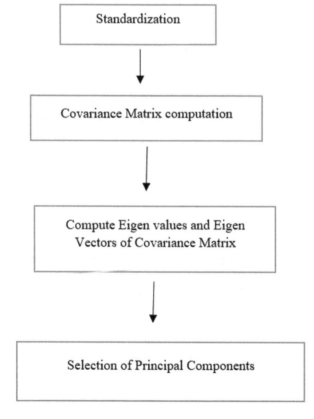

FIGURE 1.1   Principal Component Analysis.

1.6   METHODOLOGY

1.6.1   Calculation of Eigenfaces Using PCA

1.6.1.1   Step 1: Standardization

The aim of the first step is to standardize the input variables so that each of them contributes equally to the analysis. This step is useful as the input variables may have large differences between themselves and the variables with low value can be ignored when calculated with the higher ones. Transforming the data to comparable scales can prevent this problem. Standardization is used as:

$$\Psi = \frac{1}{M} \sum_{n-1}^{M} \Gamma_n \tag{1.1}$$

$$\Phi_i = \Gamma_i = \Psi \tag{1.2}$$

This can be done by subtracting the mean from their value. This converts all the input variables to the same scale.

1.6.1.2   Step 2: Covariance Matrix Computation

The main aim of this step is to understand how the variables of the input set differ from the mean and among themselves, and to find relationships between them. Sometimes, when these variables are highly correlated, they contain redundant information. Therefore, in order to identify these relations, the Covariance matrix is computed.

To find the Covariance matrix of Z matrix, firstly find its transpose matrix and then multiply it with the original Z matrix.

$$C = \frac{1}{M} \sum_{n-1}^{M} \Phi_n \Phi_n^T \tag{1.3}$$

$$C\,(Z) = Z \times Z' \tag{1.4}$$

1.6.1.3   Step 3: Compute the Eigenvectors and Eigenvalues of the Covariance Matrix

The Eigen Vectors and Eigen Values of the Covariance matrix are used to determine the Principal Components of the data.

Principal Components of the data are the new variables which are constructed as a linear combination or mixture of initial variables. The new variables contain the maximum of the input set information which is stored in such a way: a ten-dimensional data contains ten Principal Components in which the first one has the maximum possible information and the second one has the remaining maximum information, and so on. The dimensionality is reduced by discarding the variables that have low information and considering the remaining variables as Principal Components.

This way of storing information in variables is done through Eigen Vectors and Eigen Values. Eigen Vectors are the direction of axes with high information and the Eigen Values are the coefficients of the Eigen Vectors. Principal Components represent the direction of data that has a maximum amount of variance. The greater the variance, the higher is the dispersion of data and it has the maximum information.

In this step, the eigenvectors (eigenfaces) of the corresponding eigenvalues should be calculated. The eigenvectors (eigenfaces) must be normalized so that they are unit vectors.

1.6.1.4 Step 4: Selection of Principal Components

From M eigenvectors (eigenfaces), only the most important ones should be chosen, those which have the highest eigenvalues. The higher the eigenvalue, the more characteristic features of a face the particular eigenvector describes. Eigenfaces with low eigenvalues can be omitted, as they explain only a small part of characteristic features of the face. After these eigenfaces are determined, the "training" phase of the algorithm is finished.

1.7 RESULT AND ANALYSIS

These are the original images used for face detection. A total of 400 images are taken from which ten images are of the same person, clicked in different angles, some with spectacles and some without, and a lot more variation is created by the change in facial expressions. The image features are found on the basis of these images, and these features are compared to find the images of the same people.

Figure 1.2 is the graph which shows how many features store which amount of the data, and it can be seen that 50% of the data was retained by only ten Principal

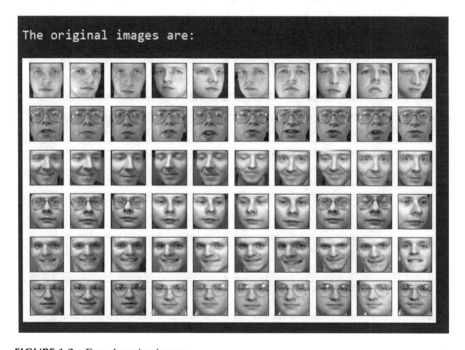

FIGURE 1.2 Face detection images.

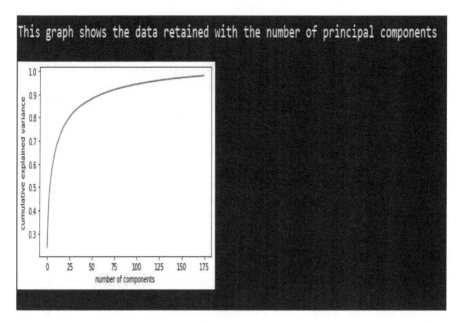

FIGURE 1.3   Data retained by PCA.

Components. The scope slowly decreased at 25 components which stored 80% of the data. For the maximum features to be retained, a total of 175 Principal Components are taken, which gives 98% accuracy of detection (Figure 1.3).

Figure 1.4 shows the Eigen faces which are formed after applying PCA to the original images. Here the features differing are highlighted and can be seen in the

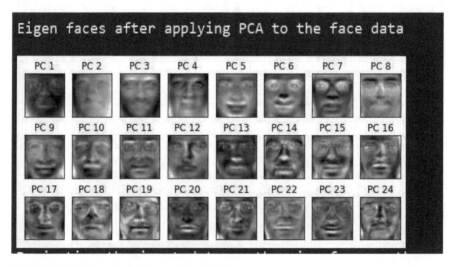

FIGURE 1.4   Eigen faces after applying PCA.

images; in some images the eyes, spectacles, or moustaches are highlighted because they differ in those parts. Through these eigen images, the detection is done.

1.7.1 EVALUATION PARAMETERS

The precision is defined as the number of true positives over the number of true positives plus the number of false positives.

$$Precision = \frac{tp}{tp + fp} \qquad (1.5)$$

Recall is defined as the number of true positives over the number of true positives plus the number of false negatives.

$$Recall = \frac{tp}{tp + fn} \qquad (1.6)$$

The f1-score gives the harmonic mean of precision and recall.

$$f1 = 2 \cdot \frac{precision.recall}{precision + reca} \qquad (1.7)$$

The accuracy is the number of samples of the true response that lie in that class.

$$Accuracy = \frac{tp + tn}{tp + tn + fp + f} \qquad (1.8)$$

The macro averages are calculated simply by adding total values to the number of values.

$$\textbf{\textit{Macro Average Precision}} = \frac{\textbf{\textit{Sum of all Precision}}}{\textbf{\textit{No. of Precision}}} \qquad \textbf{(1.9)}$$

$$Macro\,Average\,Recall = \frac{Sum\,of\,all\,Recall}{No.of\,Recall} \qquad (1.10)$$

$$Macro\,Average\,F1\,Score = \frac{Sum\,of\,all\,F1\,Score}{No.of\,F1\,Score} \qquad (1.11)$$

$$Macro\,Average\,Support = \frac{Sum\,of\,all\,Support}{No.of\,Support} \qquad (1.12)$$

The Weighted Average is calculated as each precision* its weight sum divided by the total number of precisions.

$$Weighted\ Average\ Precision = \frac{P1 + W1 + P2 * W2 ...}{No.of\ Precisions} \qquad (1.13)$$

$$Weighted\ Average\ Recall = \frac{R1 + W1 + R2 * W2 ...}{No.of\ Recalls} \qquad (1.14)$$

$$Weighted\ Average\ F1 - Score = \frac{F11 + W1 + F1 * W2 ...}{No.of\ F1 - Scores} \qquad (1.15)$$

$$Weighted\ Average\ Support = \frac{S1 + W1 + S2 * W2 ...}{No.of\ Supports} \qquad (1.16)$$

The graph (Figure 1.5a) clearly shows that 98% of the faces are detected correctly using the 175 principal components instead of using 4,096 features. This clearly shows how Principal Component Analysis can be used for increasing the speed as well as reducing the space or memory required for facial detection.

```
Projecting the input data on the eigenfaces orthonormal basis
Predicting people's names on the test set
            precision    recall  f1-score   support

        0      1.00       0.50     0.67        2
        1      1.00       1.00     1.00        2
        2      1.00       0.67     0.80        3
        3      1.00       1.00     1.00        3
        4      1.00       1.00     1.00        1
        5      1.00       1.00     1.00        3
        6      1.00       1.00     1.00        4
        7      1.00       1.00     1.00        5
        8      1.00       1.00     1.00        4
        9      1.00       1.00     1.00        2
       10      1.00       1.00     1.00        3
       11      1.00       1.00     1.00        3
       12      0.33       1.00     0.50        1
       13      1.00       1.00     1.00        3
       14      1.00       1.00     1.00        2
       15      1.00       1.00     1.00        4
       16      1.00       1.00     1.00        2
       17      1.00       1.00     1.00        2
       18      1.00       1.00     1.00        2
       19      1.00       1.00     1.00        1
       20      1.00       1.00     1.00        1
       21      1.00       1.00     1.00        1
       22      1.00       1.00     1.00        5
       23      1.00       1.00     1.00        1
       24      1.00       1.00     1.00        4
       25      0.50       0.50     0.50        2
```

FIGURE 1.5a Result based on above dataset.

26	1.00	1.00	1.00	3
27	1.00	1.00	1.00	7
28	1.00	0.80	0.89	5
29	1.00	1.00	1.00	3
31	1.00	1.00	1.00	1
32	1.00	1.00	1.00	1
34	1.00	1.00	1.00	2
35	1.00	1.00	1.00	2
36	1.00	1.00	1.00	3
37	1.00	1.00	1.00	2
38	0.75	1.00	0.86	3
39	1.00	1.00	1.00	2
accuracy			0.96	100
macro avg	0.96	0.96	0.95	100
weighted avg	0.98	0.96	0.96	100

FIGURE 1.5b   Result based on above dataset.

1.8   CONCLUSION

PCA is used to reduce the number of features used for detecting faces (Figure 1.5b). As the number of selected features in PCA increases, this also increases the level of recognition. But this increases the calculation burden. This method is chosen because of its simplicity, speed and learning ability. One of the simplest and most effective PCA methods used in face recognition programs is the eigenface approach.

Facial recognition is a very effective process for many types of applications such as biometric security, voter websites to reduce duplicate registration, a digital photo of a person that can be used as a password and many other important functions. The purpose of this project is to implement a reliable Principal Component Analysis program based on facial knowledge and to evaluate its effectiveness using standard factual information data.

BIBLIOGRAPHY

Abdullah, Manal, Majda Wazzan, and Sahar Bo Saeed. "Optimizing face recognition using PCA." *arXiv preprint arXiv:1206.1515* (2012).

Faruqe, Md. Omar, and Md. Al Mehedi Hasan. "Face recognition using PCA and SVM." *2009 3rd International Conference on Anti-counterfeiting, Security, and Identification in Communication.* IEEE, 2009.

Gosavi, Ajit P., and S. R. Khot. "Facial expression recognition using principal component analysis." *International Journal of Soft Computing and Engineering (IJSCE)* 3.4 (2013): 2231–2257.

Karamizadeh, Sasan, et al. "An overview of principal component analysis." *Journal of Signal and Information Processing* 4.3B (2013): 173.

Karim, Tahia Fahrin, Molla Shahadat Hossain Lipu, Md. Lushanur Rahman and F. Sultana, "Face recognition using PCA-based method," *2010 IEEE International Conference on Advanced Management Science (ICAMS 2010)*, 2010: 158–162, doi: 10.1109/ICAMS.2010.5553266

Kaur, Ramandeep, and Er Himanshi. "Face recognition using principal component analysis." *2015 IEEE International Advance Computing Conference (IACC)*. IEEE, 2015.

Khan, Abdul Samad, and Lawang Khan Alizai. "Introduction to face detection using eigenfaces." *2006 International Conference on Emerging Technologies*. IEEE, 2006.

Kshirsagar, V. P., M. R. Baviskar, and M. E. Gaikwad. "Face recognition using Eigenfaces." *2011 3rd International Conference on Computer Research and Development*. Vol. 2. IEEE, 2011.

Lata, Y. Vijaya, et al. "Facial recognition using eigenfaces by PCA." *International Journal of Recent Trends in Engineering* 1.1 (2009): 587.

Navaz, AS Syed, T. Dhevisri, and Pratap Mazumder. "Face recognition using principal component analysis and neural networks." *March 2013, International Journal of Computer Networking, Wireless and Mobile Communications* 3 (2013): 245–256.

Oommen, Abin Abraham, C. Senthil Singh, and M. Manikandan. "Design of face recognition system using principal component analysis." *Int. J. Res. Eng. Technol* 3.1 (2014): 6–10.

Paul, Liton Chandra, and Abdulla Al Sumam. "Face recognition using principal component analysis method." *International Journal of Advanced Research in Computer Engineering & Technology (IJARCET)* 1.9 (2012): 135–139.

Quintiliano, Paulo, Renato Guadagnin, and Antonio Santa-Rosa. "Practical procedures to improve face recognition based on eigenfaces and principal component analysis." *Pattern recognition and image analysis C/C of raspoznavaniyeobrazovianalizizobrazhe nii* 11.2 (2001): 372–375.

Saha, Rajib, and Debotosh Bhattacharjee. "Face recognition using eigenfaces." *International Journal of Emerging Technology and Advanced Engineering* 3.5 (2013).

Sandhu, Parvinder S., et al. "Face Recognition Using Eigenface Coefficients and Principal Component Analysis." *International Journal of Electrical and Electronics Engineering* 3.8 (2009): 498–502.

Slavković, Marijeta, and Dubravka Jevtić. "Face recognition using eigenface approach." *Serbian Journal of Electrical Engineering* 9.1 (2012): 121–130.

Turk, Matthew A., and Alex P. Pentland. "Face recognition using eigenfaces." *Proceedings. 1991 IEEE computer society conference on computer vision and pattern recognition*. IEEE Computer Society, 1991.

Turk, Matthew, and Alex Pentland. "Eigenfaces for recognition." *Journal of Cognitive Neuroscience* 3.1 (1991): 71–86.

Xie, Xiaohui. "Principal component analysis." Wiley Interdisciplinary Reviews (2019).

Yu, Y. L. "Face recognition with eigenfaces." *Proceedings of 1994 IEEE International Conference on Industrial Technology-ICIT'94*. IEEE, 1994.

Zafaruddin, G. Md., and H. S. Fadewar. "Face recognition using eigenfaces." *Computing, Communication and Signal Processing*. Springer: Singapore, 2019, 855–864.

2 A Systematic Exploration of Blockchain-Based Healthcare Systems

Himanshi Sharma and Tabrez Nafis
Jamia Hamdard

2.1 INTRODUCTION

Blockchain was recognized as the era of issued ledgers after the Bitcoin White Paper was issued in October 2008. As the underlying era of Bitcoin, the main use of blockchain is to allow the exchange of electronic coins between paid community participants without the overhead of a centralized trusted third party. Transactions involving the exchange of electronic currencies between individuals or groups have historically relied on subordinate third parties, including financial institutions, as intermediaries. A trusted third party can also malfunction, fail or be maliciously infringed, making financial products unusable or unsafe. As a result, it can damage the device as a single point of failure and can also set the price of the transaction and introduce some transaction delays. Therefore, the incentive behind Bitcoin is to overcome the obstacles associated with the dependence of digital transactions on a third party (Figure 2.1).

A year after the publication of the famous Bitcoin White Paper, the code was introduced as an open supply that others could modify and also extend to create an exclusive generation of blockchain-based program. You could now create technology.

The blockchain is considered a ledger system that helps process and store records on instances of pound blocks that work primarily in a decentralized way over any computer network and cryptographic links. The blockchain functions brought into the field of fintech have a wider range of possibilities. However, the location of the software and the design of an effective solution have not yet been developed.

The growing interest in blockchain and its adoption by its own government agencies and industry has made healthcare a symbol of key locations where some use cases of blockchain software have been identified. But blockchain is a particularly new era, with lots of hype in the press, and gray guides in the form of opinion pieces, commentary, blog posts, interviews and more. There are many false statistics, inferences and uncertainties about blockchain capacity usage in the healthcare industry. What are the challenges and limitations of primarily blockchain-based healthcare packages, how are these difficult situations currently being addressed and which regions need to be developed? This chapter outlines a systematic exploration that is being conducted to address all the above issues.

DOI: 10.1201/9781003190301-2

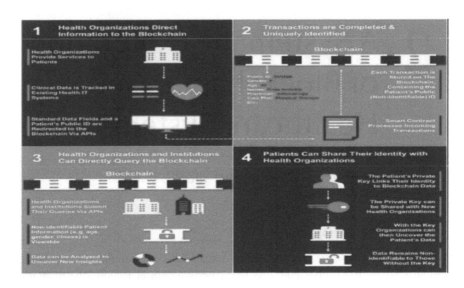

FIGURE 2.1   Blockchain in healthcare.

Our approach follows in this review by following the recommendations for systematic literature reviews and systematic mapping of systems, and the recommended report gadgets for conducting and reporting systematic reviews and meta-analysis (PRISMA) compliant assessments. Our systematic assessment is primarily based on well-designed research protocols, ensuring an overall and impartial sampling of all published peer-reviewed articles that may be relevant to a particular situation. We have obtained the related articles from legitimate academic databases, primarily based on this protocol. We will classify this into various classes and reveal the actual areas of on-going research on the application of the blockchain era in healthcare.

2.2   OVERVIEW OF BLOCKCHAIN

Blockchain is a type of paid ledger technology that allows records to be stored, shared and validated under a paid peer-to-peer network. In addition, participating nodes can maintain a common ledger in a coordinated manner by contributing to information validation efforts through encryption. The blockchain can be thought of as a continuous list of transactions that can be added in chronological order to the previous transaction. This technique is completed with the contribution of collaborative nodes to solve crypto puzzles. This increases the difficulty of making malicious operations and changes. In this sense, all transactions are visible to all parties, immutable, and provide an audit trail and statistical integrity. In addition, connected era smart contracts can be deployed on blockchain-based systems to guide or implement certain desirable tactics. Smart contracts are laptop protocols intended to execute contract terms or contracts. In reality, smart contracts can be coded in a laptop language, interacted with each other, and realized through real-life activities. When provided on blockchain machines, these attributes can also facilitate business decisions and process automation.

Blockchain improves transparency, security, privacy, traceability and acceptance between players through specific distributed schemas and immutable shared ledgers. This means that blockchain not only connects convenient isolated databases through distributed management, but also the environment surrounding healthcare professionals. However, this can lead to particularly complex supply–demand relationships and interactions between actors who operate their organizations in an originally centralized way.

2.3 THE NEED FOR BLOCKCHAIN IN HEALTHCARE

As far as healthcare is concerned, the urgency of development is increasing at an astonishing rate, faster than ever before. Today, we need a good health center backed by great new technology. This is where blockchain can play an important role in the restructuring of healthcare areas. In addition, the panorama of fitness equipment is shifting to a patient-centric approach that focuses on two of the most important factors: accessible products and always-appropriate health resources. Blockchain will enable healthcare companies to provide adequate patient care. Trading fitness facts is another time-consuming and repetitive system that brings overhead to the fitness industry, which is rapidly being organized in this generation. Leveraging the blockchain generation, citizens can also participate in fitness research applications. Similarly, better research and shared facts on public welfare will improve the remedies for unique groups. A centralized database is used to operate the entire healthcare system and business.

So far, the main issues facing the use of blockchain are interoperability in controlling data security, sharing and population fitness. This unique issue can be addressed by using blockchain. This generation improves security, data changes, interoperability, integrity and real-time updates and access, while running efficiently. There are also serious data security concerns, especially in the areas of custom medicine and wearables. Patients and medical staff need a safe and easy way to record, send and retrieve information over the network without protection issues. Therefore, blockchain technology can be applied to solve these problems.

2.3.1 BLOCKCHAIN IN HEALTH

The characteristics of blockchain, its decentralized nature, openness and lower requirement for permission, paves the way for certain aspects of healthcare. In the healthcare sector, there is a growing demand for blockchain development (Figure 2.2). Blockchain immutability is the ultimate option for Healthcare Factors. You can save fitness information, the effects of medical research and ensure regulatory compliance.

Similarly, the application of blockchain will impact the expansion of pharmacies' supply chains and countermeasures against counterfeit capsules. While the development of modern pills has high costs associated with research assessing drug protection and efficacy, smart contracts make the method of informed consent easier, detection control and statistics (see Figures 2.3 and 2.4). It can also integrate the consent process while preserving the privacy of individual medical records by providing access for patients to manage their personal choices.

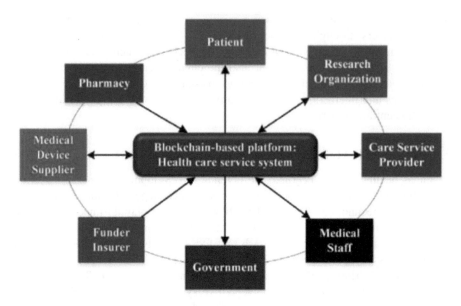

FIGURE 2.2   Blockchain-based healthcare.

Benefits of blockchain to healthcare applications.

Decentralization	The very nature of healthcare, in which there are distributed stakeholders, requires a decentralized management system. Blockchain can become that decentralized health data management backbone from where all the stakeholders can have controlled access to the same health records, without any one playing the role of a central authority over the global health data.
Improved data security and privacy	The immutability property of blockchain greatly improves the security of the health data stored on it, since the data, once saved to the blockchain cannot be corrupted, altered or retrieved. All the health data on blockchain are encrypted, time-stamped and appended in a chronological order. Additionally, health data are saved on blockchain using cryptographic keys which help to protect the identity or the privacy of the patients.
Health data ownership	Patients need to own their data and be in control of how their data is used. Patients need the assurance that their health data are not misused by other stakeholders and should have a means to detect when such misuse occurs. Blockchain helps to meet these requirements through strong cryptographic protocols and well-defined smart contracts.
Availability/robustness	Since the records on blockchain are replicated in multiple nodes, the availability of the health data stored on blockchain is guaranteed as the system is robust and resilient against data losses, data corruption and some security attacks on data availability.
Transparency and trust	Blockchain, through its open and transparent nature, creates an atmosphere of trust around distributed healthcare applications. This facilitates the acceptance of such applications by the healthcare stakeholders.
Data verifiability	Even without accessing the plaintext of the records stored on blockchain, the integrity and validity of those records can be verified. This feature is very useful in areas of healthcare where verification of records is a requirement, such as pharmaceutical supply chain management and insurance claim processing.

FIGURE 2.3   Benefits of blockchain in healthcare.

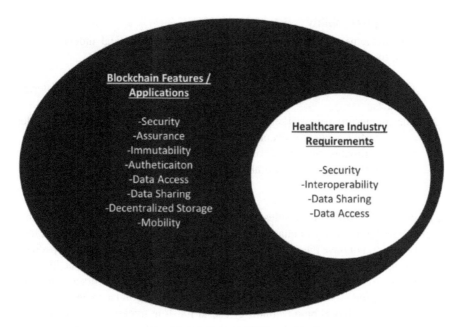

How Blockchain meets Healthcare Requirements.

FIGURE 2.4 Healthcare requirements.

2.3.2 FEATURES OF BLOCKCHAIN FOR THE HEALTHCARE DOMAIN

Many companies are now offering specific blockchain-focused solutions for healthcare organizations (see Figure 2.5). Listed below are two major areas that can greatly benefit from advances in blockchain technology.

FIGURE 2.5 Features of blockchain for Healthcare Domain.

2.3.2.1 Drug Traceability

Counterfeit medicines are a major problem in the pharmaceutical industry. Some indicators of the Health Research Funding Organization are:

1. 10% to 30% of medicines sold in developing countries are counterfeit products.
2. The counterfeit drug market is worth US $200 billion annually. Internet sales of counterfeit medicines account for US $75 billion of the total market.
4. WHO estimates that 16% of counterfeit medicines contain the wrong ingredients, while 17% inevitably contain the wrong amount of ingredients (see Figure 2.6).

The main problem with fake capsules is not the fact that they are fake, but the fact that they can differ significantly in quantity and quality from the original product. In fact, many of them do not have the active ingredients they claim to have. This is especially dangerous for patients taking counterfeit medicines, as they do not treat illnesses designed to be treated by legitimate medicines. In addition, if the factors and dosages are unique, the product can have sudden, potentially fatal, secondary effects.

A key feature of blockchain technology useful for drug tracking is security. Each new transaction added to a block is immutable and time stamped, making it easier to track products and make information immutable. To ensure the authenticity and traceability of a drug, the company that registers the product on the blockchain must be trusted.

Blockchain technologies help with two main issues when it comes to drug traceability: first, it allows companies to track their products down the supply chain, creating an airtight circuit, impermeable to counterfeit products. Secondly, it also allows stakeholders, and especially laboratories, to take action *a posteriori* in case of a problem by identifying the exact location of their drugs.

They do this by the process in which, when a drug is produced, a hash is generated that contains all the relevant information about the product. Each time the drug moves from one entity to another (e.g., from the manufacturer to the distributor), the information is stored on the blockchain, making it easy to track the drug. If a

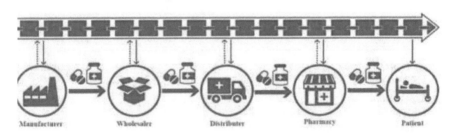

Blockchain Based Pharmaceutical Supply Chain Management System

FIGURE 2.6 Supply chain.

problem is detected and a batch has to be withdrawn from the market, blockchain technologies make it easier for the company to find their products and hence avoid any complications.

In many countries around the world, the importance of drug history tracking (tracking and tracing) is being emphasized and made mandatory. For example, the U.S. Drug Supply Chain Security Act (DSCSA) requires the pharmaceutical industry to develop interoperable electronic systems to identify and track prescription drugs distributed in the United States. Drug traceability has therefore become an integral part of the drug supply chain as it aims to establish authenticity and trace product supply chains throughout the drug supply chain.

2.4 CLINICAL TRIALS

Inside the pharmaceutical industry, medical trials are designed to check the tolerance and effectiveness of a product on a collection of patients on the way to validate or invalidate hypotheses. Commonly they take several years, and the consequences are critical for the destiny of the drug. All through medical trials, a large quantity of facts are produced; protection and exceptional reports, information, blood checks, surveys, clinical imagery and large numbers of human beings are concerned, making it difficult to manage everyone. Hence, mistakes can be made in the process, a few by accident and others not. Blockchain can offer evidence of lifestyles for any record and permit anyone to verify the authenticity of the stated file.

In order to add new information to a transaction form, most node users must agree that it is completely legal and consistent with the blockchain record. Therefore, to extend the current record, it is necessary to transform the statistics of the majority of users of computer systems within the network.

2.5 DRUG/PHARMACEUTICAL SUPPLY CHAIN

Substandard drug supply can have serious consequences for patients, but it is a common problem facing the pharmaceutical industry. Blockchain generation has been diagnosed as being able to solve this problem. Several companies are working on using blockchain to prevent prescription drug fraud. Companies include Nuco, HealthChainRx and Scalamed. The general idea is to report all prescription transactions in a blockchain community where all stakeholders (manufacturers, distributors, doctors, patients and pharmacists) are connected. This makes it possible to detect changes to recipes or malicious modifications by both parties.

2.6 BIOMEDICAL RESEARCH AND EDUCATION

Blockchain has interesting applications in biomedical research and education. In medical trials, blockchain can help eliminate falsification of information and underestimation or exclusion of unwanted medical research findings. It was originally stat-encoded. The immutability of blockchain properties also confirms the integrity of information gathered via blockchain for scientific research. The transparent and public nature of blockchains also makes it easier to copy research from blockchain-based statistics. These are some of the reasons blockchain is expected to revolutionize biomedical research.

2.6.1   REMOTE PATIENT MONITORING (RPM)

Remote patient tracking uses body proximity sensors (or IoT devices) and mobile devices to collect biomedical facts to remotely display a patient's condition outside of normal healthcare settings, including healthcare facilities. Blockchain has been proposed as a way to store, share and retrieve remotely collected biomedical statistics.

2.6.2   HEALTH INSURANCE CLAIMS

Medical insurance claim processing can benefit from blockchain's transparency, decentralization, immutability and verifiability of stored statistics. Many articles see insurance claim processing as a very promising place for blockchain software in healthcare. However, examples of implementing prototypes of these structures are very limited. The only example we can find is MIStore (a garage car fully powered by blockchain-based car insurance) deployed on the Ethereum blockchain platform.

2.6.3   HEALTH DATA ANALYTICS (HDA)

Blockchain also presents a unique opportunity to harness the power of a variety of emerging technologies, including deep familiarity and familiarity strategy shifts, to enable predictive health information analytics and improve precision medicine research. This blockchain use case is also flagged, while at the same time providing a comprehensive roadmap of how to discover it. Junja and Marefat conducted a pilot study to classify arrhythmias using blockchain in a deep learning framework.

2.7   CASE STUDY

A number of innovative solutions have been proposed for the use of blockchain-centric applications in the medical field. These ever-growing solutions are primarily designed to help healthcare professionals and patients make decisions about treatment, management and administrative readiness to support services. Here's an example:

- The company Nebula Genomics (https://nebula.org) uses blockchain technology to improve the security of genomic data, enabling buyers to efficiently acquire genomic data and solve large genomic data challenges.

2.8   RESEARCH METHODOLOGY

In undertaking and reporting this assessment, we adopted the recommendations for systematic literature assessment and the procedure for systematic mapping observation, as well as the tips described in the PRISMA announcement. As defined, the intention of a scientific mapping examination is to get an outline of the studies location, and to complement this by way of investigating the kingdom of evidence in specific topics. In this example, the effects of the mapping examination could assist us to identify and map the blockchain use instances in healthcare, and to understand the quantity to which blockchain-based total applications were developed on the subject of the identified use cases. They could also help us to discover areas of feasible studies gaps. The systematic assessment would again allow us to analyze the contemporary traits in terms of the technical methods, methodologies and concepts employed in growing blockchain-based total healthcare programs. The timeframe for the analysis was selected from the first reference to blockchain in 2008 and continued till the paper online guide in 2019. This is because of the reality that most of the complete research has been done in current years going beyond the huge conversations or online blogs.

I have employed qualitative and quantitative tactics on content evaluation and similarly to review the chosen papers, which was accomplished using an enter-process-output perspective. This technique has been extensively used in prior research and is primarily based on analyzing inputs and outputs and understanding the underlying methods. In undertaking and reporting this assessment, we adopted the recommendations for systematic literature assessment and the procedure for systematic mapping observation, as well as the tips described in the PRISMA announcement. As defined in the introduction, the intention of a scientific mapping examination is to get an outline of the studies location, and to complement this by way of investigating the kingdom of evidence in specific topics. In this example, the effects of the mapping examination could assist us to identify and map the blockchain use instances in healthcare, and to understand the extent to which blockchain-based total applications were developed about the identified use cases. They could also help us to discover areas of feasible studies gaps. The systematic assessment would again allow us to analyze the contemporary traits in terms of the technical methods, methodologies and concepts employed in growing blockchain-based total healthcare programs. Next, we will look at a systematic mapping method.

We reviewed the scientific literature on education and enterprise guidance from 2008 to 2019 to evaluate the potential of blockchain in healthcare, explore applications and identify implementation challenges. Considering the progressive nature of blockchain and the long timeframe for review and guidance of research papers, we focused on analyzing publications with open-source Google students. This provided confidence in the research. We also reviewed the corporate manual to ensure that the rapidly changing nature of blockchain is adequately addressed in the selected training course. The timeframe for the analysis was selected from the first reference to the blockchain in 2008 and persevered till the paper online guide in 2019. It is the reality that most of the complete research has been in current years going beyond huge conversations or online blogs. The preliminary consequences confirmed that very confined large courses had been available earlier than 2016, however in addition evaluation protected all selected papers (Figure 2.7).

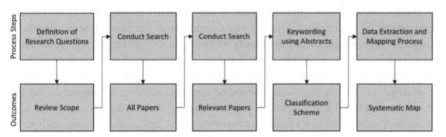

The systematic mapping process steps.

FIGURE 2.7 Mapping process.

2.8.1 FINDINGS FROM EARLIER PAPERS

Analysis of the results revealed that 136 documents diagnosed with the most recent sample came from specific medical fields. In general, courses are offered in three main subject areas including era, life sciences, biomedical sciences and social sciences.

Most of our guides are from the US and China. While the unique craze for blockchain is inspired by American characteristics, China's sophisticated leap forward is of particular interest. As of November 2018, there are 263 undeveloped blockchain projects registered in China, accounting for more than 25% of the international operations. These projects include well-connected Chinese-speaking groups, including Baidu, Alibaba and Tencent, each of which has an interest in healthcare programs. China is also considered a leader in blockchain patents, accounting for more than half of the total patent package in 2017. Blockchain development has received strong support from the Chinese authorities through the improvement of the Blockchain Improvement Center and an e-book containing a list of goals that will inspire the emergence and standardization of the blockchain era in 2018. Although the Chinese government has added numerous bans on the purchase, sale and use of cryptocurrencies, blockchain technology is advancing at various levels. For example, China's 13th Five-Year Plan has been proven to include hyperlinks to domestic and foreign sources, helping to invest in blockchain work and engage in blockchain-related activities on the global stage.

2.8.2 CONCLUSIONS

The blockchain era has developed from the time it was introduced to the world thru Bitcoin into a fashionable era, with use cases in lots of industries including healthcare. To recognize the modern-day application of present day blockchain generation in healthcare, we carried out a systematic evaluation in which we created a modern map of all applicable studies using the systematic mapping look at method. Specifically, the targets that the modern day looks at have been to understand blockchain generation use cases in healthcare, the example applications that have been developed for these use cases, the demanding situations and barriers contemporary with blockchain primarily based healthcare packages, the modern processes used in growing these programs and regions for destiny studies. Our seek and paper selection protocol produced 65 papers which we analyzed to deal with the study questions. Our study shows that blockchain has many healthcare use cases consisting of the control of contemporary digital medical records, capsules and pharmaceutical supply chain control, biomedical studies and education, remote patient tracking and health information analytics, amongst others. A modern blockchain-based healthcare program was developed as a prototype based on a growing blockchain paradigm that includes smart contracts, permissioned block chains, advanced chain storage and more. However, more research is still needed to better understand, present and evaluate the application of the modern blockchain generation. Further research was also intended to complement ongoing efforts to address the advanced scalability, latency, interoperability, security and privacy issues associated with the use of blockchain generation in healthcare.

As mentioned earlier, blockchain creation can be used to improve case management, particularly tracking and insurance intervention technologies, thus accelerating clinical travel with optimized information updates. This ubiquitous era will greatly adorn the way patients and clinicians view and use scientific statistics and has the potential to revolutionize and improve health care sooner or later.

2.8.3 CHALLENGES AND LIMITATIONS OF BLOCKCHAIN-BASED APPLICATIONS

Some of the challenges identified for improving blockchain-based end-to-end packages include interoperability, security and privacy, scalability, speed and patient engagement.

On the subject of the security and privateness of blockchain-based healthcare applications, there may be a problem that notwithstanding the encryption techniques used it could still be viable to expose the identification of an affected person in a public blockchain through linking collectively sufficient facts that are associated with that patient. In addition, there is also the danger of security breaches that might come from intentional malicious assaults to the healthcare blockchain by means of crooked corporations or even authorities' companies that might compromise the privacy of the sufferers. There have been several instances of reported attacks on the blockchain networks.

Because the immutability of blockchain ensures that data once saved to the blockchain can't be deleted or altered, it is able to prove counterproductive with its ability to completely wipe out the scientific history of a patient. The scalability of blockchain- based healthcare solutions is a major assignment, especially when it comes to the volume of data concerned. It is not most useful, or maybe potential in some cases, to shop the high-volume biomedical data on blockchain, as this is bound to cause serious performance degradation. There's additionally the hassle of pace as blockchain-based total processing can introduce significant latency.

One extra venture is how to have interaction with patients inside the management of their statistics on blockchain.

3 Smart Parking for Smart Drivers Using QR Codes

Naveed Habib[1], Muhammad Waseem Iqbal[1], Muhammad Arif[1], Toqir A. Rana[2] and Syed Khuram Shahzad[3]
[1]Superior University, Lahore, Pakistan,[2]The University of Lahore, Lahore, Pakistan, [3]University of Management and Technology, Lahore, Pakistan

3.1 INTRODUCTION

A Smart Parking System obviously impacts a driver's action by the amount of time they spend to find open parking spots, the impedance of the urban traffic stream and the corruption of urban organization, as displayed by 30% of traffic jams made up of vehicles looking to leave. In this specific circumstance, early realization of the accessible parking spots would resolve this issue. Reenacted insight strategies would be the best gadgets for anticipating this with amazing precision. Inside the setting of the internet on things, finding the answers for the space of leaving free structures depends upon the execution of methods that can recognize the climate (of the current situation for the presence of vehicles) and send this information to a focal expert for additional execution (for example through a radio channel). Confirmation of a sensible sensor gadget for separating vehicle evidence rather relies on the basics of the leaving structure, centering on approaches that have high precision while reducing the general expense [1].

To make a city smart we must do many things that can be developed using the internet of things, and smart parking is one of these. Car parking is a need in every metro city. Using the internet of things smart parking can be built, in which a person can book their parking slot using a mobile device and can find parking. Further, the study is intended to model a plan of refreshed leaving to framework an endless supply of craftsmanship videos dealing with procedures which will be significant in giving vehicles leaving a number open at the segment point. This methodology permits a relentless dictation, which is a long way from the target of wise assessment, which plans to expect consistency. The producers introduced another technique subject to critical learning with a spasmodic neural relationship to manage the stopping inhabitance rate check [2].

A Smart Parking System shows the driver is permitted to utilize a screen to get data about the parking area, and see the generally available spots. The Smart Parking System is directed to control regions near the accessibility of parking spots by utilizing sensors. In addition, the far off sensors make open district applications really testing. Upkeep and control of sensors in open locales are very intriguing.

DOI: 10.1201/9781003190301-3

The assessment of the progress of Smart Parking System inhabits affirmation. The introduced affirmation utilizes the situation of accessible Parking places ending the board framework, and bases the choices exclusively on the sensor's status. Smart Parking Systems are changing the world's way of discovering calculations to merge multi-specialists, (drivers), increase the problems and lessen the compensation from sharp ending structures. The construction proposed isolates open parking space data from the foundation [3].

The makers focused on decreasing the difficult times for drivers, where the time spent cruising per smart Parking System decreases, the demand for available parking spaces being raised. In a Smart Parking System, stacks of proposals exist in the design, which is based on the responsiveness of parking spaces, its revelation, and the supervisors. In this structure, leaving meters are used to pick the extent of usage by parked vehicles and change arrangements of issues for choices rather than drivers. The bound closure spaces address an issue to individuals for the most part [4].

The Smart Parking System to generate traffic and urban adaptability is one of the troublesome issues of the urban turn of events. They face various difficulties of reasonable convenience in the face of expanding requests for Smart Parking Systems, particularly those identified with the basic cutoff of the city's vehicle, traffic and leaving structures. One of the customary marvelous cities follows the use of public vehicle applications and the arrangement of custom information plans to clients, which intend to work with Smart Parking System that creates answers to work on the individual satisfaction of its inhabitants and their relationship with government subject matter experts [5].

The Smart Parking System must show that a reliable parking system in indoor spotting. The interest in a Smart Parking System is developing, particularly in complex indoor environments, such as underground mines, retail outlets, and so on. Because of the deterrent of GPS (Global Position two or three degrees of progress like WiFi, Zigbee and RFID can be applied in indoor situations. Recently, indoor orchestrating with mix progression is a demanding appraisal theme [6].

The Smart Parking System on the Internet of Things has increased remarkable applications in the fields of human living space. The Internet of Things is based on keen sensors and middleware among customers and terminal gadgets. It can give people, by and large, fascinating data about different things passed on in the general climate. Specifically, the ending framework is one of the fundamental undertakings for the Internet of Things. To deal with this issue, sharp sensors and middleware for supplying them are required. The Smart Parking System by which vehicles leave a locale has been proposed utilizing RFID systems. In this, the drivers need to get a RFID tag for the parking area. The Smart Parking System gives the vehicle district association to drivers through the RFID precursor of a parking spot. Regardless, this framework is genuinely arranged considering the way that the driver should get the RFID tag. Furthermore, payment for the RFID tag is required [7].

In different large organizations the Smart Parking System (including business districts), void stopping space is amazingly hard to track down. As the number of vehicles expands, it is more dangerous and saves more work to discover accessible openings. The parking issue isn't just happening on the streets but also in the final locale where the parking spot is found. The city plans of different nations, including Pakistan, require sharp stopping associations that can assist clients with finding an accessible place to diminish time and traffic issues. By a wide margin the greater part of the ending framework is viewed as an "important stopping structure (IPS)" as opposed to a "sharp ending framework (SPS)," considering the way that it just provides data about the space of the ending locale and the measure of void spaces in that ending locale, but it can't find the specific space of the void stopping space [8].

In older day's a large portion of the ending regions are overseen by human work and there is no change in construction to deal with the ending region completely. There is an outstanding relationship when a driver enters any of the places he should search for a data board that tells him about the situation with the parking locale, whether it is completely included, somewhat included or void. On a vast majority of occasions, the drivers' need to circle around the final region looking for the Smart Parking System [9].

Additionally, in indoor vehicle parking, more often than not time is squandered looking for a vacant space, which makes a traffic jam. The circumstance is more regrettable when there are numerous leaving spaces in each leaving path. One more issue is the air contamination brought about via vehicles in the end, be it left in the outside or indoor. What's more, a large portion of the populace utilize their own vehicles for voyaging, which prompts more congestion in urban communities and postpones the method of tracking down an abandoned parking spot for the remainder of the drivers. The IoT furnishes the ability to manage such difficulties, as it is intended to catch sensors information for observing focal points in urban areas [10].

3.2   BACKGROUND STUDY

In a Smart Parking System stopping the vehicle structure is confined into two subsystems. The first vehicle detection system is the VDS and the second the Vehicle Management System (VMS). The VDS perceives the situation with the Smart Parking System and sends the aggregated data to the VMS subsystem to accommodate drivers. The percentage according to predicting time and date is 89.43% and shows that the user can easily park in this place at this time without harming traffic. Data from various sensors is dispatched from a focal expert in a limited time. Two or three creators, for example, made a model utilizing a sensor circuit, Radio Frequency Identification (RFID) and the Internet of Things to see the vehicle subtleties, and in this manner utilized IR sensors to discover the presence of the vehicle with the objective that all subtleties are obtained distantly through the Internet of Things. The RFID-based framework has also been utilized by to encourage traffic signal association in vigilant cities, but the issue of presumption will stay with this turn of events [1].The study produces a comparison between various hardware components that can be used to build a Smart Parking System. The methodology permits a relentless dictation which is a long way from the target of wise assessment which plans to expect consistency. The producers introduced another technique subject to critical learning. with a spasmodic neural relationship to manage the stopping inhabitance rate check [2].

The study clarifies a CPS (Cyber-Physical-Social) system based on unbelievable stopping structures which are proposed to assist drivers with holding or discovering a Smart Parking System. Such awesome leaving structures use cameras at the passage of leaving using parts to identify every vehicle, and notice a driver's consistent comings and goings, which is ideal for leaving the shut region. Likewise, the impressive stopping structures send ultrasonic or infrared markers for each parking spot to discover if the spaces are free. With these kinds of dissipated sensors, every vehicle's careful appearance time, pulling out time, leaving time and leaving positions can be observed [3].

According to the study, the parking system by which the Smart Parking System is used manages the issues of time consumption and fuel wastage. In this plan, a three-layer system sensor, correspondence and application were used. The specialist helped the drivers with finding the best place and sent an available space bearing to them. An emerging headway called the clouds of things (COT) was introduced [4].

The proposed system in the real-time environment used ultrasonic sensors and some predefined boundaries. The predefined boundaries include a 3Km radius area, taking into account the transmission power of raspberry pi, and two time zones, one in low traffic for a Sparse Region and the other in high traffic for the Dense Region. The study has verified the performance of the proposed system using two scenarios. The study proposes iERS, which predict and guide the users to the best available parking slots in the nearest vicinity [5].According to the paper, a Smart Parking System is proposed, including three parts: the parking space detection module, the WiFi indoor positioning module and a background server. The success rate of the parking space detection module is as high as 98%, after many tests. The result of the indoor positioning module in our system is greatly improved compared with the ordinary KNN algorithm, the comparison of cumulative error probabilities of 2m and 5m are increased by 19% and 6% respectively [6]. The Smart Parking System in which vehicle leaving locale association has been proposed utilizing RFID tagging. In this the drivers need to get an RFID tag for the parking area. The Smart Parking System gives the vehicle district association to drivers through the RFID precursor of the parking spot [7].

An IoT-based Smart Parking System can provide more than just information about vacant spaces, it can also help a driver to locate an available parking slot in order to reduce traffic problems in the parking area. The system will detect the vehicle plate number and use it to inform the driver where their car is parked and is also for the purpose of security monitoring. This system is designed using hardware and software based on an IoT concept and mobile application, the driver can easily check parking information and use mobile payment to pay the parking fee. The goal of our study is to improve the parking process by reducing the time that is required to park a car [8].The accuracy of the proposed algorithm is found to be 100%, 98%, 96% and 94%. The results show that when the captured images of the parking lot are not clear because of poor lighting or occlusions, the efficiency decreases and the accuracy for detection declines. It was observed that the average performance is 99.5% and is very high compared with other parking lot detection applications [9].This study has proposed a Smart Parking System that enhances saving users time to locate an appropriate parking space and reduces the general costs for moving to a chosen parking space. The most obvious finding to emerge from this study is that we proposed a Smart Car Parking system that will ensure the reduction of transmitted data through the network, saving energy in the perception layer [10].

This chapter presents a complete investigation on significant viewpoints for planning a brilliant stopping framework such as sensor determination and an ideal situation for sensor sending for a precise location. At first, two generally normal sensors, a Light Dependable Resistor (LDR) sensor that deals with shadow discovery head and an Infra-Red (IR) sensor which works on an object location instrument are utilized. The exhibition investigates the exactness of recognition of empty leaving spaces and vehicle location under various conditions [11].This study gives an easy way to all users of finding a parking lot, because it monitors and gives information before the drivers (users) get into the parking lot. The testing of this Smart Parking System was done using 4 HC–SR04 ultrasonic sensor(s), assembled in each parking lot, the sensors detect the parking slot, which will be filled by the car. The data obtained from the ultrasonic sensor will be managed by Arduino mega 2560 located in the monitor area and then sent to the monitoring area using the Wireless Sensor Network Xbee-Pro S2 communication. The parking slot area available or already filled by a car will be displayed [12].

The survey that has been conducted shows positive behavioral intention toward using SPS. All the four hypotheses are accepted; and it is found that perceived usefulness with a highest coefficient value (0.374) has most influence on behavioral intention toward using SPS. It can be concluded that more guidance and information are required by drivers inside the parking lots. The limitation of this study is that there is a lack of information about smart parking bay detection systems [13]. For parking status detection, we propose a cost–effective solution that utilizes mobile phone sensors such as GPS, accelerometer and Bluetooth sensors. Furthermore, the parking status detection algorithm may piggy-back on pay-by-phone for parking transactions [14],[15].

This chapter introduces mechanism design principles to allocating parking slots to heterogeneous demanding drivers, where drivers value the same slot differently and any two slots can be valued differently by the same driver. We showed that welfare-maximizing allocation, coupled with payment equivalent to a driver's externality induces truth telling and achieves the social optimum allocation outcome. The investigation was then extended to dynamic parking slot assignment, where each driver is assumed to report arrival, latest waiting and departure times in addition to valuation. Assuming that the parking manager does not have information about future arrivals, a myopic optimal allocation rule and a new price scheme were put forward to elicit truthful information reporting from drivers. A variant of the dynamic mechanism when valuation was reported on a per-unit-time basis was further considered, for which we showed that drivers' truth telling holds as well [16]. A paper analysis of the statistic survey was conducted, which showed the SCPS has not gained any significant ground in Nigeria and people barely know about this innovative technology.

From the analysis of the questionnaires, out of a total of 80 (100%) participants, 51 (63.8%) are staff of NDDC, 1 (1.3%) work with the Federal Ministry of Internal Affairs, 15 (18.8%) are staff of Ken-Poly, 1 (1.3%) works with Total while 2 (2.5%) are staff of Destiny Made Real Foundation. Ten (12.5%) worked with Port Harcourt Polytechnic [17].

This paper studied the problem of assigning prices to available parking slots to incentivize travelers to choose parking slots in a way that helps the system and environment. The paper presented the system optimal assignment and the Nash equilibrium assignment of vehicles to parking slots. According to simulations that were run, this type of pricing scheme can lead to improvements in total distance traveled of up to 23%. In a big city like Chicago, this leads to improvements of up to 39,000,000 vehicle miles traveled [18].The paper has proposed a Smart Parking System that exploits technologies for parking space availability detection and for driver localization and optimally allocates and reserves parking spots to drivers instead of only supplying guidance to them [19].

The paper has proposed a method that allows high recall (98.4%) and high precision (99.3%) at the parking slot recognition stage and gives a low error rate (0.9%) at the slot occupancy classification stage. The proposed method effectively detects available parking slots using AVM images. Visual analysis is used during both parking slot recognition and slot occupancy classification; the parking slot recognition stage generates available parking slots using the corners of parking slot markings. In this stage, guidelines are detected through feature extraction and classification [20]. The paper has designed a wireless sensor node, i.e., a smart parking system using IoT, employing two sensors and a Raspberry Pi for detection of parking slot availability. Inbuilt Wi-Fi (IEEE standard 802.11) is used as the communication module. Also, a heterogeneous network is proposed to implement different Wireless Sensor Networks (WSNs) where the different wireless sensor nodes send their data to a master or centralized node implemented by use of a Raspberry Pi (RPi). A database is created at all nodes (master and slaves). Various Quality of Service (QoS) parameters are also evaluated for the proposed system [21].

The congested traffic of metropolitan areas is usually caused by the number of cars that are cruising for parking. Existing studies mainly focus on the allocation of open parking spaces and the minimization of total travel time. In some realistic settings, our proposed mechanisms can almost realize cost savings of 60% and make more than 50% of agents better off. There is no private parking slot sharing in the benchmark case. Overall, this paper opens the door to the solutions of a host of price-compatible matching problems [22]. To this purpose, a Hybrid Sensing Network (HSN) has been deployed. It is able to combine the communication capability of a WSN, with the identification features of the RFID technology. On the client side, we developed two Android and iOS mobile apps, called DriverApp and TrafficApp. By using the DriverApp, a driver can find the parking spaces available in a given area, get the right directions to the selected parking spot, pay the parking fee, check the remaining parking time and receive notifications when the purchased time is expiring [23].

This paper has proposed a Smart Parking System. By using the secured wireless network and sensor communication, Smart Parking is an intelligent parking service application, as well as a novel security/privacy aware infrastructure. First, vehicles on the road can view and reserve a parking spot. The parking process can be an efficient and non-stop service [24]. The proposed architecture for a parking detection system would decrease the searching time for empty spaces, as all the data of the parking center is stored in the main server. It has figured out how to access and map the status of parking spaces from any remote area through a mobile application. The system will help the user to find the parking slots, giving priority to find the user desired parking location. The proposed system considered full automation, high energy efficiency, and cost–effectiveness. The system can decrease traffic jams and human effort as well as most importantly it can minimize the carbon footprint in the atmosphere [25].

In this paper, a Distributed Ledger Technology (DLT) and Directed Acyclic Graph (DAG) based parking lot allocation model is discussed. The DLT technique helps in creating a secure peer-to-peer network of the users, parking lot owners, garages and free spaces. Anyone with a free parking slot can register in the network and can securely utilize the resources for monetary benefits. The hash graph or DAG technique used for network and transaction creation gives a unique consensus timestamp for all the parking reservation requests, thereby ensuring the best possible service to the users in a cost-optimal way. An adaptive pricing model is discussed to generate a unique price for each parking request based on multiple parameters. The pricing model proves to be equally beneficial both for the users and the PL owners. The users get the best available parking slot in less time and at less cost, whereas the PL owners get the best utilization for their resources at the best possible prices [26].

3.3   METHODOLOGY

3.3.1   UCD Process Model

The philosophy of User Centered Design (UCD) is proposed to analyze the usability and validity of mobile device interfaces according to user contexts [27]. User centered design (UCD) is a methodology that focuses on high usability and low-cost products for understanding of needs, tasks, environments, preferences and limitations in a user's context [28]. Recent studies in the domain of healthcare awareness among children through video games are mostly scenario-based. Health awareness video games discussed in the background study were based on puzzle themes, story-telling themes and clinic scenario themes. In this study, the run and grab theme has been used. It is a novel approach that has not been discussed in previous studies. The character of the game will run and grab healthy foods for promoting oral hygiene practices among children.

Figure 3.1 shows the iterative model for User Centered Design (UCD), the prototype has passed through this process to fulfill the driver's requirement. The first phase is understanding the requirement of drivers to develop the prototype after evaluation with the driver to check if it fulfills the driver needs or not and then update it according to feedback or requirements. This process repeats again and again until the requirements of drivers are not fulfilled.

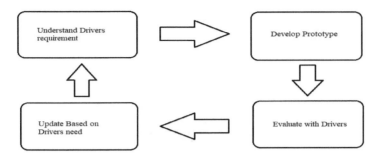

FIGURE 3.1   User centered design.

3.3.2 PROTOTYPE DEVELOPMENT

A prototype is developed for the Smart Parking System. It has two interfaces. The first interface is for the drivers, the main screen of the driver's interface shows two options. The first is to find parking and the other is to check the charges for parking. If you click on the first option to get a parking place it will show you the QR code which is unique for every driver, you have to scan it from the QR code scanner to get a parking slot. Once you have scanned the QR code, you will get the allotted slot along with the parking charges. You can park your car in the allotted slot; in case some one's car is already parked on your allotted slot you can request a new slot by clicking on "Someone is parked on my parking" and you will get a new allotted slot where you park your car. For exit just click on "Exit Parking," the QR code will be generated for exit, and you can scan it by the QR code scanner machine and pay your charges.

Figure 3.2 shows the main screen where the drivers have two options. The first option is to get a parking slot and the second option is to check the parking charges. After clicking the first option the driver moves to Figure 3.3 which shows the unique QR code to get a parking slot. Once the QR code is scanned the driver gets the

FIGURE 3.2   Main screen.

FIGURE 3.3   QR Code to get Parking Slot.

FIGURE 3.4   Allocated Parking Slot

parking slot (Figure 3.4) which shows the allocated slot and shows the charge. When the driver clicks on exit parking, the screen changes to Figure 3.5, which shows the unique QR code for exit parking; this QR code has the record of the driver, such as the allocated slot number, time and charges.

The second interface is for administration. The main screen of the admin interface is the login page where the admin is authenticated, then it moves to dashboard where the admin shows five options. The first option is where admin manages the parking slots and parking floors. The second option is where admin manages the parking charges and also manages fines like "wrong parking". The third option is where admin manages the employees. The admin has privileges to create and delete the employees. The fourth option is where admin gets the parking complaints from drivers like "wrong parking". Admin has the option to skip the complaints or fine the

FIGURE 3.5   QR Code to exit Parking.

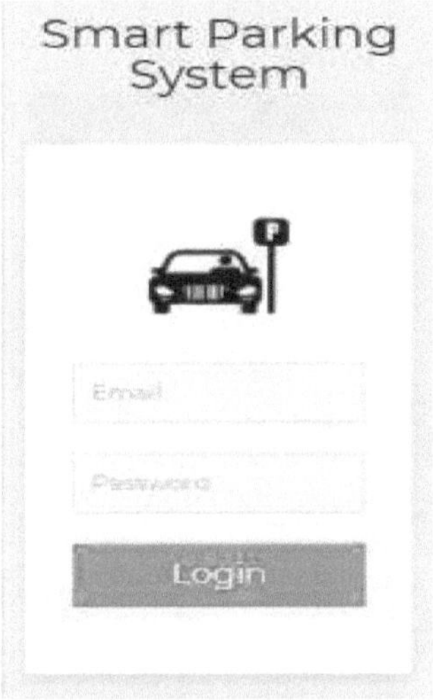

FIGURE 3.6   Login screen.

drivers who wrongly parked their car. The charges will be collected when the driver is exiting the parking. The fifth option is where admin manages his/her password.

Figure 3.6 shows the login screen for admin where the admin is logged in with their email and password to manage the parking. After logging in successfully the admin redirects to the dashboard (Figure 3.7), it shows the options which admin have for the management of parking; if admin wants to manage the parking floors it simply clicks the first option and it redirects to Figure 3.8 which shows the floor name, slot from and slot to, here admin add the parking floors and define the slots, and also manage the existing floors by updating or deletion.

FIGURE 3.7 Dashboard.

FIGURE 3.8 Parking floors.

3.3.3 USABILITY EVALUATION

3.3.3.1 Effectiveness

This measures how effectively a user completes the specific goal. Effectiveness is calculated on the basis of the number of tasks completed successfully. It is calculated using a simple equation of completion rate metrics [29].

3.3.3.2 Efficiency

What resources are consumed to attain a specific goal? Efficiency is measured on the basis of task time. The task time is calculated with a simple equation that is time-based efficiency [29].

3.3.3.3 Satisfaction

How much a user is satisfied after using the system and what is their feedback [29]? The system you are presenting is suitable or not for the user and provides the solution to the user or not.

3.3.3.4 Proposed Model

Figure 3.9 shows the proposed model of parking prototype in which when the car enters the parking, a barrier has been used to restrict the driver. QR code scanners and screens are connected with a database and placed close to the barriers. The driver opens the prototype and will get the QR Code by clicking on "Find Parking" which they will scan by the scanner to get a parking slot. Once the QR code scans, a slot is allocated to the driver. If a slot is available, the screen shows the allocated slot, otherwise it shows a message "Parking is full try after some time". For exit parking a barrier is used to restrict drivers exiting without scanning a QR code. When the driver clicks on "Exit Parking" from the prototype, they get the QR code which will be scanned by the scanner to exit. Once the QR code scans, the screen shows the thank you message and changes the status of slot allotted to available.

3.4 DATA COLLECTION AND EVALUATION

We performed multiple tasks from drivers and categorized their results in tables by age to check how many drivers could easily use this prototype and complete their task in a given time.

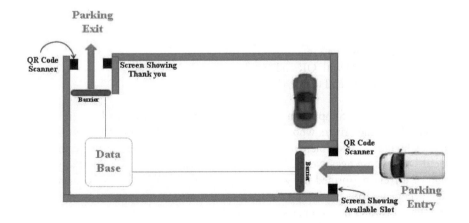

FIGURE 3.9 Proposed model.

3.4.1 SAMPLING

We took 220 drivers and categorized them on the basis of their genders. After categorization we got 110 male and 110 female drivers, then we created two groups for each male and female drivers to get better results. Groups are divided on the basis of age. The age limit of first group is 21–30 years. The age limit of second group is 31–40 years. We then had four groups. Two groups for male and two groups for female; in each group were 55 drivers. We provided them with prototypes and performed multiple tasks which are discussed below.

3.4.2 DEFINED TASKS

We defined three tasks, and the results of these tasks show the performance of drivers. We have discussed these tasks step by step with screenshots.

Task 1:
1. Click on "Find parking".
2. Scan QR code with QR code reader to get parking slot.
3. Get the parking slot.
4. Click on "Exit parking".
5. Scan QR Code with QR code reader to Exit Parking.
6. Payment and Exit.

Task 2:
1. Click on "Find parking".
2. Scan QR code with QR code reader to get parking slot.
3. Get the parking slot; if your parking is already taken then click on "Someone Parked on my parking" to get new parking slot.
4. Click on "Exit parking".
5. Scan QR code with QR code reader to Exit Parking.
6. Payment and Exit.

Task 3:
1. Click on "Find parking".
2. Scan QR code with QR code reader to get Parking Slot.
3. Parking is full and then Exit.

Graph 3.1 shows the comparison of male drivers based on tasks and age limits. The blue line shows the drivers who completed their task, and the orange line shows the drivers who failed to complete their tasks. We performed tasks from two categorized male drivers whose ages were 21–30 and 31–40; the graph shows that the younger group of drivers performed it well as compared to elders but in task 3 there was a 100% accuracy result.

Graph 3.2 shows the comparison of female drivers on the basis of tasks and age limits, the same as in Graph 3.1. The blue line shows the drivers who completed their task and the orange line shows the drivers who failed to complete their tasks. We

Comparison Graph Male Drivers

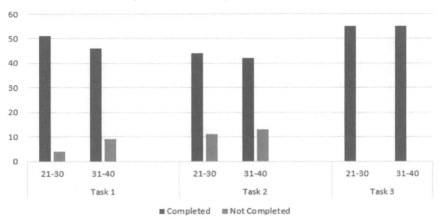

GRAPH 3.1 Comparison of male drivers.

Comparison Graph Female Drivers

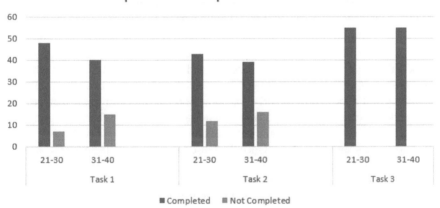

GRAPH 3.2 Comparison of female drivers.

performed tasks from two categorized female drivers whose ages are 21–30 and 31–40; the graph shows that the younger group of drivers performed it well as compared to elders but in task 3 100% accuracy resulted.

3.5 EXPERIMENTATION

3.5.1 SELECTION OF PROTOTYPE INTERFACE

The prototype interface passes through the process of UCD for better interaction with drivers and try to remove all the needs of drivers regarding parking. The prototype is simple, using light colors to avoid irritation of the eyes, and is easy to use; even a new driver can use it first time.

3.5.2   Sample Size

For the experimentation, we took 110 male drivers and 110 female drivers under the following conditions.

1. Driver age should be between 21–40.
2. Driver must have driving experience of more than one year.
3. Driver must be a smart phone user for one year.

3.5.3   Allocated Tasks

We categorized participants of male and female drivers by age limits and performed multiple tasks from them as shown in the table.

Table 3.1 shows the group for male and female drivers with the age limit between 21–40 years. It also shows the multiple tasks and evaluates them with ASQ. The ASQ technique is used for post evaluation. It contains three questions on a seven point scale (strongly disagree=1, disagree=2, somewhat disagree=3, neither agree nor disagree=4, somewhat agree=5, agree=6, strongly agree=7).

Task 1

In task 1 the driver clicks on "Find Parking" and gets the unique QR code which is scanned by the QR code scanner to get a parking slot. Once the QR code is scanned, the parking slot allocated to the driver is shown on the screen of the prototype. The driver parks their car on the allocated slot and also checks the parking charges. Then the driver clicks on exit parking and gets the same QR code to exit which is scanned by the QR code scanner machine. Once the QR code is scanned, the charges show on the screen of prototype.

Figure 3.10 shows the task 1 prototype testing from a male driver. The name of the Driver is Khalil Ikram. The testing conducted date is 08-Sep-2021 and the place of testing is the Mall of Sialkot.

Figure 3.11 shows the task 1 prototype testing from a female driver. The name of the driver is Zainab Butt. The testing conducted date is 09-Sep-2021 and the place of testing is the Mall of Sialkot.

We provided Samsung Galaxy A51 and Samsung Galaxy J3 Pro devices to the drivers. In this device the prototype was installed. First, we mentioned the purpose of this prototype to them, and then we provided them with a short demo of how you can use this prototype. We assigned 180 seconds for this task. Most of them completed the task without getting support and gave a positive response.

Task 2

In task 2 the driver clicks on "Find Parking" and gets the unique QR code which is scanned by the QR code scanner to get a parking slot. Once the QR code is scanned,

TABLE 3.1
Tasks Allocated to Drivers

Participants	Gender	Age	Task 1	Task 2	Task 3	Post Evaluation
55	M	21–30	Scan QR Code get allocated slot, park on it and then exit	Scan QR Code get allocated slot, someone park on your slot, request for another slot, park on it and then exit	Scan QR Code parking is full and again try after some time	ASQ
55	F	21–30	Scan QR Code get allocated slot, park on it and then exit	Scan QR Code get allocated slot, someone park on your slot, request for another slot, park on it and then exit	Scan QR Code parking is full and again try after some	ASQ
55	M	31–40	Scan QR Code get allocated slot, park on it and then exit	Scan QR Code get allocated slot, someone park on your slot, request for another slot, park on it and then exit	Scan QR Code parking is full and again try after some time	ASQ
55	F	31–40	Scan QR Code get allocated slot, park on it and then exit	Scan QR Code get allocated slot, someone park on your slot, request for another slot, park on it and then exit	Scan QR Code parking is full and again try after some time	ASQ

FIGURE 3.10   Task 1 Prototype testing from male drivers.

FIGURE 3.11   Task 1 Prototype testing from female drivers.

the parking slot allocated to the driver is shown on the screen of the prototype. If someone's car was already parked on the allocated slot then the driver clicks on the "Someone parked on my parking". Once the driver clicked, a new parking slot was allocated to the driver. The driver parks their car on the allocated slot and also checks the parking charges. Then the driver clicks on the exit parking and gets the same QR code to exit, which is scanned by the QR code scanner machine. Once the QR code is scanned, the charges show on the screen of the prototype.

Figure 3.12 shows task 2 prototype testing from a male driver. The name of the driver is Fahad Ali. The testing conducted date is 10-Sep-2021 and the place of testing is the Mall of Sialkot.

Figure 3.13 shows task 2 prototype testing from a   female driver. The name of the driver is Amna Raza. The testing conducted date is 10-Sep-2021 and the place of testing is the Mall of Sialkot.

We provided Samsung Galaxy A51 and Samsung Galaxy J3 Pro devices to drivers with the prototype installed. First, we told them the purpose of this prototype and then we provided them with a short demo of how you can use this prototype. We assigned

FIGURE 3.12   Task 2 Prototype testing from male drivers.

FIGURE 3.13   Task 2 Prototype testing from female drivers.

240 seconds for this task. Most of them completed the task without getting support and gave a positive response.

Task 3

In task 3 the driver clicks on "Find Parking" and gets the unique QR code which is scanned by a QR code scanner to get a parking slot. Once the QR code is scanned, the message shows on the screen of the prototype "Parking is full". The driver exits the parking lot.

Figure 3.14 shows task 3 prototype testing from a male driver. The name of the Driver is Khawaja Azan. The testing conducted date is 14-Sep-2021 and the place of testing is the Mall of Sialkot.

Figure 3.15 shows the task 3 prototype testing from a female driver. The name of the driver is Ajar Javaid. The testing conducted date is 13-Sep-2021 and the place of testing is the Mall of Sialkot.

We provided Samsung Galaxy A51 and Samsung Galaxy J3 Pro devices to drivers with the prototype installed. First, we told them the purpose of this prototype and then

FIGURE 3.14   Task 3 Prototype testing from male drivers.

FIGURE 3.15   Task 3 Prototype testing from female drivers.

we provided them with a short demo on how you can use this prototype. We assigned 240 sec for this task. Most of them completed the task without getting support and gave a positive response.

3.6   USABILITY EVALUATION

There are three parameters to measure the performance of usability: effectiveness, efficiency and satisfaction. The ISO 9241-11 standard is used to measure the effectiveness and efficiency, whereas After Scenario Questionnaire (ASQ) is chosen for the post task evaluation to measure the driver's satisfaction [28].

3.6.1 Effectiveness

Effectiveness is the number of goals achieved and it is measured as:

$$\text{Effectiveness} = \frac{\text{Total number of tasks completed successfully}}{\text{Total number of tasks undertaken}} * 100$$

Effectiveness for male drivers.

Task 1	Task 2	Task 3
88.1%.	78.1%	100%

Effectiveness for female drivers.

Task 1	Task 2	Task 3
80%.	74.5%	100%

Effectiveness for male drivers with the age limit of 21–30 years.

Task 1	Task 2	Task 3
92.7%.	80%	100%

Effectiveness for male drivers with the age limit of 31–40 years.

Task 1	Task 2	Task 3
83.6%.	76.3%	100%

Effectiveness for female drivers with the age limit of 21–30 years.

Task 1	Task 2	Task 3
87.2%.	78.1%	100%

Effectiveness for female drivers with the age limit of 31–40 years.

Task 1	Task 2	Task 3
72.2%.	70.9%	100%

3.6.2 EFFICIENCY

Resources such as time, money or mental efforts that have to be expended to achieve the intended goals, called efficiency, can be measured as:

$$\text{Time based Efficiency} = \frac{\sum_{j=1}^{R} \sum_{i=1}^{N} \frac{n_{ij}}{t_{ij}}}{NR}$$

Where:
N = The total amount of tasks (goals)
R = The number of users

nij = The result of task *i* by user *j*; if the user successfully completes the task, then *Nij*= 1, if not, then *Nij* = 0.*tij* = The time spent by user *j* to complete task *i*. If the task is not successfully completed, then time is measured until the moment the user quits the task.

Efficiency for male drivers.

Task 1	Task 2
48%.	32%

Efficiency for female drivers.

Task 1	Task 2
44%.	31%

Efficiency for male drivers with the age limit of 21–30 years.

Task 1	Task 2
51%.	33%

Efficiency for male drivers with the age limit of 31–40 years.

Task 1	Task 2
46%.	31%

Efficiency for male drivers with the age limit of 21–30 years.

Task 1	Task 2
48%.	32%

Efficiency for male drivers with the age limit of 31–40 years.

Task 1	Task 2
40%.	29%

3.6.3 SATISFACTION

Satisfaction is measured by the amount a driver finds the use of the prototype acceptable. Usability is dependent on the context of use and on the specific circumstances in which a prototype is used. The context of use consists of the driver's task, hardware, software and material. There are many post-task evaluation techniques available (e.g., SEQ, UME, SMEQ), but in this study satisfaction is measured through the ASQ technique.

The ASQ is a short questionnaire which takes little time, is easy to understand and has tremendous practical considerations for participants in usability studies. It contains three questions on a seven point scale (strongly disagree=1, disagree=2, somewhat disagree=3, neither agree nor disagree=4, somewhat agree=5, agree=6, strongly agree=7), with important aspects of driver satisfaction with system usability. The first question shows the aspect of ease in task completion, the second question provides the aspect of time to complete a task while the third question analyzes the satisfaction level on the capability of the support information [28].

3.7   RESULTS AND DISCUSSION

The study reflects that the prototype can be used to address parking slot issues. The effectiveness, efficiency and satisfaction have been calculated from drivers. The results are presented by organizing three usability parameters.

Graph 3.3 shows the effectiveness comparison for male and female drivers with an age limit of 21–30 years. It shows a substantial difference between male and female drivers. The overall gap of effectiveness measures based on gender is also considerable where the female group showed lower effectiveness compared to the male group. In task 1 (92.7%) of male drivers completed the task and (87.2%) of female drivers completed the task. In task 2 (80%) of male drivers completed the task and (78.1%) of female drivers completed the task and in task 3 (100%) of male and female drivers completed the task.

Graph 3.4 shows the effectiveness comparison for male and female drivers with an age limit of 31–40 years. It shows a substantial difference between male and female drivers. The overall gap of effectiveness measures based on gender is also considerable where the female group showed lower effectiveness compared to the male group. In task 1 (83.6%) of male drivers completed the task and (72.2%) of female drivers completed the task. In task 2 (76.3%) of male drivers completed the task and (70.9%)

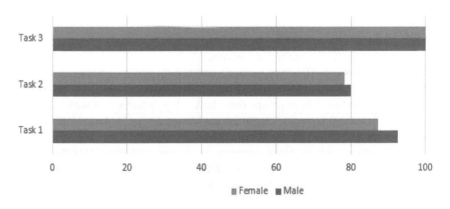

GRAPH 3.3   Effectiveness comparison for male and female drivers age limit of 21–30 years.

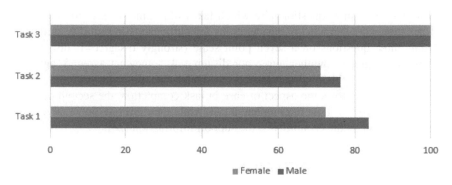

GRAPH 3.4   Effectiveness comparison for male and female drivers age limit of 31–40 years.

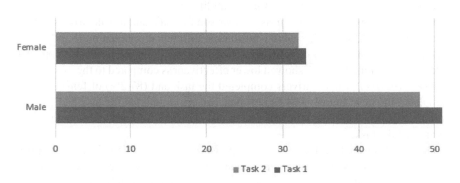

GRAPH 3.5   Efficiency comparison for male and female drivers age limit 21–30.

of female drivers completed the task and in task 3 (100%) of male and female drivers completed the task.

Graph 3.5 shows the efficiency for male and female drivers with an age limit of 21–30 years. The efficiency for female drivers recorded low in task 1 as compared to male drivers, but in task 2 both groups don't have a big difference. In task 1 it was (51%) for male drivers and (48%) for the female drivers. In task 2 it was (33%) for male drivers and (32%) for the female drivers.

Graph 3.6 shows the efficiency for male and female drivers with an age limit of 31–40 years. The efficiency for female drivers recorded low in task 1 as compared to male drivers, but in task 2 both groups don't have a big difference. If we see in task 1 it was(46%) for male drivers and (40%) for the female drivers. In task 2 it was (31%) for male drivers and (29%) for the female drivers.

Graph 3.7 shows the usability comparison in terms of driver satisfaction for adaptive and non-adaptive environments. The evaluation had been taken through ASQ to measure the satisfaction of drivers. The graph shows that 90% of male drivers are satisfied to adopt the prototype and 10% of male drivers are not satisfied, while 70% of female drivers are satisfied to adopt the prototype and 30% of female drivers are not satisfied. Overall 80% of drivers are satisfied to adopt the prototype and 20% of drivers are not satisfied.

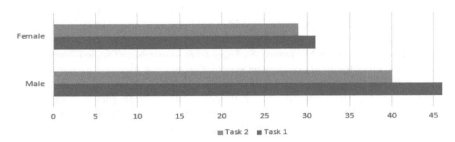

GRAPH 3.6 Efficiency comparison for male and female drivers age limit 31–40.

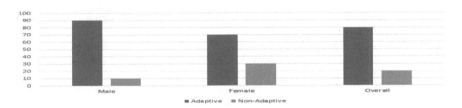

GRAPH 3.7 Usability comparison for adaptive and non-adaptive prototype.

3.8 CONCLUSION AND FUTURE WORK

This study has proposed a smart parking prototype, which reduces parking issues and saves time for drivers by allocating them a parking slot on entrance and notifying the parking charges. The prototype has gone through a process of User Centered Design (UCD) to fulfil the needs of drivers in a sense of functionality and design perspective. We performed tasks from drivers to check the prototype performance and showed the results in table and graphical views. Furthermore, this prototype also helps the management to manage their parking. By using this prototype, management can easily manage their parking slots, parking charges and their employees. In addition, the presented paper will help in future work, reduces the more issues of drivers regarding parking, and expand this prototype to become more mature and more helpful. Finally, the future step would be the deployment of this prototype for drivers to find available parking slots and guide them.

REFERENCES

[1] Tekouabou, S. C. K., Cherif, W., & Silkan, H. (2020). Improving parking availability prediction in smart cities with IoT and ensemble-based model. *Journal of King Saud University-Computer and Information Sciences.*

[2] Rupani, S., & Doshi, N. (2019). A review of smart parking using internet of things (IoT). *Procedia Computer Science*, 160, 706–711.

[3] Perković, T., Šolić, P., Zargariasl, H., Čoko, D., & Rodrigues, J. J. (2020). Smart parking sensors: state of the art and performance evaluation. *Journal of Cleaner Production*, 262, 121181.

[4] Kizilkaya, B., Caglar, M., Al-Turjman, F., & Ever, E. (2019). Binary search tree based hierarchical placement algorithm for IoT based smart parking applications. *Internet of Things*, 5, 71–83.

[5] Chauhan, V., Patel, M., Tanwar, S., Tyagi, S., & Kumar, N. (2020). IoT Enabled real-time urban transport management system. *Computers & Electrical Engineering*, 86, 106746.

[6] Yuan, C., Fei, L., Jianxin, C., & Wei, J. (2016). A smart parking system using WiFi and wireless sensor network. Paper presented at the 2016 IEEE International Conference on Consumer Electronics-Taiwan (ICCE–TW).

[7] Lee, C., Han, Y., Jeon, S., Seo, D., & Jung, I. (2016). Smart parking system for Internet of Things. Paper presented at the 2016 IEEE International Conference on Consumer Electronics (ICCE).

[8] Lookmuang, R., Nambut, K., & Usanavasin, S. (2018). Smart parking using IoT technology. Paper presented at the 2018 5th International Conference on Business and Industrial research (ICBIR).

[9] Bibi, N., Majid, M. N., Dawood, H., & Guo, P. (2017). Automatic parking space detection system. Paper presented at the 2017 2nd International Conference on Multimedia and Image Processing (ICMIP).

[10] Alsafery, W., Alturki, B., Reiff-Marganiec, S., & Jambi, K. (2018). Smart car parking system solution for the internet of things in smart cities. Paper presented at the 2018 1st International Conference on Computer Applications & Information Security (ICCAIS).

[11] Bachani, M., Qureshi, U. M., & Shaikh, F. K. (2016). Performance analysis of proximity and light sensors for smart parking. *Procedia Computer Science*, 83, 385–392.

[12] Sahfutri, A., Husni, N. L., Nawawi, M., Lutfi, I., Silvia, A., & Prihatini, E. (2018). Smart parking using wireless sensor network system. Paper presented at the 2018 International Conference on Electrical Engineering and Computer Science (ICECOS).

[13] Kianpisheh, A., Mustaffa, N., See, J. M. Y., & Keikhosrokiani, P. (2011). User behavioral intention toward using smart parking system. Paper presented at the International Conference on Informatics Engineering and Information Science

[14] Srisura, B., Wan, C., Sae-lim, D., Meechoosup, P., & Win, K. M. (2018). User preference recommendation on mobile car parking application. Paper presented at the 2018 6th IEEE International Conference on Mobile Cloud Computing, Services, and Engineering (MobileCloud).

[15] Xu, B., Wolfson, O., Yang, J., Stenneth, L., Philip, S. Y., & Nelson, P. C. (2013). Real-time street parking availability estimation. Paper presented at the 2013 IEEE 14th International Conference on Mobile Data Management.

[16] Zou, B., Kafle, N., Wolfson, O., & Lin, J. J. (2015). A mechanism design based approach to solving parking slot assignment in the information era. *Transportation Research Part B: Methodological*, 81, 631–653.

[17] Anderson, E. C., Obayi, A., & Okafor, K. (2017). Awareness analysis of smart car parking system in heterogeneous high-density clusters. Circulation in Computer Science–Special Issue Disruptive Computing, Cyber-Physical Systems (CPS), and Internet of Everything (IoE), USA, 22–26.

[18] Ayala, D., Wolfson, O., Xu, B., DasGupta, B., & Lin, J. (2012). Pricing of parking for congestion reduction. Paper presented at the Proceedings of the 20th International Conference on Advances in Geographic Information Systems.

[19] Geng, Y., & Cassandras, C. G. (2013). New "smart parking" system based on resource allocation and reservations. *IEEE Transactions on Intelligent Transportation Systems*, 14(3), 1129–1139.

[20] Chen, J.-Y., & Hsu, C.-M. (2017). A visual method for the detection of available parking slots. Paper presented at the 2017 IEEE International Conference on Systems, Man, and Cybernetics (SMC).

[21] Balhwan, S., Gupta, D., & Reddy, S. (2019). Smart parking—a wireless sensor networks application using IoT. Paper presented at the Proceedings of 2nd International Conference on Communication, Computing and Networking.

[22] Xu, S. X., Cheng, M., Kong, X. T., Yang, H., & Huang, G. Q. (2016). Private parking slot sharing. *Transportation Research Part B: Methodological*, 93, 596–617.

[23] Mainetti, L., Patrono, L., Stefanizzi, M. L., & Vergallo, R. (2015). A Smart Parking System based on IoT protocols and emerging enabling technologies. Paper presented at the 2015 IEEE 2nd World Forum on Internet of Things (WF-IoT).

[24] Yan, G., Yang, W., Rawat, D. B., & Olariu, S. (2011). Smart Parking: A secure and intelligent parking system. *IEEE Intelligent Transportation Systems Magazine*, 3(1), 18–30.

[25] Al Maruf, M. A., Ahmed, S., Ahmed, M. T., Roy, A., & Nitu, Z. F. (2019). A proposed model of integrated smart parking solution for a city. Paper presented at the 2019 International Conference on Robotics, Electrical and Signal Processing Techniques (ICREST).

[26] Hassija, V., Saxena, V., Chamola, V., & Yu, F. R. (2020). A parking slot allocation framework based on virtual voting and adaptive pricing algorithm. *IEEE Transactions on Vehicular Technology*, 69(6), 5945–5957.

[27] Iqbal, M. W., Ahmad, N., Shahzad, S. K., Feroz, I., & Mian, N. A. (2018). Towards adaptive user interfaces for mobile phone in smart world. *International Journal of Advanced Computer Science and Applications*, 9(11), 77.

[28] Iqbal, M. W., Ahmad, N., & Shahzad, S. K. (2017). Usability evaluation of adaptive features in smartphones. *Procedia Computer Science*, 112, 2185–2194.

[29] Shehzad, R., & Ahmad, N. (2017). Web usability and user trust on e-commerce websites in Pakistan. *International Journal of Advance Computer Science and Applications*, 8(12).

4 Impact of Gamification in Children's Health Awareness

Khowla Khaliq[1], Muhammad Waseem Iqbal[1], Misbah Noor[1], Toqir A. Rana[2] and Muhammad Arif[1]
[1]Superior University, Lahore, Pakistan, [2]The University of Lahore, Lahore, Pakistan

4.1 INTRODUCTION

Sports and games have been very essential in learning among children since the beginning of time. Play enables children to learn ethics, social norms, behavioral skills, physical skills, health benefits and many other things while playing [1]. Some children suffer from chronic diseases which may affect their social, emotional and physical capabilities. These chronic diseases require an intensive care routine for the children affected. Games can be helpful for children to achieve health awareness while having fun [2].

With the advent of technology, games have transferred from physical games to video games. Multimedia video games are very popular among children because of their interfaces and content [3]. According to a survey conducted of 2,000 people including children and teenagers (8 years to 18 years), most of them spent 7 hours and 38 minutes playing video games daily [4].

Multimedia devices play a very important role in the motivation, enhancing imagination and learning of children. Such games have the same impact as computer-assisted instruction to train children about multiple aspects of their lives [5].

Nowadays, children spend hours on mobile devices playing video games, therefore video games can be utilized as a means of raising awareness of healthcare problems among children. Healthcare games are very popular in STEM games to teach children daily life practices to maintain their health. Moreover, mobile games are providing digital medical solutions for the physical and mental rehabilitation of children [6].

4.1.1 GAMES PROMOTE MEDICAL EDUCATION

Some games are developed to maximize medical education, and programs like Cogmed have been proven to enhance cognitive results in childhood cancer survivors [7]. Playing games may promote adherence to essential therapy processes because they are very interesting and motivating. As a result, video games can be a useful

DOI: 10.1201/9781003190301-4

supplement to conventional therapies. The game Re-Mission was the first to demonstrate improved treatment compliance through the use of video games [8].

4.1.2 HUMAN–COMPUTER INTERACTION (HCI) AND COMPUTER GAMES

Human–computer interaction (HCI) corresponds to how humans and computers interact with one another. Because of the increased interaction of computers in businesses and homes, the scope of HCI has expanded to include social, organizational and cognitive aspects related to computer use [9]. HCI can help with child behavior prediction and the growth of psychosocial skills. Furthermore, advances in virtual simulation technology allow for the development of games that improve children's organizational skills. Children can also learn problem-solving and reasoning skills by playing video games. The more those who make mistakes trying to accomplish a project in the game, the more they will try again and again until they succeed [10].

Children's behavior toward games has shifted dramatically as a result of modern technologies. By the age of 21, the average 8–14-year-old child has spent more than one hour each day playing video games, accumulating at least 10,000 hours of play. Applied games are video games that are used for objectives other than entertainment [11]. They have enormous promise for training and teaching new ways of thinking and doing (see Figure 4.1), as well as addressing specific behavioral domains. Indeed, applied games have been shown to effectively reduce anxiety and depression symptoms in teenagers in recent research [12].

4.1.3 GAMING IMPACTS ON CHILDREN'S PROGRESS

Games can have an impact on a child's social, emotional and cognitive development. Today's games use an immersive social backdrop to assist players learn social skills and pro-social behavior quickly [14]. Indeed, playing a pro-social game has

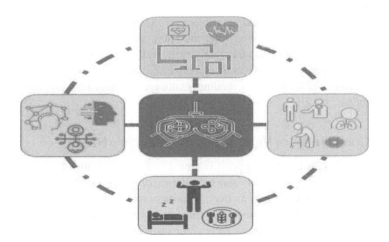

FIGURE 4.1 HCI computer games for health awareness [13].

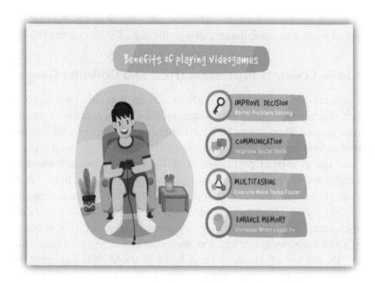

FIGURE 4.2   Benefits of playing video games for children [18].

been found to improve help, collaboration, empathy and emotional awareness over time. Individuals who participated in a cooperative game demonstrated more pro-social behavior in a dilemma task than those who had participated in a competitive game, implying that these behaviors could be transmitted to their social and family connections outside of the game world. Playing video games has been shown to alter both positive and negative emotional processing [15]. Video games, like ordinary play, may be realistic enough to make goal attainment meaningful, while also being safe enough to exercise skills for controlling or modulating unpleasant emotions to reach those goals. Even though there are reasons for believing that gaming can benefit a person's development and peer connection, little has been understood about gaming's long-term effects on feelings and emotions [16]. Several studies, for example, have found that people's moods improve after they play games. Playing video games can improve problem-solving skills and creativity, as well as improving focus and spatial skills. A recent study on the effects of video games found that they have a favorable impact on intellectual functioning, reading, math, spelling and academic accomplishment (Figure 4.2) [17].

4.1.4   Good Effects of Video Games on Children's Health

Regular video games can have a positive impact on patient health because they can be used to divert patients' minds and help them cope with the side effects of therapies such as nausea, vomiting, anxiety, weariness and pain. Frequent playing may be used to help clients participate in and enhance physical exercise and the effects of medication [19]. Playing computer games, for instance, has been shown to decrease stimulated nausea in sick children, as well as decreasing anxiety when they were permitted to play with a Gameboy just before and during anesthesia induction. These findings imply that games can improve children's and teenagers' mental health and well-being [20].

4.1.4.1 Examples

The video game "SPARX" (Figure 4.3) was found to be useful in reducing depression symptoms in adolescents in research. It was concluded that it could be utilized to fulfill some of the unmet treatment requests for adolescents with depressive symptoms in primary care as an alternative to standard therapy. Mind light has recently been found to considerably reduce anxiety in children with problems [21]. However, no research has looked into the influence of applied games on depressive or anxiety symptoms in children with chronic diseases, even though applied games and the usage of apps are receiving more attention in the pediatric environment. Other games, such as Need for Speed 2 and Power Boat Racer, encourage people with physical disabilities to be more active, increasing their chances of successful treatment in a systematic study on chronic pediatric disease [22].

Technological advances have also found a new type of playing games in which participants are obligated to participate in physical activity as an element of the play. The Nintendo Wii, for example, with particular gadgets, requires users to be physically active in order to complete certain game objectives. Although some games cannot be compared to legitimate physical activity, such as sports, it has been demonstrated that they result in higher energy consumption, especially in comparison to non-active and passive games [23].

FIGURE 4.3   SPARX game for mental therapy [24].

4.1.5 Types of Health Awareness Games for Children

4.1.5.1 Serious Games

Serious games, which are games with fun activities and useful goals like education and experience, have grabbed the interest of the world's largest gaming communities. They have been used effectively in a variety of disciplines. Games in education, health, simulation, environmental sciences, ecology, rehabilitation, business economics, tourism, marketing and psychiatry can be found [25]. These games improve reasoning, prediction and problem-solving abilities. Because serious games can also be used for teaching and modeling, the military sector was the first to be very involved with them. The United Nations had also created several serious games to raise awareness about important global concerns including the effects of the war in Darfur (e.g., "Darfur is Dying"), Cytomegalovirus (e.g., fast car game), as well as the COVID19 disease outbreak [26].

4.1.5.2 Arcade Games

The 1970s and 1980s were when the ultimate examples of arcade gaming arrived. Moreover, as desktop and PlayStation games have become more popular, the popularity of these gameplays started to decline. Arcade games have recurring frameworks that necessitate kinesthetic awareness and quick actions concerning time. Arcade-style games have been typically organized by stages, highest score, or tasks, and lack the idea of glory struggles [27]. As a result, their use can end up making the games simpler and more appealing, keeping the participant involved for a prolonged period.

A category in the gaming community is characterized as a sequence of interface standards and game element experiences of a group of labels. Furthermore, a game category is considered as a particular cluster of games that are linked by comparable game design attributes. Moreover, categories are decided by the games, user interface, key dynamics, a common struggle, as well as other attributes, instead of the channel of the game or the actual information of the game [28]. Furthermore, categories can include a variety of games, which tends to result in more particular classifications known as sub-categories. The most successful video game categories are action-based games, sports-based games and cooperative learning games. Educational video games seem to be distinct sorts of games that are designed purely to launch fresh ideas through interactive media, and are thus categorized as instructional-oriented gaming platforms or instructional activity arcade games [29].

Arcade games seemed to be identified in public areas and were controlled by coins input into the machine. Electromechanical games, pinball and computer games are instances of arcade games [30].

4.1.5.3 Diabetes Prevention Video Games

Every year, more than 79,000 children are diagnosed with diabetes. They consult medical clinics and health centers on a routine basis to initiate examinations such as blood sugar tests, weight and eye diseases [31]. The expense of follow-up care is incredibly high, and techniques should be implemented to mitigate the stress on health care facilities and clinics [32]. Afterward, we must devise a strategy to minimize diabetics' reliance on medical practitioners even more, while also motivating them to take charge of their health. Diabetes is a lifelong condition that can cause other signs such as vision loss, organ damage, social isolation and psychological problems. Diabetes disease management necessitates long-term tracking of blood sugar, nutrition, insulin consumption and lifestyle [33]. Educational video games are a method for increasing diabetes knowledge and understanding. Such games can affect diabetic children's behavior, enhance their knowledge, and inspire individuals to eat a healthy diet, take part in physical tasks, and self-manage their well-being. Diabetic children need to learn about the disorder and adopt a new way of life to be helped [34].

It is essential to understand the relationship between diabetes, food consumption and physical exercise. In the research, several diabetes games have already been created [35].

4.1.5.4 Obesity Awareness Games

Child obesity has become a major concern in New Zealand's public health system, and around the globe. According to the World Health Organization (WHO), the amount of extremely obese young children nearly doubled from 32 million in 1990 to 1.4 billion in 2016 [36], [32].

Furthermore, if current trends continue, the worldwide number of children who are overweight could reach 70 million [37]. Trying to combat this problem early in a child's growth will undoubtedly be very advantageous; failure to intervene means that children who are obese will stay that way as they reach maturity into adolescence and then adulthood [38]. According to the latest statistics from the American National Center for Health, 80% of the overweight children in America will continue to stay obese into their adult years. Obesity has an impact not just on the well-being of a child, but also on their learning and standard of living [39].

Obesity is linked to more frequent episodes of obstructive sleep apnea (stopped breathing while sleeping), musculoskeletal disorders (pain in joints, ligaments, tendons, nerves and muscle structures that support the body) and asthma [40]. Obesity is also influenced by psychological issues, which can lead to low self-esteem in children, and which can eventually lead to depression. Obesity puts children at risk because they are more likely to inherit health and mental problems during childhood and in the rest of their life. Obesity that persists into adult years increases the risk of developing long-term diseases like diabetes, heart disease, chronic pain, mental illness and some cancers, which is why intervention measures should be implemented early in a child's life [41].

One of the factors that contribute to child obesity is a lack of education for children about having a healthy diet and recognizing the consequences of those decisions. It is indeed essential for children to eat a balanced diet instead of high-energy foods with no nutritional content [42].

4.1.5.5 Mental Therapy Games

A variety of therapeutic games for children are based on mental therapy. Mental therapy is a method of treatment that has been shown to successfully treat a range of mental health issues in the overall population. An intellectual therapy program, in a nutshell, describes the link between opinions, emotions, and behavior [43]. Individuals are then questioned to recognize and verify their negative thinking, as well as to explain the relationship between the opinions, their own emotions, and their behavior. Individual basic assumptions are also described as the possible cause of (negative) thoughts and emotions, and people who receive mental therapy are encouraged to rethink their troublesome core faith [44].

4.1.5.6   Oral Health Awareness Games

Games can be used to replicate crucial moments involving danger, the decision-making process, or the availability of innovative abilities [45]. They can be used in learning to simulate scenarios where the use of understanding is required for the game's progression. Teaching and learning can be merged in certain situations to recreate scenarios in which you gain knowledge for use in human psychology on societal issues. As a result, oral health is a vital area in which games and simulation models can be used [46].

Implants Training, established by the company BreakAway in collaboration with the Medical College of Georgia in the United States, is an instance of a serious game for dental health. This game imitates situations and simulates patients through the use of enjoyment [47]. The simulated service users can be selected at random, letting students communicate with them by inquiring regarding their health information and virtually inspecting them. The virtual service users in the game have different characteristics to look like individuals, and the students can implement the diagnosis based on the psychological, physical and sentimental characteristics of patients. Despite the three-dimensional setting, this game doesn't employ a haptic machine for communication [48].

4.1.5.7   Smoking Prevention Games

There is a need for an effective tool to show the effects of smoking among primary school children to encourage them to avoid smoking. Nowadays, strategies on the risks of smoking are conducted through forms of media such as broadcast TV, radio and newspaper articles, but their effect is less efficient since the percentage of smokers within and between primary school children is rising [49]. This is directly attributable to the campaigns lack of use of persuasive technologies including smartphones and interactive tasks [50].

Although most schoolchildren love playing simulators and many own handheld platforms, a mobile game using persuasive technology could be used to distribute awareness about the risks of smoking to them. Persuasive technology can also be used to persuade and socially affect users to update their thoughts and behaviors. Using persuasive technology fundamentals to create a mobile game for young kids should be taken into account, since it has the potential to mobilize and change children's attitudes and behaviors [51].

In this chapter, firstly I have analyzed previous studies in the domain of health awareness among children using video games. Video games have played a crucial role in developing awareness regarding multiple health domains, such as hygiene awareness games, obesity awareness games, physical activity awareness games, diabetes awareness games, mental therapy games, oral hygiene games, smoke prevention games, etc. Afterward, a novel oral hygiene game "ToothPower" is proposed about oral health through play and learning techniques that raise awareness about oral hygiene. The game's main avatar will be a tooth icon that will run and chase healthy food while ignoring unhealthy food.

The paper consists of five categories i.e., (i) Background of the Study, (ii) Proposed Solution and Methodology, (iii) Results of the Experiments, (iv) Discussion and (v) Conclusion and Future Works.

4.1.6 PROBLEM STATEMENT

Nowadays, an unhealthy lifestyle is very common among children. Most of them eat unhealthy food and don't play enough physical games which results in various health issues among them. Common health problems because of an unhealthy lifestyle are obesity, mental pressure, heart problems, diabetes, etc. Moreover, most children in today's age spend hours on mobile games and desktop games. Such games can be beneficial for children to play and learn simultaneously. To overcome these health problems, children must be involved in game-based learning programs to adopt a healthy lifestyle and avoid unhealthy lifestyles.

4.1.7 OBJECTIVES

- To identify the impact of games on children to improve health awareness.
- To develop a game for oral hygiene awareness.

4.2 BACKGROUND STUDY

Health awareness in children using video games is a wide field. Learning a healthy lifestyle through playing is very attractive for children. They not only enjoy playing video games, but also learn healthy habits through them. Numerous researchers developed multiple video games in this domain.

Carmen Soler et al. developed a mobile-based game "Molarcropolis", consisting of a puzzle theme, to educate the children about oral hygiene practices and the risks of not maintaining their oral hygiene. While playing the game, the player took the character of Strico bacteria and Philusa bacteria, the two main characters of the game. The game was developed using Flash CS3 and Action Script 3 was used for writing the game. To observe the effectiveness of the developed game, a sample of children aged between 11 years to 20 years was specified. Lastly, the game proved effective and educating [46].

Mohammad Hafiz bin Ismail et al. worked on school children smoking with persuasive technology. The main aim of their work was to provide a new medium for campaiging on the danger of smoking and proposed a conceptual framework based on Bandura's "Social Learning Theory and Fogg" Behavior Model. Their work applied the principles of persuasive technology immersive with the mobile game to influence children's behavior to reject smoking at an early age (Loureiro et al., 2010).

David Farrell et al. worked on the e-bug computer game based on hygiene practices regarding handwashing and respiratory problems. This game consists of several levels that promote knowledge, delivered by way of game mechanics. This game was designed for the target ages of children i.e., junior school children aged 9–12 years and senior school children aged 13–15 years. The research was made in three schools which involved 62 children of schools and 1,700 online players to evaluate the results of the game. However, an evaluation demonstrated statically significant effectiveness as the knowledge of the students changed (Farrell et al., 2011).

Lamboglia et al. reviewed the previous research work in the domain of video games and physical activities. The goal of this systematic review was to look at how gaming can be used as a key approach in the struggle against childhood overweight and obesity. Knowledge was obtained from multiple database systems in English and French, using the search terms "e-games," "exergames," "exergaming," "new generation of video games," "active video games," "energy expenditure," "body composition" and "physical activity." The inclusion criteria were met by nine articles. Exergaming has been shown to continue increasing activity levels, energy expended, maximum possible oxygen uptake, heartbeat and the ratio of physical exercise participation, as well as to decrease waist size and physically inactive screen time [12].

Herbert F. Rodrigues and Ana Maria G. Valença developed a serious oral hygiene game TouchBrush to integrate multiple oral hygiene games through haptic systems. For the development of the game the process model "Serious Game Unified Process" was adapted which was presented by Rodrigues. The process model was based on the computational aspects of the game and contents of the game and integrated multiple areas of different games. The game was developed using the Adobe Flash platform and was compatible with Windows, Linux, Android and IOS operating systems. Moreover, the game was more usable and effective than previous versions [47].

I. H. Pouw developed a game for monitoring and guiding diabetic children regarding carbohydrate intake. Firstly, an online survey was made to check their prior knowledge about carbohydrates. In pilot testing, primary school children were selected to evaluate the effectiveness of the game. Afterward, the real test was examined through diabetic children. They filled out a written test before and after playing the game. The game was proved effective and entertaining [33].

Andreea Molnar and Patty Kostkova in their work presented a mobile game "MicrobeQuest", aimed to make children between the age of 9–12-years-old aware of microbiology including antibiotic use and hand hygiene. The main challenge of their application was to transfer the desktop version into the mobile app. An assessment was also made on the educational evaluation basis and the impacts of the game (Molnar & Kostkova, 2015).

Nilufar Baghaei et al. worked on developing a diabetes awareness game (Diabetic Mario Bros) to engage diabetic children in a healthy lifestyle. The developed game was android-based. The effectiveness of the game was evaluated through the heuristic method by introducing four heuristics. The game proved effective and usable [35].

Andreea Molnar and Patty Kostkova in their research work presented an educational game "Interactive Digital Storytelling". The authors presented an Interactive Digital Storytelling (IDS) conceptual model that illustrated the IDS logic limitation in their research. To enable the development of IDS-based games, this has been executed in a video game, and a writing and editing tool was developed. Through using suggested generators and content development tools, they formed numerous IDS-based games. Furthermore, in their study, they served as case reports. They also discussed some of the difficulties experienced after integrating the games and the solutions to overcome those (Molnar & Kostkova, 2016).

Simon Mayr et al. in their research work presented a game framework Aquamorras for obese children, using their decisions and experiences for achieving awareness regarding obesity and a healthy lifestyle. The presented game was developed using the Unity Game Engine, as well as 2D hand-made drawing, and was compatible with android and IOS operating systems. It was the first game that not only made children aware of obesity, but also treated obese children. The game proved effective and informative [36].

Sotiris Michael et al. reviewed the mobile video games that were available for obese children and also presented their own game, NutritionBuddy. The objective of the game was to make children aware of healthy and nutritious food and prevent them from becoming obese. The developed game was based on platform games and used a database to store the data. The users of the game included children aged between 8 years to 12 years and proved effective and informative [42].

Dias et al. reviewed the literature to examine the efficiency of video games for obese children. The studies were gathered from various database systems. The descriptors were video games and obesity, with game design as the key phrase. Criteria for inclusion included studies classified as Randomized Clinical Trials written in English, Spanish or French and involving children as subjects. In the initial search, 2,722 studies have been found, with six remaining in the final sample. The papers emphasized encouraging behavioral changes in players, such as increased physical activity and better eating habits. According to the studies, games are indeed a promising option for promoting positive people coping with child obesity [52, p. 1].

Hidde van der Meulen et al. mentioned their continued development of the design and assessment of Pesky gNATs, a cognitive behavioral therapy computer game, in their study. Furthermore, concepts were used to explain complicated concepts such as negative automatic thoughts (NAT) and basic assumptions: prickly living beings identified as Pesky gNATs affected a child's patterns of thinking. Pesky gNATs was a 3D game that used the same analogies as before. The game was developed to use something during the treatment program. The study sample comprised of children ranging in age from 9 to 17 years. The game was both appealing and usable [43].

Thomas Bailey et al. made an android-based game FoodKnight for controlling obesity among children. The game was more interesting than typical teaching methods. Moreover, the game could engage the children in different activities for making physical movements and losing weight. Major platforms for developing the game were Android Studio, Unity and Bitnami Parse API. The game used many healthy and unhealthy food icons to teach children that they should consume healthy food and avoid unhealthy food. The FoodKnight has a feature which counts the steps of registered persons. For the effectiveness of the game, a survey was conducted among children, parents and adults. The overall rating of the effectiveness was 4.1 out of 5 points [53].

Lisa Afonso et al. developed an android-based application Fammeal for children aged 3–6 years and their caregivers for promoting healthy eating habits. They presented a framework to aid in the management and cure of children in health care facilities. The development was based on a creative platform when tried to compare someone else because: (a) it guided both caregivers and children, and tended to involve them via customizing and gaming techniques; (b) it was intended to prevent or assist the care by trying to promote guardian's' abilities to alter their way of life; and (c) it was designed for use in medical centers. The game has proven usable and effective [40].

Ju-Hui Wu et al. worked on examining the effectiveness of a serious game Virtual Dental Clinic (VDS) through a three-step process including development of the game, validation of the game and application of the game. Both qualitative and quantitative analyses were observed to record the effectiveness of the game. The testing sample consisted of 92 persons including clerkship students. The game was developed using Unity Game Engine and proved effective [45]. Table 4.1 compares the technologies used and addresses health areas in the above-mentioned papers.

4.3   METHODOLOGY

The proposed model is about making children aware of dental hygiene practices. Children spend most of their time on video games so they can learn hygiene practices while playing video games. For this purpose, the conceptual model of a novel oral hygiene game "ToothPower" is developed.

4.3.1   Research Gap

Recent studies in the domain of healthcare awareness among children through video games are mostly scenario-based. Health awareness video games discussed in the background study were based on puzzle themes, story-telling themes and clinic scenario themes. In this study, the run and grab theme has been used. It is a novel approach that has not been discussed in previous studies. The character of the game will run and grab healthy food for promoting oral hygiene practices among children.

4.3.2   Significance of the Study

In the era of modern technology, every individual is exposed to internet facilities and provided services belonging in every domain of daily life. In the domain of human health care, specific applications are designed and developed by the experts for the ease of mankind. The correct use of technology in the domain of health care systems is beneficial for both developing and developed countries. Developing countries like Pakistan and India are now applying today's technology like the online system as online healthcare apps such as oral health care applications specifically designed for oral hygiene awareness in the community and especially to children by giving them knowledge regarding oral hygiene practices through video games.

The present study promotes awareness specifically to children through video games by raising unhygienic and hygienic oral practices. Tooth care is a necessary

TABLE 4.1
Comparison of Technologies, Parameters Achieved and Health Issues

Sr. No.	Authors	Title	Technology Used	Parameters Achieved	Addressed Health Area
1	Soler et al. (2009)	Molarcropolis: a mobile persuasive game to raise oral health and dental hygiene awareness	Flash CS3 and Action script 3	Effectiveness	Oral Care
2	Loureiro et al. (2010)	Smoking Habits: Like Father, Like Son, Like Mother, Like Daughter?	Persuasive Technology	Effectiveness	Smoking Prevention
3	Farrell et al. (2011)	Computer games to teach hygiene: an evaluation of the e-Bug junior game	Android Studio	Effectiveness	Hygiene
4	Lamboglia et al. (2013)	Exergaming as a Strategic Tool in the Fight against Childhood Obesity: A Systematic Review	Survey Based	Effectiveness	Physical Activity
5	Rodrigues et al. (2014)	Applying Haptic Systems in Serious Games: A Game for Adult's Oral Hygiene Education.	Adobe Flash	Effectiveness	Hygiene
6	Molnar &Kostkova (2015)	Mind the Gap: From Desktop to App	Android Studio	Usability Effectiveness	Hygiene
7	Pouw (2015)	You are what you eat: Serious gaming for type 1 diabetic persons	Android Studio	Effectiveness	Diabetes
8	Molnar &Kostkova, (2016)	Interactive Digital Storytelling Based Educational Games: Formalise, Author, Play, Educate and Enjoy!–The Edugames4all Project Framework	IDS Game	Effectiveness	Mental Health
9	Baghaei et al. (2016)	Diabetic Mario: Designing and Evaluating Mobile Games for Diabetes Education	Android Studio	Effectiveness	Diabetes
10	Mayr et al. (2016)	A serious game to treat childhood obesity	Unity Game Engine	Effectiveness, Usability	Obesity
11	Michael et al. (2018)	NutritionBuddy: a Childhood Obesity Serious Game	Platform Games	Effectiveness	Obesity

(Continued)

TABLE 4.1 (Continued)
Comparison of Technologies, Parameters Achieved and Health Issues

Sr. No.	Authors	Title	Technology Used	Parameters Achieved	Addressed Health Area
12	Dias et al. (2018)	Serious games as an educational strategy to control childhood obesity: a systematic literature review	Survey Based	Effectiveness	Obesity
13	Van Der Meulen et al. (2018)	Including End-Users in Evaluating and Designing a Game that Supports Child Mental Health	Android Studio	Effectiveness, Usability	Mental Health
14	Thomas Bailey et al. (2019)	FoodKnight: A mobile educational game and analyses of obesity awareness in children	Android Studio, Unity, Bitnam Parse API	Effectiveness	Obesity
15	Afonso et al. (2020)	Fammeal: A Gamified Mobile Application for Parents and Children to Help Healthcare Centers Treat Childhood Obesity	Android Studio	Effectiveness, Usability	Obesity
16	Wu et al. (2021)	Development and questionnaire-based evaluation of virtual dental clinic: a serious game for training dental students	Unity Game Engine	Effectiveness, Usability	Oral Care

part of human life, so this study will create awareness among younger students and children through the presented model. In the present time of the pandemic of COVID-19, children are highly exposed to video games and spend hours playing video games. Therefore, this oral hygiene game must be helpful for children's awareness and in grooming their hygiene practices.

4.3.3   PROBLEM STATEMENT

In these hectic times in the world, health is much more important than the development of the country. Technology will always provide benefits. An unhealthy lifestyle is very common among children and youngsters. Most of the community have an unhealthy food intake like junk food, and do not take part in physical exercises i.e., play enough physical games which results in various health issues among children. Common health problems because of an unhealthy lifestyle are tooth decay, muscle weakness, joint pain, obesity, mental pressure, heart problems, diabetes, etc. Most of today's children spend hours on mobile and desktop games. We must lead the children to the right path by educating them through internet use by developing education games such as oral care. Such games can be beneficial for children to play and learn simultaneously. To overcome these health problems, children must be involved in game-based learning programs to adopt a healthy lifestyle and avoid unhealthy lifestyles.

4.3.4   SCOPE OF STUDY

The proposed framework is based on the dental care game "ToothPower," which raises awareness about oral hygiene. The game is based on educational content for children. "ToothPower" is a novel idea that will enable students to learn and play together. Nowadays, children are used to consuming unhealthy and junk food. Moreover, they spend hours playing video games. Therefore, "ToothPower" as a video game can play a very important role in teaching children oral hygiene practices.

4.3.5   OBJECTIVES

*   To identify the impact of games on children to improve health awareness.
*   To develop a game for oral hygiene awareness among children.
*   To enable children to play and learn together.

4.3.6   PROPOSED MODEL

The proposed framework is based on the dental care game "ToothPower," which raises awareness about oral hygiene. The game is based on educational content for children. The game's main avatar is a tooth icon that will run and chase healthy food while ignoring unhealthy food. For unhealthy foods, there would be icons of chocolates, candies, doughnuts and soda, and for healthy foods, there would be icons of apples, milk and bread. When the Tooth icon consumes any unhealthy food, the tooth begins to decay, and the tooth's life would be reduced. On the other hand, when the tooth icon consumes nutritious foods, it will earn points. Some power boosters, such as toothbrushes, mouthwash and dental floss, will also be added to the framework to

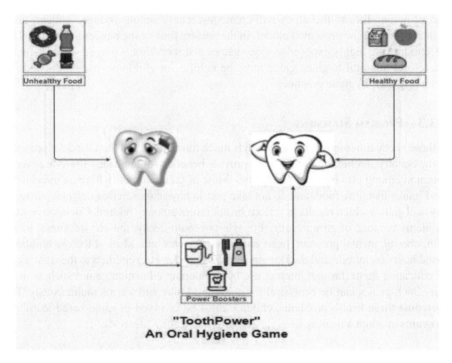

FIGURE 4.4   Proposed model of "ToothPower".

prevent tooth decay and save the tooth's life. Figure 4.4 illustrates the flow and conceptual design of the "ToothPower" game.

"Moqups" (Figure 4.5) is used for the development of the conceptual model of "ToothPower". "Moqups" is a prototyping tool that is available online as well

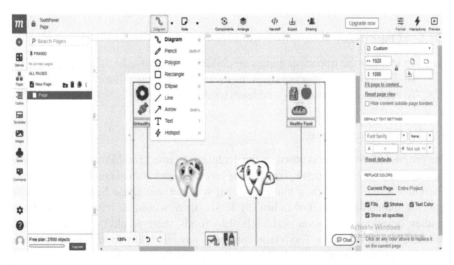

FIGURE 4.5   "Moqups" web-based prototyping tool for developing the conceptual model.

as offline for PCs. In this research work, the online web version of "Moqups" has been used.

4.3.7 UCD Model

The conceptual design of "ToothPower" is based on user-centric design (Figure 4.6). It is comprised of multiple phases including:

- **Research**: In the first phase, research has been done on previous studies in the domain of health awareness among children through video games. Numerous methodologies and design ideas were explored to design "ToothPower".
- **Scope**: In this phase, the context of the use of "ToothPower" was examined. The scope phase proved that "ToothPower" would be beneficial in making children aware of oral hygiene. Moreover, children would be able to learn and play together.
- **Analyze**: This phase analyzed user requirements and examined whether those requirements are feasible, acceptable and affordable or not.
- **Design**: In the design phase, all possible designs were carried out, and the best suitable design for "ToothPower" was chosen.
- **Prototype**: In this phase, the conceptual prototype of "ToothPower" was developed using the "Moqups" web version. The developed prototype was then evaluated to mitigate possible errors in the prototype.
- **Delivery**: At the final stage, the developed prototype of "ToothPower" was delivered.

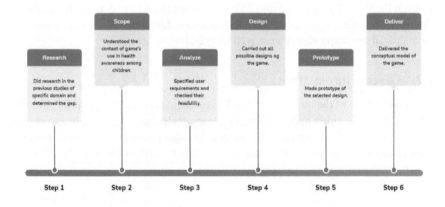

FIGURE 4.6 UCD model of "ToothPower".

4.4 RESULTS AND DISCUSSION

This study aimed to evaluate the impact of gamification on children's health awareness. In the previous chapter, the research methodology of the study has been discussed. In this chapter, the outcomes of the study have been discussed based on data gathered from the survey questionnaires. The result outcomes discussed were based on the questionnaire design, which was divided into three sections. The first section of the questionnaire contains the personal information of the respondent. The second section contains general information regarding the use of video games, and children's interests in the type of educational video games including puzzle games, human health-related games and creative games. The third section contains oral hygiene awareness information among children. A total number of 120 survey questionnaires were conducted during this research.

4.4.1 PERSONAL INFORMATION

These findings and discussion chapter are based on the results of a completed questionnaire survey from children aged 5 to 16 years; the first section covers the respondent's personal information, such as their name, age and gender. Questions about personal information are listed next.

4.4.1.1 Age and Gender

The first question was about personal information related to the respondent's age and gender (Figure 4.7). The ages of the respondents were further divided into age groups of 5 to 8 years, 9 to 12 years and 13 to 16 years. The results of the questionnaire showed the age group of the respondents; 25% were from the 5 to 8 year group, 57% were from the 9 to 12 year group and 38% were from the 13 to 16 group (Figure 4.8). In the case of gender, most of the respondents were female (70%) and at least 30% were male. All the respondents were well aware of video games.

4.4.2 GENERAL INFORMATION

The second section of the questionnaire asks broad questions about children's interest in different types of video games. Creative games, instructional games, health-related games and puzzle-solving games were among the titles provided. The questionnaire's second component included questions about using mobile or tablet devices to play

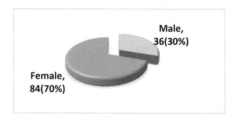

FIGURE 4.7 Percentage data.

FIGURE 4.8   Age data.

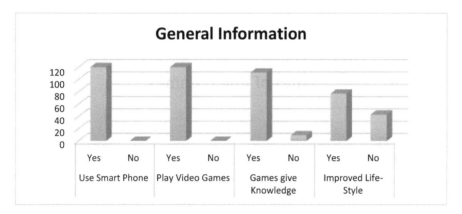

FIGURE 4.9   Lifestyle data.

video games, game frequency (how often they play games per day), children's interest in gaming types, and obtaining information from video games. The results of this part revealed that everyone in the household owns a smartphone, with 120 respondents owning either a smartphone or a computer to play video games. While 111 out of 120 people agreed with the statement about instructional video games increasing awareness and providing information, 77% of respondents agreed that their lifestyle has improved (Figure 4.9), whereas 43% of respondents disagreed with the statement. According to the findings of the survey, youngsters spent 69% of their time playing video games for two to three hours per day, 38% for three to five hours, and 13% percent for five to seven hours per day (Figures 4.10 and 4.11). This contributes to the success of the research project.

4.4.3   AWARENESS LEVEL IN CHILDREN REGARDING ORAL HYGIENE

This section dealt with children's levels of awareness, particularly with oral hygiene (Figure 4.12). The findings revealed that 87% of respondents agreed with the question concerning tooth decay being an illness, while 33% disagreed. Only 21 respondents clean their teeth twice a day, while the remaining 99 respondents brush their teeth once a day. A very high 93% of respondents do not prefer to attend dentists or dental

FIGURE 4.10   Hourly data.

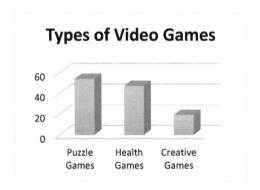

FIGURE 4.11   Game activity data.

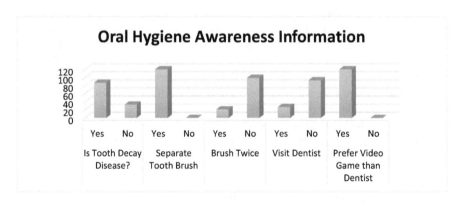

FIGURE 4.12   Oral hygiene data.

clinics, while only 27% prefer to do so regularly. According to this study, 100% of children would rather play instructional video games than go to the dentist.

4.5 CONCLUSION

The impact of gamification on children's health awareness was examined in this chapter. Using video games, numerous research studies in various aspects of healthcare awareness have been conducted. Children of this generation are good with technology and spend hours playing video games. As a result, instructional video games can be an excellent source of health knowledge among today's youth. A survey was undertaken to see how gamification affected children's health awareness. The study's sample included 120 children aged 5 to 15, with 70% of females and 30% of males participating. The findings revealed that the vast majority of respondents (100%) preferred to increase health knowledge through gamification over visiting doctors for medical care. A recommended framework for improving healthy behaviors among youngsters was presented as an innovative oral hygiene game called "ToothPower." Only the conceptual design of "ToothPower" is discussed in this study, which will be handled in the future.

REFERENCES

[1] T. Baranowski, R. Buday, D. I. Thompson, and J. Baranowski, "Playing for Real," Am. J. Prev. Med., vol. 34, no. 1, pp. 74–82. e10, Jan. 2008, doi: 10.1016/j.amepre.2007.09.027

[2] S. L. Nijhof et al., "Healthy Play, Better Coping: The Importance of Play for the Development of Children in Health and Disease," Neurosci. Biobehav. Rev., vol. 95, pp. 421–429, Dec. 2018, doi: 10.1016/j.neubiorev.2018.09.024

[3] A G. LeBlanc et al., "Active Video Games and Health Indicators in Children and Youth: A Systematic Review," PLoS ONE, vol. 8, no. 6, p. e65351, Jun. 2013, doi: 10.1371/journal.pone.0065351

[4] A. M. Moosa, N. Al-Maadeed, M. Saleh, S. A. Al-Maadeed, and J. M. Aljaam, "Designing a Mobile Serious Game for Raising Awareness of Diabetic Children," IEEE Access, vol. 8, pp. 222876–222889, 2020, doi: 10.1109/ACCESS.2020.3043840

[5] College of Medicine–University of Diyala–Diyala–Iraq, M. Faiq Jamel, W. Saadoon Shafiq, and S. Sh Abdul-wahid, "The Impact of Computer–Based Video-games Devices on the Children's Health," Diyala J. Med., vol. 16, no. 1, pp. 94–100, Apr. 2019, doi: 10.26505/DJM.16014200801

[6] A. Molnar and P. Kostkova, "Learning about Hygiene and Antibiotic Resistance through Mobile Games: Evaluation of Learning Effectiveness," in Proceedings of the 2018 International Conference on Digital Health, Lyon France, Apr. 2018, pp. 95–99. doi: 10.1145/3194658.3194682

[7] J. McDougall and M. J. Duncan, "Children, video games and physical activity: An exploratory study," Int. J. Disabil. Hum. Dev., vol. 7, no. 1, Jan. 2008, doi: 10.1515/IJDHD.2008.7.1.89

[8] A. S. Luet al., "The Narrative Impact of Active Video Games on Physical Activity Among Children: A Feasibility Study," J. Med. Internet Res., vol. 18, no. 10, p. e272, Oct. 2016, doi: 10.2196/jmir.6538

[9]   C. O'Donovan, E. F. Roche, and J. Hussey, "The energy cost of playing active video games in children with obesity and children of a healthy weight: Energy cost of active video game play," Pediatr. Obes., vol. 9, no. 4, pp. 310–317, Aug. 2014, doi: 10.1111/j.2047-6310.2013.00172. x

[10] F. Laamarti, M. Eid, and A. El Saddik, "An Overview of Serious Games," Int. J. Comput. Games Technol., vol. 2014, pp. 1–15, 2014, doi: 10.1155/2014/358152

[11] L. Lanningham-Foster, R. C. Foster, S. K. McCrady, T. B. Jensen, N. Mitre, and J. A. Levine, "Activity-Promoting Video Games and Increased Energy Expenditure," J. Pediatr., vol. 154, no. 6, pp. 819–823, Jun. 2009, doi: 10.1016/j.jpeds.2009.01.009

[12] C. M. G. F. Lamboglia et al., "Exergaming as a Strategic Tool in the Fight against Childhood Obesity: A Systematic Review," J. Obes., vol. 2013, pp. 1–8, 2013, doi: 10.1155/2013/438364

[13] A. Tlili et al., "Game-Based Learning for Learners with Disabilities—What Is Next? A Systematic Literature Review from the Activity Theory Perspective," Front. Psychol., vol. 12, 2022, Accessed: Feb. 13, 2022. [Online]. Available at: www.frontiersin.org/article/10.3389/fpsyg.2021.814691

[14] K. B. Adamo, J. A. Rutherford, and G. S. Goldfield, "Effects of interactive video game cycling on overweight and obese adolescent health," Appl. Physiol. Nutr. Metab., vol. 35, no. 6, pp. 805–815, Dec. 2010, doi: 10.1139/H10-078

[15] P. M. Kato, "Video Games in Health Care: Closing the Gap," Rev. Gen. Psychol., vol. 14, no. 2, pp. 113–121, Jun. 2010, doi: 10.1037/a0019441.

[16] V. Unnithan, W. Houser, and B. Fernhall, "Evaluation of the Energy Cost of Playing a Dance Simulation Video Game in Overweight and Non-Overweight Children and Adolescents," Int. J. Sports Med., vol. 27, no. 10, pp. 804–809, Oct. 2006, doi: 10.1055/s-2005-872964

[17] B. H. Aboul-Enein, J. Bernstein, and J. Kruk, "Fruits and vegetables embedded in classic video games: a health-promoting potential?" Int. J. Food Sci. Nutr., vol. 70, no. 3, pp. 377–385, Apr. 2019, doi: 10.1080/09637486.2018.1513995

[18] Ndb. Admin, "Ten Benefits of Playing Video Games–NewsDeskBlog.Com," Sep. 12, 2020. https://newsdeskblog.com/benefits-of-playing-video-games/ (accessed Feb. 13, 2022).

[19] C. Ndulue and R. Orji, "Gender and the Effectiveness of a Persuasive Game for Disease Awareness Targeted at the African Audience," in Adjunct Proceedings of the 29th ACM Conference on User Modeling, Adaptation and Personalization, Utrecht Netherlands, Jun. 2021, pp. 318–324. doi: 10.1145/3450614.3464625

[20] D. Farrell et al., "Computer games to teach hygiene: an evaluation of the e-Bug junior game," J. Antimicrob. Chemother., vol. 66, no. Supplement 5, pp. v39–v44, Jun. 2011, doi: 10.1093/jac/dkr122

[21] W. Peng, J. C. Crouse, and J.-H. Lin, "XX(X) 1–22 © 2012 Society for Public Health Education Reprints and permission: sagepub.com/journalsPermissions.nav DOI: 10.1177/1090198112444956 http://heb.sagepub.com," Health Educ., p. 22.

[22] R. Orji and K. Moffatt, "Persuasive technology for health and wellness: State-of-the-art and emerging trends," Health Informatics J., vol. 24, no. 1, pp. 66–91, Mar. 2018, doi: 10.1177/1460458216650979

[23] A. M. Morais, H. F. Rodrigues, L. S. Machado, and A. M. G. Valença, "Planning Serious Games: Adapting Approaches for Development," in Entertainment for Education. Digital Techniques and Systems, vol. 6249, X.   Springer Berlin Heidelberg, 2010, pp. 385–394. doi: 10.1007/978-3-642-14533-9_40

[24] "SPARX app review | Health Navigator NZ." www.healthnavigator.org.nz/apps/s/sparx/ (accessed Feb. 13, 2022).

[25] A. L. Penko and J. E. Barkley, "Motivation and Physiologic Responses of Playing a Physically Interactive Video Game Relative to a Sedentary Alternative in Children," Ann. Behav. Med., vol. 39, no. 2, pp. 162–169, May 2010, doi: 10.1007/s12160-010-9164-x

[26] E. Brox, L. Fernandez-Luque, and T. Tøllefsen, "Healthy Gaming–Video Game Design to promote Health," Appl. Clin. Inform., vol. 02, no. 02, pp. 128–142, 2011, doi: 10.4338/ACI-2010-10-R-0060

[27] M. J. M. Chin APaw, W. M. Jacobs, E. P. G. Vaessen, S. Titze, and W. van Mechelen, "The motivation of children to play an active video game," J. Sci. Med. Sport, vol. 11, no. 2, pp. 163–166, Apr. 2008, doi: 10.1016/j.jsams.2007.06.001

[28] L. Kauhanen et al., "Active video games to promote physical activity in children with cancer: a randomized clinical trial with follow-up," BMC Pediatr., vol. 14, no. 1, p. 94, Dec. 2014, doi: 10.1186/1471-2431-14-94

[29] L. Foley and R. Maddison, "Use of Active Video Games to Increase Physical Activity in Children: A (Virtual) Reality?" Pediatr. Exerc. Sci., vol. 22, no. 1, pp. 7–20, Feb. 2010, doi: 10.1123/pes.22.1.7

[30] C. Ni Mhurchu, R. Maddison, Y. Jiang, A. Jull, H. Prapavessis, and A. Rodgers, "Couch potatoes to jumping beans: A pilot study of the effect of active video games on physical activity in children," Int. J. Behav. Nutr. Phys. Act., vol. 5, no. 1, p. 8, 2008, doi: 10.1186/1479-5868-5-8

[31] G. Chen, N. Baghaei, A. Sarrafzadeh, C. Manford, S. Marshall, and G. Court, "Designing games to educate diabetic children," in Proceedings of the 23rd Australian Computer-Human Interaction Conference on–OzCHI'11, Canberra, Australia, 2011, pp. 72–75. doi: 10.1145/2071536.2071546

[32] T. B. Talbot, "Virtual Reality and Interactive Gaming Technology for Obese and Diabetic Children: Is Military Medical Technology Applicable?" J. Diabetes Sci. Technol., vol. 5, no. 2, pp. 234–238, Mar. 2011, doi: 10.1177/193229681100500205

[33] I. H. Pouw, "You are what you eat: Serious gaming for type 1 diabetic persons," p. 54, (2015) (Master's thesis, University of Twente).

[34] M. Belghali, Y. Statsenko, and A. Al-Za'abi, "Improving Serious Games to Tackle Childhood Obesity," Front. Psychol., vol. 12, p. 657289, May 2021, doi: 10.3389/fpsyg.2021.657289

[35] N. Baghaei, D. Nandigam, J. Casey, A. Direito, and R. Maddison, "Diabetic Mario: Designing and Evaluating Mobile Games for Diabetes Education," Games Health J., vol. 5, no. 4, pp. 270–278, Aug. 2016, doi: 10.1089/g4h.2015.0038

[36] S. Mayr, L. Ledit, P. Petta, C. Eichenberg, and B. Sindelar, "A serious game to treat childhood obesity," in 2016 IEEE International Conference on Serious Games and Applications for Health (SeGAH), Orlando, FL, USA, May 2016, pp. 1–6. doi: 10.1109/SeGAH.2016.7586258

[37] F. Gonçalves, V. Carvalho, and D. Matos, "Design and Development of a Serious Game to Fight Childhood Obesity," Int. J. Mechatron. Appl. Mech., vol. 1, no. 4, Nov. 2018, doi: 10.17683/ijomam/issue4.35

[38] J. D. Latner, J. K. Rosewall, and M. B. Simmonds, "Childhood obesity stigma: Association with television, videogame, and magazine exposure," Body Image, vol. 4, no. 2, pp. 147–155, Jun. 2007, doi: 10.1016/j.bodyim.2007.03.002

[39] D. Thompson, "What Serious Video Games Can Offer Child Obesity Prevention," JMIR Serious Games, vol. 2, no. 2, p. e8, Jul. 2014,doi: 10.2196/games.3480

[40] L. Afonso et al., "Fammeal: A Gamified Mobile Application for Parents and Children to Help Healthcare Centers Treat Childhood Obesity," IEEE Trans. Games, vol. 12, no. 4, pp. 351–360, Dec. 2020, doi: 10.1109/TG.2020.3015804

[41] N. G. del Rio, C. S. G. Gonzalez, R. M. Gonzalez, V. N. Adelantado, P. T. Delgado, and Y. B. Fleitas, "Gamified educational programme for childhood obesity," in 2018 IEEE Global Engineering Education Conference (EDUCON), Tenerife, Apr. 2018, pp. 1962–1668. doi: 10.1109/EDUCON.2018.8363476

[42] S. Michael, P. Katrakazas, O. Petronoulou, A. Anastasiou, D. Iliopoulou, and D. Dionisios Koutsouris, "NutritionBuddy: a Childhood Obesity Serious Game," in 2018 Second World Conference on Smart Trends in Systems, Security and Sustainability (WorldS4), London, Oct. 2018, pp. 5–8. doi: 10.1109/WorldS4.2018.8611473

[43] H. van der Meulen, G. O'Reilly, and D. Coyle, "Including End-Users in Evaluating and Designing a Game that Supports Child Mental Health," in Proceedings of the 2018 Annual Symposium on Computer-Human Interaction in Play Companion Extended Abstracts, Melbourne VIC Australia, Oct. 2018, pp. 655–659. doi: 10.1145/3270316.3271546

[44] O. A. David, R. Predatu, and R. A. I. Cardoş, "Effectiveness of the REThink therapeutic online video game in promoting mental health in children and adolescents," Internet Interv., vol. 25, p. 100391, Sep. 2021, doi: 10.1016/j.invent.2021.100391

[45] J.-H. Wu, J.-K. Du, and C.-Y. Lee, "Development and questionnaire-based evaluation of virtual dental clinic: a serious game for training dental students," Med. Educ. Online, vol. 26, no. 1, p.1983927, Jan. 2021, doi: 10.1080/10872981.2021.1983927

[46] C. Soler, A. Zacarías, and A. Lucero, "Molarcropolis: a mobile persuasive game to raise oral health and dental hygiene awareness," in Proceedings of the International Conference on Advances in Computer Entertainment Technology–ACE '09, Athens, Greece, 2009, p. 388. doi: 10.1145/1690388.1690468

[47] H. F. Rodrigues, L. S. Machado, and A. M. G. Valença, "Applying Haptic Systems in Serious Games: A Game for Adult's Oral Hygiene Education," J. Interact. Syst., vol. 5, no. 1, p. 1, Jul. 2014, doi: 10.5753/jis.2014.639

[48] A. Hegde, V. Gopikrishna, S. B. Kulkarni, N. N. Bhaskar, S. K. Gangadharappa, and J. Jacob, "Recharging Smiles: Strategies for Using Mobile Phones in Dental Public Health," J. Mob. Technol. Med., vol. 7, no. 2, pp. 60–65, Oct. 2018, doi: 10.7309/jmtm.7.2.9

[49] E. Biddiss and J. Irwin, "Active Video Games to Promote Physical Activity in Children and Youth: A Systematic Review," Arch. Pediatr. Adolesc. Med., vol.164, no. 7, Jul. 2010, doi: 10.1001/archpediatrics.2010.104

[50] M. L. Loureiro, A. Sanz-de-Galdeano, and D. Vuri, "Smoking Habits: Like Father, Like Son, Like Mother, Like Daughter? *: Smoking habits," Oxf. Bull. Econ. Stat., vol. 72, no. 6, pp. 717–743, Dec. 2010, doi: 10.1111/j.1468-0084.2010.00603. x

[51] A. Molnar and P. Kostkova, "Interactive Digital Storytelling Based Educational Games: Formalise, Author, Play, Educate and Enjoy!–The Edugames4all Project Framework," in Transactions on Edutainment XII, vol. 9292, Z. Pan, A. D.Cheok, W. Müller, and M. Zhang, Eds. Berlin, Heidelberg: Springer, Berlin, Heidelberg, 2016, pp. 1–20. doi: 10.1007/978-3-662-50544-1_1

5 Road Lane Detection System

Muhammad Khurram Zahur Bajwa[1] and Muhammad Arif[2]
[1]University of Central Punjab, Lahore, Pakistan,
[2]Superior University Lahore, Pakistan

5.1 INTRODUCTION

According to the Pakistan Bureau of Statistics "Traffic accidents kill an average of 15 people in Pakistan daily" [1], which is quite horrific. The accident is often a result of a driver's bad judgement regarding the traffic environment. ADAS (advanced driver-assistance systems) in this regard are very helpful, as they create possibilities in which accidents can be avoided or their effect can be minimized. ADAS can be defined as the link between driver, vehicle and traffic environment which helps the driver in life-saving decisions smartly, efficiently and very quickly.

Self-driving cars in the near past have received a lot of attention and lane detection is considered as one of the key objectives. Once lanes are detected, there are many applications such as assisting the driver so that if he loses his focus while driving, there must be someone who can alert the driver by different alarms and feedback messages. Furthermore, detection of lane boundaries plays a vital role in avoiding accidents and informing the driver if some other vehicle has entered its lane or not. In this regard, an algorithm was developed for the detection of lanes using a video feed from a mobile phone. The final product was developed in the form of an android app that could be installed in any android phone, which can then be attached to the wind-screen of the vehicle, capturing the video feed from the front view. The app will detect lanes from that feed and show them to the driver in real-time.

5.2 LITERATURE REVIEW (FIGURE 5.1)

5.2.1 Lane Detection

In lane detection there is the problem of locating road markings without prior knowledge of the road geometry [2]. That's why this area is highly active in research, and several algorithms have been introduced over the years [3],[4],[5],[6]. Driving assistance systems and the research of autonomous vehicles require information about lanes to decide the driving routes of vehicles [7]. Vision systems are used to install in vehicles to detect lanes. Furthermore, lane detection plays a vital role in obstacle detection, lane changing, avoiding accidents and monitoring driver's intent.

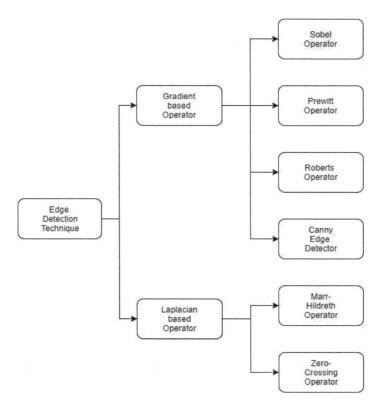

FIGURE 5.1   Literature Review 1[3].

Although after so much research in this field this is a problem that might seem simple but applying these algorithms on varying road conditions is still quite a challenge.

Edge detection and Hough line transformation play a key role in identifying lanes, a brief description for both follows.

5.2.1.1 Edge Detection

Any sudden change which causes discontinuities in an image is called an edge [3]. In an image, edge or boundary play a vital role, as with the help of edge detection filters, useless information can be removed. Hence, it saves a lot of extra processing before it happens. Edge detectors are categorized in two main branches.

5.2.1.1.1 Gradient-Based Operator

As is obvious from the name, these are first order operators, as edges are detected in this technique by extracting local maxima and minima [4]. The gradient of an image can be calculated by the following formula:

$$\partial I(x, y) \quad \partial I(x, y)$$

$$\nabla I = x + y \quad \partial x \partial y$$

Where ∂x is the gradient in x direction () and ∂y is the gradient in y direction (Gy), The magnitude of the gradient can be calculated as $|G| = ((G_y)^2 + (G_x)^2)^{1/2}$ and the direction of the gradient vector can be found as $theta = tan^{-1}[Gy/Gx]$.

The most commonly used list of gradient based operators are:

- Prewitt Operator.
- Sobel Operator.
- Robert's Cross Operator.
- Canny Edge Detector.

Prewitt Operator

The Prewitt Operator is a 3×3 matrix, which determines the value of the pixel gradient with the eight points around it [2]. Moreover, this filter is basically used for horizontal or vertical edge detection. To get the resultant output, both the filters are added together such that $P = (Px2 + Py2)1/2$, where P is the final pixel value, while Px and Py are two template convolutions. It is normally used to remove low frequency noise.

$$\begin{pmatrix} 1 & 1 & 1 \\ 0 & 0 & 0 \\ -1 & -1 & -1 \end{pmatrix} \qquad \begin{pmatrix} -1 & 0 & 1 \\ -1 & 0 & 1 \\ -1 & 0 & 1 \end{pmatrix}$$

Horizontal   Vertical

Sobel Operator

The Sobel Operator is just the same as the Prewitt Operator, as it's also a derivative mask which detects edges in both vertical and horizontal directions. It performs a 2-D spatial gradient measurement on an image and so emphasizes regions of high spatial frequency that correspond to edges (Wang, Yong Chuan and Chong Qing, 2009). This is also a pair of 3×3 convolutional kernels.

$$\begin{pmatrix} 1 & 2 & 1 \\ 0 & 0 & 0 \\ -1 & -2 & -1 \end{pmatrix} \qquad \begin{pmatrix} -1 & 0 & 1 \\ -2 & 0 & 2 \\ -1 & 0 & 1 \end{pmatrix}$$

Horizontal   Vertical

This operator is specially designed to make the filter more sensitive to horizontal and vertical edges. The ultimate result in this case is the summation of horizontal and vertical kernels such that $P = (Px2 + Py2)1/2$, where Px and Py are convolutional along horizontal and vertical dimensions and P is the resultant value of the pixel.

Robert Cross Operator

The Robert Cross Operator is quite a simple but fast 2D spatial gradient convolutional based operator used for detecting edges in vertical and horizontal dimensions in digital images. High spatial regions which are often edges can be easily extracted by applying this filter. As it consists of two 2×2 kernels it takes grayscale images as input to work on [8].

$$\begin{pmatrix} 1 & 0 \\ 0 & -1 \end{pmatrix} \qquad \begin{pmatrix} 0 & 1 \\ -1 & 0 \end{pmatrix}$$

Horizontal   Vertical

Canny Edge Detector

The Canny Edge Detector (Figure 5.2) is based on three basic objectives: low error rate, good localization, and single edge point response [9,10]. These can be segmented down to six steps.

  i.   Gaussian filtering for removing noise.
  ii. Extracting the derivatives using the Sobel Operator.
  iii. Calculating gradient magnitude and direction to filter out desired gradients.
  iv. Applying an image thinning process also known as Non-Maximum Suppression (NMS).
  v.   Applying double thresholds such as high and low thresholding, to filter out required gradients.
  vi. Applying Hysteresis thresholding to connect weak edges with strong edges.

This technique is widely used for edge detection of gray-scaled images due to its flexibility of a double thresholding step which can be modified easily according to the user's requirement.

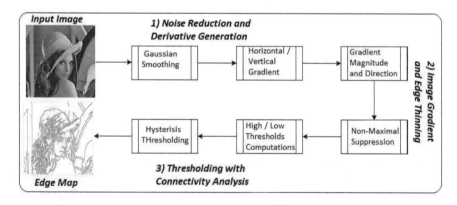

FIGURE 5.2   Image processing.

5.2.1.1.2 Laplacian Edge Detector

Unlike gradient based operators, these operators basically use second order differentials to find edges in the images which are also known as second order operators. Moreover, these are isotropic filters which means these are invariant to rotation such that the result will be the same whether the filter is applied directly or at 90° [11]. The second order derivative for Laplacian would be:

$$\nabla 2f = \partial\partial 2xf2 + \partial\partial y2f2.$$

The following two are the most commonly used edge detectors in the Laplacian edge detector domain:

1. Marr-Hildreth
2. Zero Cross

Marr-Hildreth

Being a Laplacian based operator, Marr-Hildreth uses a second order differential to extract edges at different scales [12]. Firstly, Gaussian filtering is applied to smoothen the image such that response to noise is improved and then the differential of that smoothed image is taken, due to which it's also known as Laplacian of Gaussian (LoG).

Zero Cross

This operator is basically used to look for Laplacian where it crosses zero such that when the sign of Laplacian is changed these points can be referred to as edges. In a nutshell, these are points where huge differentials are found or points where the intensity of the image changes rapidly [13]. In general, Laplacian of Gaussian (LoG) is applied first then at those zero crossings where the LoG is quite influential, smoothing is applied. That's how a limited number of zero crossings can be achieved with higher scale smoothing alongside.

5.2.1.2 Hough Line Transformation

Hough line transformation is an interesting technique based on feature extraction used to detect straight lines by a voting procedure introduced by Richard O. Duda and Peter E. Hart as "Use of the Hough Transformation to Detect Lines and Curves in Pictures" [14]. The equation of a line in the xy-cartesian plane can be written as $y = ax + b$, which can be represented by a single point in a, b space and *vice a versa* as shown in Figure 5.3.

In Hough Line Transformation, lines are represented in a polar system, thus the equation of a line becomes $r = xcos\theta + ysin\theta$ where r is the smallest distance between the origin and the line and θ is the angle between the smallest distance between the line and x-axis elaborated in Figure 5.4.

If the image space contains several lines intersecting on a single point, then their corresponding points in the Hough space will form a sinusoidal, [15] as shown in Figure 5.5.

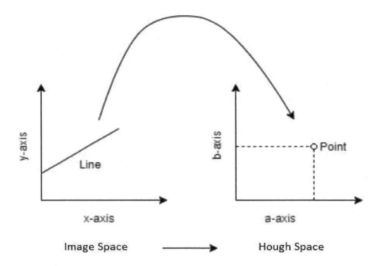

FIGURE 5.3   Hough Line plot.

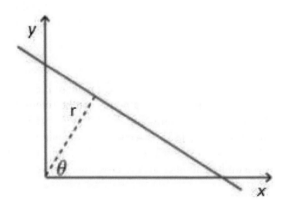

FIGURE 5.4   Hough Line plot.

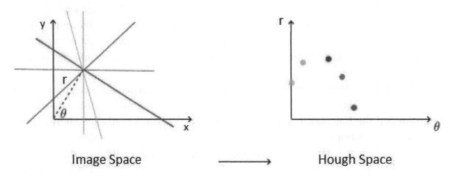

FIGURE 5.5   Hough space plot.

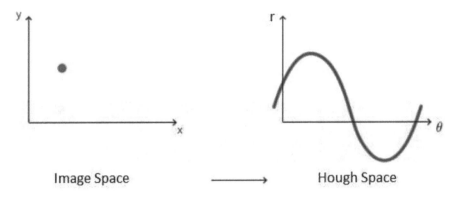

Image Space   ⟶   Hough Space

FIGURE 5.6   Hough Line plot.

This means that if an infinite number of lines are being drawn in an image space which intersect at a single point, then a complete sinusoidal waveform will appear in the Hough space. In other words, a single point in an image space will be equal to a sinusoidal in the Hough space, illustrated in Figure 5.6 [15].

Hence, if more sinusoidals intersect at the same point in a Hough space, then this illustrates that more points in the image space are representing a line. In short, a threshold representing the minimum number of intersections can be set to detect a line.

5.3   REQUIREMENT AND ANALYSIS

As the whole project was to develop an algorithm and there was no hardware directly involved in it, thus the requirements for this project are totally algorithm based:

- In order to develop the algorithm, first of all python was selected as a programming language, which upon discussion with the supervisor was changed to C++ , because C++ is a lower-level language as compared to python. Hence, in order to develop the algorithm in an efficient way, it was a compulsory step.
- For camera calibration, the Zhang camera calibration tool for MATLAB was used, as it was considered as the most accurate source for calibrating the camera.
- As it's a vision-based project, and image processing (Figure 5.7) was used extensively in its development, OpenCV was used as a reference library for using different computer vision algorithms already included in this library.
- While developing the algorithm, edge detection was the first key step, and in order to deliver this step efficiently, many edge detection techniques were tested using MATLAB. The one with more informative results was selected, namely canny edge detector. One can easily analyze from Figure 5.7, that canny is better than its competitors which are required for detecting Hough Lines for further processing.

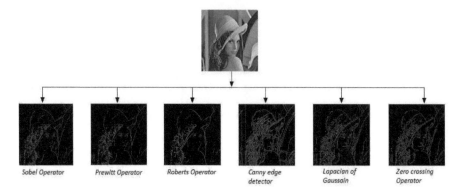

FIGURE 5.7   Image Operator.

5.4   DESIGN AND IMPLEMENTATION

5.4.1   ALGORITHM

In order to attain the objective, i.e., to detect the lane markers on the road, initially an algorithm was developed. To get an abstract view of that approach, the flowchart shown in Figure 5.8 would definitely help.

5.4.1.1   Step 1–Parsing Video to Frames

First of all, the video obtained from the camera feed is parsed to frames. This is because a video is nothing but a set of continuous frames. Furthermore, in the field of computer vision, an individual frame is considered as a matrix that we play with to get the desired results, thus to perform image processing on any video, some individual frames are used to perform the required operation as was done here.

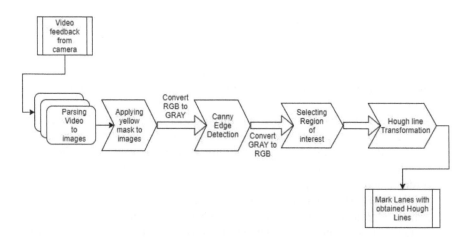

FIGURE 5.8   Methodology–Flowchart of Initial Approach.

5.4.1.2   Step 2–Applying Yellow Mask

As the color used for marking lanes over the whole world is either white or yellow, a filter was developed in such a way that it filters out all the colors from the frame except for yellow or white to ensure that we're not losing the critical information as well as removing undesired information which would eventually decrease the time in future processing as it is always easier to process smaller amounts of information as compared to larger.

In practical terms, as an image is basically a 3-channel (BGR) matrix when stored in the memory of a computer using Open cv libraries, a range of colors from{0, 190, 190 (yellow)} to {255, 255, 255 (white)} was allowed to be left behind and the rest of the range of colors was turned black.

5.4.1.3   Step 3–Conversion of Actual Frame (Colored) to Gray Scaled Image

This step is not a successor to the last step (Step 2–Applying yellow mask) but is certainly a predecessor to Step 4–Edge Detection (Canny edge detector).

The fundamental reason behind the concept of gray scale conversion of images is to get a simpler form of image in which that image can be represented, which is again to analyze and process the operations on the images easily. Thus, a 3-channel input image was converted to a single channel frame to make things easier for Step 4–Edge Detection (Canny edge detector).

5.4.1.4   Step 4–Edge Detection (Canny Edge Detector)

In order to detect the lane markers, the ultimate goal of the whole exercise, the first landmark was definitely edge detection, because on the basis of these edges further processing was possible. Edge detectors, as explained in detail earlier in Section 5.4.1.1, are basically in search of change in values in consecutive pixels.

After trying all sorts of edge detectors (explained in Section 5.4.1.1), canny edge detector was selected, in which 100 and 200 were set to be the lower and upper thresholds for detecting the edge in the given frame. These thresholds were set in such a way that if the difference between gray-scaled values ranging from 0–255 becomes less than 100 then don't consider that boundary of two pixels as an edge, while if the difference between two consecutive pixels gray-scaled values is more than 200 then there is a definitely an edge. On the other hand, if the difference is within the range of the upper and lower threshold and that very pixel is attached to some other edge in its surroundings, then consider it as an edge.

That's how edges of all the lane markers become clear enough for further processing.

5.4.1.5   Step 5–Extracting the Region of Interest

So far, all the required edges from the input frame are obtained, along with some unnecessary ones which should be removed but which exist naturally. Thus, to get rid of them, the best possible way so far was to shrink or crop down the region which was of interest. Therefore, an equilateral triangular region from the bottom half of the input frame was cropped and selected for further processing, which helped to avoid unwanted information such as trees and sky.

In practical terms, to crop the image, a binary image (matrix) was initialized in such a way that it contained white color in its bottom half in the shape of an equilateral triangle, and the rest of the region was black. Then bit-wise of that binary image was performed with the input frame and the required resultant cropped image was obtained.

5.4.1.6   Step 6–Creating Hough Lines

What does a Hough line mean? To get the answer see Section 5.4.1.2. To create them, an input image with edges defined on every pixel is required. Thus, after getting the Canny edge detector's output, the Hough Lines transformation's algorithm looked for edges in such a way that if at least 50 edges lie on the same line whose minimum length is set to 40 pixels with resolution of six, such that the offset of pixels in a neighbor was set to be six with a maximum of a 3° degree shift, then consider that line to be a proper Hough Line. Furthermore, a last check for maximum line gap between two Hough lines was also set to 50 pixels, as none of the two lane markers in the sample video were found as far away from each other as 50 pixels.

5.4.1.7   Step 7–Removing Unnecessary Hough Lines

So far, a lot of straight lines, including lane markers, are obtained, but without any distinguishing features. The only unnecessary information which was removed so far was that which doesn't lie within the white to yellow color range plus those which lie outside the cropped region. Thus, in order to remove those unnecessary Hough Lines which were still present in the cropped region, a filter was designed such that all vertical and horizontal lines were also removed and only lane makers were left behind.

5.4.1.8   Step 8–Line Fitting

Now, as the only lines left behind are lane lines, first of all these lines were categorized to left or right on the basis of their calculated slopes. Then, the starting and ending points of all the left and right lines were sent separately to make a second order polynomial equation from them using Cramer's rule. As a result, two second degree polynomial line equations were obtained which later on were used to draw and overlay onto the input image in red.

5.4.2   ANDROID APP

The algorithm implemented was in the form of an android application using the video feed from the rear camera of a mobile phone, lanes were detected in real time and displayed on the screen of the phone. The basic interface of the app contains a display of the real time lane detection feed, with a floating button to shift between menu and video feed.

5.4.2.1   Home Screen/UI

The main view in Figure 5.9 is the first screen that appears when the app is opened. This view has the following main features.

FIGURE 5.9   Home Screen/UI for road lane detection (lane detection app working on ring road Lahore).

Video Feed Display

The video feed received from the rear camera of the phone is processed by the algorithm to search for lanes and is displayed on the screen. The boundary of the detection colored in red is filled with a blue shade to clearly display the detected lanes.

Frame Rate Display

On the upper left corner of the display the frame rate of video is displayed in a blue color along with the quality of the video being captured.

Menu Tab

On the right corner of the view a floating tab is displayed. This tab can be used to enter the menu of the application. The menu allows access to further functionalities of the application.

5.4.2.2   Menu View

The menu view is shown in Figure 5.10.

5.4.2.3   Terms and Conditions View

The terms of use view (Figure 5.11) contains the text for terms of use of the app. The view is implemented using web view for proper formatting of the text. The web view contains text in the form of an html page to format the text. At the top left corner of the view a clickable back arrow is displayed to take the user back to the menu view.

5.4.2.4   Privacy Policy View

The privacy policy view (Figure 5.12) is also implemented using the web view. A scroll pan to the right of the view allows the user to scroll the text above and below. A similar arrow in the top left corner of the view allows the user to get back to the menu view.

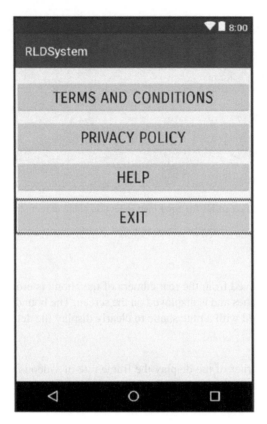

FIGURE 5.10 The menu of the app accessed form the floating button on the main view of the app contains buttons to access further information about the app including help and exit button.

5.4.2.5   Help View

The help view (Figure 5.13) shows the user necessary information regarding the app usage. It also includes information for mounting the phone on to the windscreen of the car. The information is necessary for the user to be able to use the app efficiently. The view also includes a similar back arrow on the top left corner to navigate the app back to menu view.

5.4.2.6   Exit Button

The exit button (Figure 5.14) opens a confirmation view asking the user whether he is sure he wants to exit the app. If the user presses the app the app exits, whereas on pressing "no" the user is redirected to the menu view.

5.5   RESULTS AND DISCUSSION

First of all, the video was parsed into frames. One of those parsed frames is shown in Figure 5.15.

FIGURE 5.11   Terms and conditions view.

Now, in order to detect the lane markers, the next step was to pass Results and Discussions 1 (input frame) through a filter which only allows a range of colors from white to yellow to pass from itself.

Now this image (Figure 5.16) was sent to the canny edge detector for further processing, and the result obtained after applying canny edge detector was as shown in Figure 5.17.

Just to get an idea of how much simpler the canny edge detector's output is, refer to Results and Discussions 5.4 (Figure 5.18), which was the result of applying the canny edge detector directly onto the input image without passing it through a yellow mask (Figure 5.18).

Now it had been settled that applying a yellow mask was indeed a necessity. The region of interest was selected, and the input frame cropped out. In this regard, a bit-wise AND operation was performed between the input frame and Results and Discussions 5.5 (Figure 5.19) to get Results and Discussions 5.6 (Figure 5.20). This step was performed to simplify the process of creating Hough lines.

Thus, all the steps from Sections 5.4.1.2 to 5.4.1.4 were followed by considering Results and Discussions 5.6 (Figure 5.20) as the input frame. After performing all

FIGURE 5.12 Privacy policy view.

those steps, Hough lines were created and overlaid onto input frame Results and Discussions 5.1 (Figure 5.15) as shown in Figure 5.20.

Here one thing becomes very clear that Results and Discussions 5.7 (Figure 5.21) is perfect for the line fitting step. But before any further processing, in order to realize the importance of steps 5.4.1.5 and 5.4.1.2, check the following result which was obtained without performing the above mentioned two steps and thus the output, Results and Discussions 5.8 (Figure 5.22) becomes very difficult to analyze any further.

The final step of the initial approach was to create a second degree polynomial fitted line and overlay that onto the input frame. Thus, the final result after performing step 5.4.1.8 over Results and Discussions 5.7 (Figure 5.21) is shown in Figure 5.22.

This final algorithm was then implemented into an android app. The results of app functioning on the Ring Road of Lahore are shown in Figures 5.23, 5.24 and 5.25.

FIGURE 5.13   Help view.

FIGURE 5.14   Exit view.

FIGURE 5.15   Results and Discussions 1.

FIGURE 5.16   Results and Discussions 2.

FIGURE 5.17   Results and Discussions 3.

FIGURE 5.18   Results and Discussions 4.

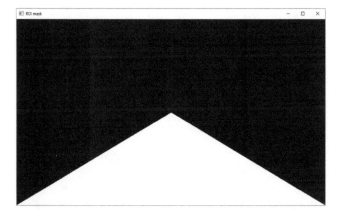

FIGURE 5.19   Results and Discussions 5.

FIGURE 5.20   Results and Discussions 6.

FIGURE 5.21 Results and Discussions 7.

FIGURE 5.22 Results and Discussions 8.

FIGURE 5.23 Results and Discussions 9.

FIGURE 5.24   Results and Discussions 10.

FIGURE 5.25   False Positive Results.

5.6   CONCLUSION

After getting results of the suggested approach mentioned in detail in Section 5.4 and analyzing their results, discussed in Section 5.5, some conclusions were made which are as follows:

In order to perform any sort of image processing or computer vision techniques on video it is mandatory to parse that video into a required number of frames.

- After analyzing Results and Discussions 5.3 and Results and Discussions 5.4, which are basically the results of canny edge detector after applying yellow mask and without yellow mask respectively, it has been concluded that the yellow mask eliminates a lot of useless information for lane marker detection.
- The upper and lower threshold of canny edge detector should be selected in such a manner that a minimum number of edges should be detected to clearly identify a lane marker so that further processing for deleting unwanted information becomes easy.
- Camera calibration plays a vital role in detecting Hough line transformation as it helps in cancelling out the effect of edges caused due to clouds, and minor errors caused due to radial and tangential noise.
- The parameters of Hough line transformation should be set in such a way that a minimum number of lines should come into existence, along with actual lane

marker lines, to simplify further processing efficiently in terms of time complexity, because when there are fewer total lines (of which actual lines are to be identified) then this process would be easier rather than collecting all sort of lines.

- The region of interest is the main thing in this puzzle of identifying lanes. This is very crucial in a lot of perspectives as if the ROI (region of interest) is smaller, it would be computationally efficient and *vice versa*, but at the same time if the ROI is smaller then there is a chance of losing some important information .Thus, ROI should be decided with special precautions, and it should never be hard coded, otherwise the same outcome would occur as happened with the initial approach discussed in Section 5.4.1. That is, it would only be able to identify lanes if there are only two lanes in the selected region, which is very difficult if the same hardcoded region is selected among different sorts of videos.
- Once the ROI is selected and left and right lines are short listed, it is better to make a second degree polynomial equation for each side of a line. This would handle curves if they occurred in the lane markers.
- Finally, it has been established now that the second approach discussed in Section 5.4.2 is better compared to the initial one, as it is more generic in terms of input video, whereas the initial approach is more efficient as less computations are being performed.

5.7   FUTURE WORK RECOMMENDATIONS

In future, an application can be made for navigational purposes which would use the algorithm developed and shared which would be able to track a user's own vehicle's current position using GPS/IMU, find available routes to the user's destination and overlay that route on the lanes identified by the algorithm developed here, and show its run time on the camera feed. A brief description for the added navigational portion that is how GPS and IMU would work is mentioned below.

5.7.1   NAVIGATION

Navigation can be seen as the theory and practice of directing the course of a vehicle from a starting point toward a desired position [16]. A number of applications in the domain of "navigation for autonomous vehicles" have been developed across the globe [17],[18],[19],[20].

The primary objective is to obtain the maximum level of accuracy while determining the current position, which has been resolved to a much better extent by integrating GPS (global positioning system) and IMU (inertial measurement unit) as the accuracy of the navigation systems is directly dependent upon the accuracy of IMU and GPS.

However, possible routes from the user's current position to the user's desired destination can be found using the Google Maps API [21].

5.7.2 GPS

The GPS or "Global Positioning System" is a satellite-based navigation system which calculates position from signals sent through its dedicated set of 24 satellites [22]. The position is calculated by the three segments of information sent from the satellite which are the satellite's number, its position in space and the time at which the signal is sent [23]. The GPS sensors used in most vehicles to track position is actually a low frequency error such that it updates the information at a very slow rate, [24] but smartphones with pre-installed GPS are very accurate within a range of 4.9 m radius (16 ft) [25]. High frequency faults arise when the GPS signals undergo multipath errors [24]. These errors will be removed using Kalman filtering which finds the most optimum averaging factor for each consequent state [25] and by integrating IMU and GPS [24].

5.7.3 IMU

IMU stands for Inertial Measurement Unit. It's a unit that measures inertia [24]. The primary advantage of using an IMU on outdoor land vehicles is that the acceleration, angular rotation, and attitude data is provided at high update rates [24]. This can be quite helpful in calculating the position of the vehicle. As IMU is a high frequency sensor, it can cause misalignment of sensor axes with respect to the local navigation frame at low frequency. That's why GPS is used to remove the low frequency faults generated by IMU.

REFERENCES

[1] 14 Dec 2017. [Online]. Available: https://www.thenews.com.pk/print/58036-traffic-accidents-kill- an-average-15-people-in-pakistan-daily.

[2] W. Dong and Z. Shisheng, "Color Image Recognition Method Based on the Prewitt Operator," 2008 International Conference on Computer Science and Software Engineering, 2018.

[3] M. Bertozzi and A. Broggi, "GOLD: a parallel real-time stereo vision system for generic obstacle and lane detection," IEEE Transactions on Image Processing, vol. 7, no. 1, pp. 62–81, 2018.

[4] C. Kreucher and K. Lakshmanan, "A Driver warning System based on the LOIS Lane detection Algorithm," Proceedings of IEEE International Conference on Intelligent Vehicles, pp. 17–22, 2018.

[5] M. Chen, J. D. and P. T., "AURORA: A Vision-Based Roadway Departure Warning System," in IEEE Conference on Intelligent Robots and Systems, 2014.

[6] B. Ran and H. Xianghong, "Development of A Vision-based Real Time Lane Detection and Tracking System for Intelligent Vehicles," Presented in Transportation Research Board, 2002.

[7] H. Wu, Y. Liu and J. Rong, "A Lane Detection Approach for Driver Assistance," in International Conference on Information Engineering and Computer Science, 2009.

[8] "Feature Detectors–Roberts Cross Edge Detector," Homepages.inf.ed.ac. uk, [Online]. Available: http://homepages.inf.ed.ac.uk/rbf/HIPR2/roberts.htm. [Accessed 15 Dec 2018].

[9]   R. K. Sidhu, "Improved canny edge detector in various color spaces," in Proceedings of 3rd International Conference on Reliability, Infocom Technologies and Optimization, 2014.

[10]   J. Lee, H. Tang and J. Park, "Energy Efficient Canny Edge Detector for Advanced Mobile Vision Applications," IEEE Transactions on Circuits and Systems for Video Technology, 2016.

[11]   S. Singh and R. Singh, "Comparison of various edge detection techniques," in 2015 2nd International Conference on Computing for Sustainable Global Development (INDIACom), 2015.

[12]   "Laplacian & Marr Hildreth Edge Detection–Computer Vision Website Header," Users.ecs.soton.ac.uk, [Online]. Available: http://users.ecs.soton.ac.uk/msn/book/new_demo/laplacian. [Accessed 21 Dec 2018].

[13]   "Feature Detectors–Zero Crossing Detector," Homepages.inf.ed.ac.uk, [Online]. Available: https://homepages.inf.ed.ac.uk/rbf/HIPR2/zeros.htm. [Accessed 13 Dec 2018].

[14]   R. Duda and P. Hart, "Use of the Hough transformation to detect lines and curves in pictures," Communications of the ACM, pp. 11–15, 1972.

[15]   "Hough Lines Transform Explained," ProggBlogg, [Online]. Available: http://tom aszkacmajor.pl/index.php/2017/06/05/hough-lines-transform-explained. [Accessed 12 Dec 2018].

[16]   D. Soares dos Santos, C. Nascimento and W. Cunha, "Autonomous navigation of a small boat using IMU/GPS/digital compass integration," in 2013 IEEE International Systems Conference (SysCon), 2103.

[17]   J. Borenstein, H. Everett, L. Feng and D. Wehe, "Mobile robot positioning sensors and techniques," Robot. Syst., pp. 231–249,2017.

[18]   R. Chatila, S. Lacroix, S. Betge-Brezetz, M. Devy and T. Simeon, "Autonomous mobile robot navigation for planet exploration," IEEE Int. Conf. Robot. Automation, 2016.

[19]   E. Krotkov, R. Simmons and F. Cozman, "Safeguarded teleoperation for lunar rovers: From human factors to field trials," IEEE Int. Conf. Robot. Automat., 2016.

[20]   R. Volpe, J. Balaram and T. Ohm, "The rocky 7 mars rover prototype," IEEE Int. Conf. Robot. Automat., 2016.

[21]   "Google Maps Directions API | Google Developers," Google Developers, [Online]. Available: https://developers.google.com/maps/documentation/directions. [Accessed 17 Dec 2018].

[22]   "An Introduction to GPS–Global Positioning System," Esds.co.in, [Online]. Available: https://www.esds.co.in/blog/an-introduction-to-gps-global positioning-system/#sthash.4UgwVBJR.dpbs.

[23]   "Introduction to Global Positioning Systems GPS," Aqua.wisc.edu, [Online]. Available: https://aqua.wisc.edu/CPR/Default.aspx?tabid=80.

[24]   Sukkarieh and Nebot, "A high integrity IMU/GPS navigation loop for autonomous land vehicle applications," IEEE Transactions on Robotics and Automation, pp. 572–578, 1999.

[25]   v. Diggelen, Frank and Enge, "The World's first GPS MOOC and Worldwide Laboratory using Smartphones," Proceedings of the 28th International Technical Meeting of The Satellite Division of the Institute of Navigation (ION GNSS+ 2015), pp. 361–369,2015.

6 Stock Price Prediction Using Artificial Intelligence Based on LSTM–Deep Learning Model

Honey Habib, Gautam Siddharth Kashyap, Nazia Tabassum and Tabrez Nafis
SEST, Jamia Hamdard, New Delhi, India

6.1 INTRODUCTION

Artificial intelligence (AI) is already changing our economy, we refer to Artificial Intelligence (AI) not only as a technology for reasoning, planning, learning and processing, but we also refer to the ability to move and manipulate objects. This relates to research on Artificial Intelligence (AI) with Cyber Physical Systems (CPS). By Cyber Physical Systems (CPS) (Radanliev et al., 2021), we refer to computerized human or autobot controlling physical processes, where physical processes affect computations and *vice versa*. One example is replacing 70% of an order in Wall Street from human to autobots or algorithms, because we are now living in the age of artificial intelligence (AI). One major replacement is going to be predicting the stock market and its prices, because it has been a long discussed topic. Much research has been done and is still going on and progressing day-by-day because it is one of the most challenging tasks to be able to control or predict the movement of the market. With the help of Artificial Intelligence (AI) it is now possible.

In the past decades, there has been an increasing interest in predicting markets among economists, policymakers, academics and market makers. The objective of the proposed work is to study and improve the supervised learning algorithms to predict the stock price. The technical objectives will be implemented in Python. The system must be able to access a list of historical prices. It must calculate the estimated price of stock based on the historical data. It must also provide an instantaneous visualization of the market index.

DOI: 10.1201/9781003190301-6

6.2   PROBLEM STATEMENT

Financial analysts investing in stock markets are not usually aware of the stock market behavior. They face the problem of trading as they do not properly understand which stocks to buy or which stocks to sell in order to attain more profits. In today's world, all the information pertaining to the stock market is available for all to access. Analyzing all this information individually or manually is tremendously difficult. As such, automation of the process is required. This is where data mining techniques can help. Understanding the analysis of numerical time series gives close results, intelligent investors use machine learning techniques to predict stock market behavior. This allows financial analysts to foresee the behavior of the stock that they are interested in, and thus act accordingly. The challenge of this project is to accurately predict the future high value of a given stock across a given period of time in the future. For this project I will use a **Long Short Term Memory network** (usually just called **"LSTMs"**) to predict the high price of one of the Tata group's shares (Tata Steel) using a dataset of historical prices. The input to our system will be a historical data price from Yahoo finance and the entire system will be implemented in Python language using open-source libraries. Hence, it will effectively be a zero-cost system, summarized as:

1. Explore stock prices.
2. Implement a basic model using linear regression.
3. Implement LSTM using keras library.
4. Compare the results and submit the report.

6.3   METHODOLOGY

As mentioned in Section 6.2, the goal of this work is to develop a predictive framework for forecasting the highest price movement of the stock. We will collect the historical price data during the period from 02 January 2012 until 06 May 2021.This is a series of data points indexed in time order or a time series. For ease of reproducibility and reusability, all data was pulled from Yahoo Finance. Particularly, we collected the stock data for the company Tata Steel. The data was collected for every day on which the National Stock Exchange (NSE) was operational during the years 2012 to 2021 (see Figure 6.1).The raw data for each stock consisted of the following variables: (i) date, (ii) open value of the stock, (iii) high value of the stock, (iv) low value of the stock, (v) close value of the stock, and (vi) volume of the stock (vii) close values of stock traded on a given day.

For the purpose of this research what matters is the high price of a stock at a particular date, and I do not need any other features or columns. Therefore, I removed all other columns at the data pre-processing step and only used two columns, date and high price. To visualize the data, I have used the matplotlib library. I have plotted the high stock price of the data from 2012 to 2021 with the number of items (number of days) available.

Figure 6.2 is the snapshot of the plotted data.

Date	High	Low	Open	Close	Volume	Adj Close
2012-01-02	329.646881	316.403839	321.929718	324.978455	4036645.0	261.415100
2012-01-03	346.605591	327.931946	328.694153	344.747742	6112021.0	277.317596
2012-01-04	350.130707	339.460052	346.796143	346.748505	5721689.0	278.927094
2012-01-05	353.941650	342.413544	347.748871	345.462311	4381464.0	277.892487
2012-01-06	350.416534	333.648376	342.032440	346.462677	4779047.0	278.697113
...	...	...	...	...	...	...
2021-04-30	1052.599976	1011.099976	1024.000000	1034.000000	28129738.0	1034.000000
2021-05-03	1069.000000	1018.500000	1031.949951	1064.750000	26484100.0	1064.750000
2021-05-04	1086.650024	1057.550049	1074.449951	1063.849976	24961628.0	1063.849976
2021-05-05	1088.349976	1047.000000	1084.000000	1070.150024	19249839.0	1070.150024
2021-05-06	1129.000000	1042.500000	1055.000000	1100.900024	46434537.0	1100.900024

2299 rows × 6 columns

FIGURE 6.1 Tata Steel historical price dataset.

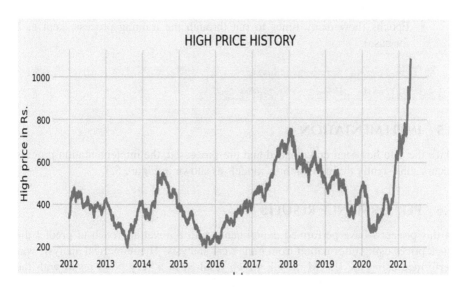

FIGURE 6.2 Tata steel high price plot (x-axis: year, y-axis: high price).

6.4 DEEP LEARNING MODEL

The goal of this project was to study time-series data and explore as many options as possible to accurately predict the stock price. Through my research I came to know about **Recurrent Neural Networks (RNN)** which are used specifically for sequence and pattern learning. They are networks with loops in them, allowing information to persist and thus having the ability to memorize the data accurately. However, Recurrent Neural Networks have a vanishing gradient descent problem which does not allow them to learn from past data as was expected. The remedy for this problem was solved in **Long-Short Term Memory Networks**, usually referred to as **LSTMs.** These are a special kind of RNN, capable of learning long-term dependencies.

In addition to adjusting the architecture of the neural network, the following full set of parameters can be tuned to optimize the prediction model:

- Input Parameters
  - Preprocessing and Normalization (see Data Preprocessing Section).
- Neural Network Architecture
  - Number of Layers (how many layers of nodes in the model).
  - Number of Nodes (how many nodes per layer).
- Training Parameters
  - Training/Test Split (how much of dataset to train versus test model on; kept constant at 80% and 20% for benchmarks and LSTM model).
  - Validation Sets.
  - Batch Size (how many time steps to include during a single training step; kept at 1 for a basic LSTM model).
  - Optimizer Function (which function to optimize by minimizing error; used **"Adam"** throughout).
  - Epochs (how many times to run through the training process; kept at 1 for base).

```
1739/1739 [==============================] - 81s 36ms/step - loss: 0.0021
<keras.callbacks.History at 0x7fdf3138e6d0>
```

6.5 IMPLEMENTATION

Once the data has been downloaded and pre-processed, the implementation process occurs consistently through all three models as shown in Figure 6.3.

6.6 PERFORMANCE RESULTS

In this project I have performed experiments with a novel approach to predict the stock prices using information from numerical analysis. The numerical analysis was performed using the LSTM model, which resulted in a very good result with the Mean Square error of 1.253737263 (Lee, 2001), which is optimized using the Adam optimizer algorithm and loss is calculated using mean square error.

In this project we studied the LSTM model in the area of Deep Learning, RNN, Time Series Forecasting, back propagation Algorithm, Adam Optimizer algorithm and about the Tensor flow library in Python. This project is wholly based on Python Language.

The model performance is shown in Figures 6.4 and 6.5 (Lee, 2001).

6.7 CONCLUSION

While most of the previous research in this field concentrated on techniques to forecast stock price based on historical numerical data such as past stock trends, there is not much research put into the textual analysis side of it. News and media have a huge influence on human beings and the decisions we take. Also, fluctuations in the

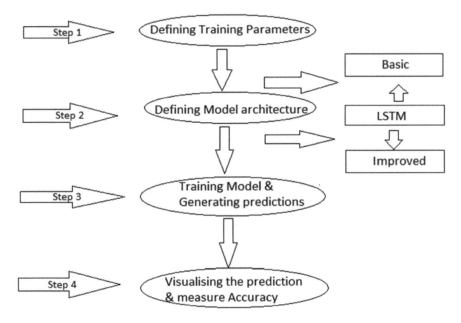

FIGURE 6.3 Implementation entity relationship diagram.

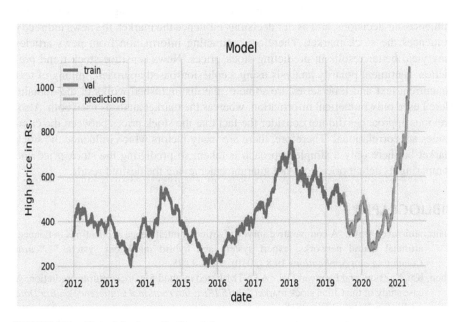

FIGURE 6.4 Plot of final result of model.

	High	predictions
Date		
2019-06-25	499.799988	506.804657
2019-06-26	512.299988	507.220917
2019-06-27	516.450012	509.431122
2019-06-28	515.650024	512.777771
2019-07-01	514.849976	516.051331
...	...	...
2021-04-30	1052.599976	954.524231
2021-05-03	1069.000000	975.280640
2021-05-04	1086.650024	996.063416
2021-05-05	1088.349976	1016.109802
2021-05-06	1129.000000	1032.519897

460 rows × 2 columns

FIGURE 6.5   Predicted high price.

stock market are a result of the trading activities of human beings. As news articles influence our decisions, and as our decisions influence the market, the news indirectly influences the stock market. Therefore, extracting information from news articles may yield better results in predicting stock prices. News sensitive stock trend prediction, sentiment polarity analysis using a cohesion-based approach, mining of text concurrent text and time series are some of the distinguished works in the domain. Here I used only numerical information, whereas the market analysts used both. Also, previous approaches did not consider the fact that the stock prices between the companies are correlational. Therefore, there are many factors which influence the stock market but here only a simple approach is taken, so predicting the stock price and comparing its actual price does not guarantee achieving the desired result.

BIBLIOGRAPHY

Bahrammirzaee, Arash. "A comparative survey of artificial intelligence applications in finance: artificial neural networks, expert system and hybrid intelligent systems." *Neural Computing and Applications* 19.8 (2010): 1165–1195.

Chen, Kai, Yi Zhou, and Fangyan Dai. "A LSTM-based method for stock returns prediction: A case study of the China stock market." *2015 IEEE International Conference on Big Data (IEEE Big Data)*. IEEE, 2015.

Denil, Misha, et al. "Predicting parameters in deep learning." *Advances in Neural Information Processing Systems* 26 (2013).

Farshadfar, Zahra, and Marcel Prokopczuk. "Improving stock return forecasting by deep learning algorithm." *Advances in Mathematical Finance and Applications* 4.3 (2019): 1–13.

Goodfellow, Ian, Yoshua Bengio, and Aaron Courville. *Deep learning*. MIT Press, 2016.

Gulli, Antonio, and Sujit Pal. *Deep learning with Keras*. Packt Publishing, 2017.

Kamalov, Firuz, Linda Smail, and Ikhlaas Gurrib. "Forecasting with deep learning: S&P 500 index." *2020 13th International Symposium on Computational Intelligence and Design (ISCID)*. IEEE, 2020.

Krollner, Bjoern, Bruce J. Vanstone, and Gavin R. Finnie. "Financial time series forecasting with machine learning techniques: A survey." *ESANN*, 2010.

Lee, J. W. (2001, June). "Stock price prediction using reinforcement learning." In *2001 IEEE International Symposium on Industrial Electronics Proceedings* (Cat. No. 01TH8570) (Vol. 1, pp. 690–695). IEEE 2001.

Li, Audeliano Wolian, and Guilherme Sousa Bastos. "Stock market forecasting using deep learning and technical analysis: a systematic review." *IEEE Access* 8 (2020): 185232–185242.

Mahmoud, Amal, and Ammar Mohammed. "A survey on deep learning for time-series forecasting." *Machine Learning and Big Data Analytics Paradigms: Analysis, Applications and Challenges*. Springer, Cham, 2021, pp.365–392.

Mehtab, Sidra, Jaydip Sen, and Abhishek Dutta. "Stock price prediction using machine learning and LSTM-based deep learning models." *Symposium on Machine Learning and Metaheuristics Algorithms, and Applications*. Springer, Singapore, 2020.

Mokhtari, Sohrab, Kang K. Yen, and Jin Liu. "Effectiveness of artificial intelligence in stock market prediction based on machine learning." *arXiv preprint arXiv:2107.01031* (2021).

Radanliev, P., D. De Roure, M. Van Kleek, *et al.* "Artificial intelligence in cyber physical systems." *AI &Soc* 36 (2021), 783–796.

Ray, R., P. Khandelwal, and B. Baranidharan. "A survey on stock market prediction using artificial intelligence techniques." *2018 International Conference on Smart Systems and Inventive Technology (ICSSIT)*, 2018, pp. 594–598, doi: 10.1109/ICSSIT.2018.8748680.

Singh, Ritika, and Shashi Srivastava. "Stock prediction using deep learning." *Multimedia Tools and Applications* 76.18 (2017): 18569–18584.

Shahi, Tej Bahadur, *et al.* "Stock price forecasting with deep learning: A comparative study." *Mathematics* 8.9 (2020): 1441.

Sunny, Md Arif Istiake, Mirza Mohd Shahriar Maswood, and Abdullah G. Alharbi. "Deep learning-based stock price prediction using LSTM and bi-directional LSTM model." *2020 2nd Novel Intelligent and Leading Emerging Sciences Conference (NILES)*. IEEE, 2020.

Vijh, M., D. Chandola, V. A. Tikkiwal, and A. Kumar, "Stock closing price prediction using machine learning techniques." *Procedia Computer Science* 167 (2020): 599–606.

7 Blockchain in Healthcare

Mohd Talib Akhtar and Tabrez Nafis
Jamia Hamdard

7.1 INTRODUCTION

Computers can learn without being explicitly programmed; this technology is known as Machine Learning. It is also called a subset of Artificial Intelligence. It learns from the experience and patterns using the dataset. Machine Learning is actively being used today, perhaps in every field such as medical, business, weather forecasting, etc. We programmed the machine by giving the precursory data and machine predicts the diseases The term Machine learning was initially used by Arthur Samuel, a pioneer of Artificial Intelligence at IBM in 1959. There is a plethora of ML algorithms which are often designated by their type of output, i.e., classification and regression, and their type of data, i.e., supervised and unsupervised.

Machine learning is used in every sector now from business to sports, hence it is important to know about its algorithms, and each algorithm has its own importance in the world of AI, and its own drawbacks too.

We will also be looking at blockchain and how it can be useful in the medical field; using blockchain we can reduce data redundancy and provide security and integrity to the patients' data.

In this project, our problem is classification, and we use supervised data. At first, we analyze the data and clean it, if there is any anomaly. We analyze the data to gain the information as much we can, this process is known as Exploratory Data Analysis (EDA). The most important and perplexing part of a ML project is to choose the algorithm for the model. To compare our algorithms, we cleave the dataset into 80% training data and 20% test data and compare the accuracy, sensitivity and specificity of the output.

7.2 PROPOSED METHODOLOGY

The goal of this project is to build a diabetes prediction model which has the best accuracy. In this part we will briefly discuss the steps that we follow to build these machine learning models:

1. Dataset: The data is collected from Kaggle which is named as Heart Disease Dataset. This dataset contains thirteen dependent features and one independent feature.

DOI: 10.1201/9781003190301-7

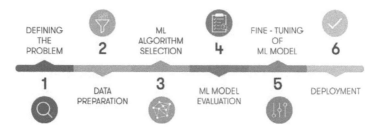

FIGURE 7.1 Workflow algorithms.

2. Data Pre-processing: Data pre-processing is a most important process. Most healthcare related data contains missing values and other impurities that can reduce the effectiveness of data. To improve quality, data pre-processing is carried out.

   a. Missing Values removal–Remove all the instances that have zero (0) as worth. Having zero as worth is not possible. Therefore, this instance is eliminated. Through eliminating irrelevant features/instances we make a feature subset; this process is called features subset selection, it reduces the dimensionality of data and enables faster working.

   b. Splitting of data–After cleaning the data, data is normalized in training and testing the model. When data is split then we train the algorithm on the training data set and keep a test data set aside. This training process will produce the training model based on logic, algorithms and values of the feature in training data. Basically, the aim of normalization is to bring all the attributes to the same scale.

3. Now that your pre-processing is done, the data is ready to be trained and hence, we apply a different Machine Learning algorithm to train this data. We use six algorithms to compare the accuracy, and these are Logistic Regression, Kernel SVM, Naïve Bayes, K-Nearest Neighbor (KNN), XG Boost and Random Forest (see Figure 7.1). We will discuss these algorithms later in this report.

4. After building the Machine Learning Algorithm we checked the accuracy of our model by using the test data on that model.

5. The last step is to deploy our model by using different platforms like Herokuor AWS.

7.2.1 LOGISTIC REGRESSION

Logistic regression is a classification procedure that uses a discrete set of classes to assign observations to. Email spam vs. non-spam, online transaction fraud vs. non-fraud, and tumor malignant vs. benign are some examples of classification issues. To return a probability value, logistic regression modifies its output with the logistic sigmoid function. The algorithm of logistic regression is based on the concept of probability and is used to do predictive analysis.

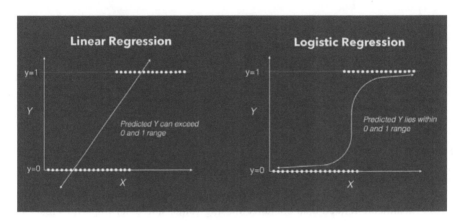

FIGURE 7.2   Linear and logistic regression: what is sigmoid function?

A Logistic Regression model is similar to a Linear Regression model, except that the Logistic Regression uses a more complex cost function, which is known as the "Sigmoid function" or the "logistic function" instead of a linear function (Figure 7.2).

The Sigmoid function is used to convert expected values to probabilities. The function converts any real number into a number between 0 and 1.

$$(x) = \frac{1}{1 + e^{-(x)}}$$

Kernel SVM

SVM techniques are based on a set of mathematical functions known as the kernel. The kernel's job is to take data and turn it into the required format. Different types of kernel functions are used by different SVM algorithms. There are various types of functions that can be used. Linear, nonlinear, polynomial, radial basis function (RBF) and sigmoid are examples.

An example of non-linear data is shown in Figure 7.3.

In this case we cannot find a straight line to separate apples from lemons. Therefore, we have to use Kernel SVM.

The basic idea is that when a data set is inseparable in the current dimensions, add another dimension, maybe that way the data will be separable. Just think about it, the example above is in 2D and it is inseparable, but maybe in 3D there is a gap between the apples and the lemons, maybe there is a level difference, so apples are on level one and lemons are on level two.

7.2.1.2   Mapping from 2D to 3D

Let's assume that we add another dimension called X3. Another important transformation is that in the new dimension the points are organized using the formula $x1^2 + x2^2$. If we plot the plane defined by the $x^2 + y^2$ formula, we will get something like is shown in Figure 7.4.

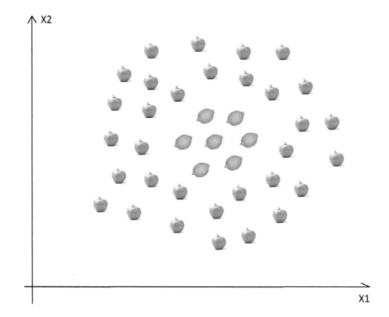

FIGURE 7.3 SVM.

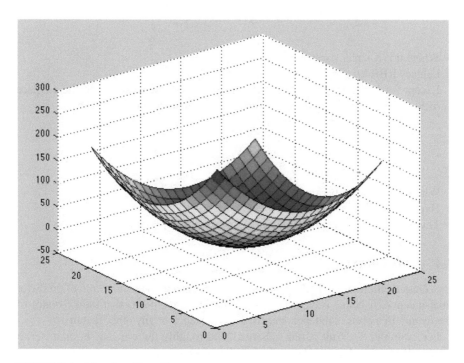

FIGURE 7.4 Mapping 2D to 3D.

Now we have to map the apples and lemons (which are just simple points) to this new space. Think about it carefully, what did we do? We just used a transformation in which we added levels based on distance. If you are in the origin, then the points will be on the lowest level. As we move away from the origin, it means that we are climbing the hill (moving from the center of the plane towards the margins) so the level of the points will be higher.

Now we can easily separate the two classes. These transformations are called kernels. Popular kernels are: Polynomial Kernel, Gaussian Kernel, Radial Basis Function (RBF), Laplace RBF Kernel, Sigmoid Kernel, Anove RBF Kernel, etc. (see Kernel Functions or a more detailed description Machine Learning Kernels).

Types of Kernels
Polynomial Kernel
It is widely used in the field of image processing.

$$\text{Equation: } (x,y) = (x^T y + 1)^d$$

here d is the degree of polynomial and where T is a use r defined scalar.

Gaussian Radial Basis Function Kernel
This is a general-purpose kernel that's employed when you don't know anything about the data.

$$\text{Equation: } (x,y) = \exp\left(\frac{\|x - y\|^2}{2\,\alpha^2}\right)$$

Where α is a scalar parameter

Laplace RBF Kernel
Except for being less sensitive to changes in the sigma parameter, the Laplace Kernel is identical to the radial basis function kernel since it is comparable.

$$\text{Equation: } (x, y) = \exp\left(\frac{\|x - y\|}{\alpha}\right)$$

Where α is a scalar parameter.

Hyperbolic Tangent Kernel
This kernel used in neural networks. Equation: $(x_i, x_j) = tanh(kx_i \cdot x_j + C)$.

7.3 NAÏVE BAYES

It's a classification method based on Bayes' Theorem and the assumption of predictor independence. A Naïve Bayes classifier, in basic words, posits that the existence of one feature in a class is independent from the presence of any other feature.

For example, if a fruit is red, spherical, and roughly three inches in diameter, it is termed an apple. Even if these characteristics are reliant on one another or on the presence of other characteristics, they all add to the likelihood that this fruit is an apple, which is why it is called "Naïve".

The Naïve Bayes model is simple to construct and is especially good for huge data sets. Naïve Bayes is renowned as it outperforms even the most advanced classification systems due to its simplicity.

We can calculate posterior probability P(c|x) from P(c), P(x) and P(x|c). Look at the equation:

$$P(c \mid x) = \frac{P(x \mid c) P(c)}{P(x)}$$

In the above equation:

- P(c|x) is the posterior probability of *class* (c, *target*) given *predictor* (x, *attributes*).
- P(c) is the prior probability of *class*.
- P(x|c) is the likelihood which is the probability of *predictor* given *class*.
- P(x) is the prior probability of *predictor*.

7.4 RANDOM FOREST

Random Forest is a well-known machine learning algorithm that uses the supervised learning method. In machine learning, it may be utilized for both classification and regression issues. It is based on ensemble learning, which is a method of integrating several classifiers to solve a complicated issue and increase the model's performance. Instead, depending on one decision tree, the random forest collects forecasts from each tree and predicts the ultimate output based on the majority votes of predictions (see Figure 7.5).

7.4.1 ASSUMPTIONS FOR RANDOM FOREST

Because the random forest mixes numerous trees to forecast the dataset's class, some decision trees may correctly predict the output while others may not.

However, when all of the trees are combined, the proper result is predicted. As a result, two assumptions for a better Random Forest classifier are as follows:

- The dataset's feature variable should have some real values so that the classifier can predict correct outcomes rather than guesses.
- Each tree's predictions must have very low correlations.

7.4.2 WORKING OF RANDOM FOREST

1. In Random Forest, n random records are chosen at random from a data collection of k records.
2. For each sample, a unique decision tree is created.
3. An output is generated by each decision tree.
4. For classification and regression, the final result is based on Majority Voting or Averaging.

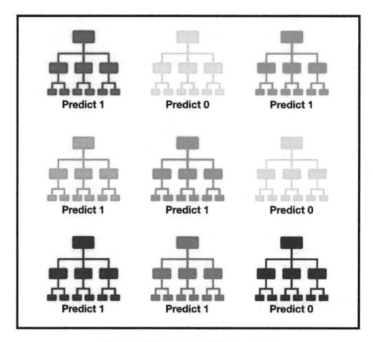

Tally: Six 1s and Three 0s
Prediction: 1

FIGURE 7.5 Predictor.

For example: consider the data in the fruit basket, as represented in Figure 7.5. Now, a number of samples are collected from the fruit basket, and each sample is given its own decision tree. As illustrated in the Figure 7.5, each decision tree will provide an output. The ultimate result is determined by a majority vote. As can be seen in Figure 7.5, the majority decision tree produces an apple rather than a banana, hence the end outcome is an apple.

7.5   K NEAREST NEIGHBOR (KNN)

The K Nearest Neighbor method is a type of supervised learning technique that is used for classification and regression. It's a flexible approach that may also be used to fill in missing values and resample datasets. K Nearest Neighbor examines K Nearest Neighbors (Data points) to forecast the class or continuous value for a new datapoint, as the name indicates.

KNN's learning:

- Instance-based learning: It uses full training instances to predict output for unknown data, rather than learning weights from training data to predict output (as in model-based algorithms).

- Lazy learning: The learning process is postponed until a prediction is required on the new instance, and the model is not learned using training data beforehand.
- Non-parametric: The mapping function in KNN does not have a preset form.

Working of KNN:

The KNN algorithm predicts the values of new datapoints based on "feature similarity", which implies that the new data point will be assigned a value depending on how closely it resembles the points in the training set.

Steps involved in its working:

- We need a data set to implement any algorithm. As a result, we must load both training and test data at the first stage of KNN.
- The value of K, i.e., the closest data points, must then be chosen. Any integer can be used as K.
- Do the following for each point in the test data:
- Calculate the distance between each row of training data and the test data using one of the following methods: Euclidean, Manhattan or Hamming distance. The Euclidean technique is the most widely used method for calculating distance.
- Sort them in ascending order depending on the distance value.
- The top K rows of the sorted array will then be chosen.
- The test point will now be assigned a class based on the most common class of these rows.

Example

Figure 7.6 is an illustration of the notion of K and how the KNN algorithm works. Let's say we have a dataset that can be plotted as in Figure 7.6.

Now we must sort the new data point with the black dot (at 60,60) into the blue or red categories. We'll assume K = 3, which means it'll find the three closest data points. It's seen in Figure 7.7.

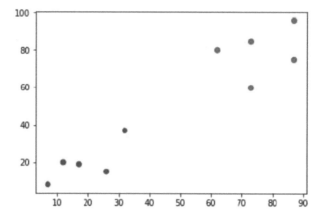

FIGURE 7.6 KNN.

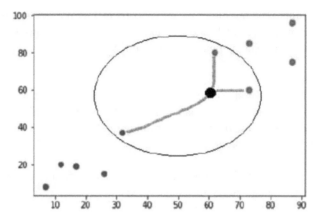

FIGURE 7.7   k = 3.

The three closest neighbors of the data point are marked with a black dot in Figure 7.7. Because two of the three belong to the red class, the black dot will be allocated to the red class as well.

7.6 XG BOOST

Extreme gradient boosting, often known as XG Boost, is a well-known gradient boosting technique(ensemble) that improves the performance and speed of tree-based (sequential decision trees) machine learning algorithms. Tianqi Chen designed XG Boost (Figure 7.8), which was first maintained by the Distributed (Deep) Machine Learning Community (DMLC). It is the most widely used algorithm for applied machine learning in competitions, and it has grown in popularity because of winning solutions in structured and tabular data. It's a free and open–source program. Previously, just Python and R packages were available for

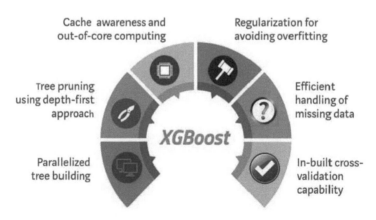

FIGURE 7.8   XG Boost.

XG Boost, but it has since been expanded to include Java, Scala, Julia and more languages.

Algorithm enhancements:

Regularization: To avoid overfitting, it penalizes more complicated models using both LASSO (L1) and Ridge (L2) regularization.

Sparsity Awareness: By automatically "learning" the optimum missing value based on training loss, XG Boost naturally accommodates sparse features for inputs and handles different sorts of sparsity patterns in the data more efficiently.

Weighted Quantile Sketch: The distributed weighted Quantile Sketch approach is used by XG Boost to discover the best split points across weighted datasets.

7.7 BLOCKCHAIN

Blockchain (Figure 7.9) is a common, permanent record that works with the method involved with recording exchanges and following resources in a business organization. A resource can be unmistakable (a house, vehicle, money, land) or theoretical (protected innovation, licenses, copyrights, marking). For all intents and purposes anything of significant worth can be followed and exchanged on a blockchain network, diminishing the gamble and reducing expenses for all included.

Business runs on data. The quicker it's obtained and the more exact it is, the better. Blockchain is great for conveying that data since it gives quick, shared and totally straightforward data on a changeless record that can be accessed exclusively by network individuals with permission.

A blockchain organization can follow orders, instalments, records, creation and considerably more. What's more, since individuals share a solitary perspective on reality, you can see all subtleties of an exchange start to finish, giving you more noteworthy certainty, as well as new efficiencies and amazing open doors.

7.7.1 HOW BLOCKCHAIN WORKS

As every exchange happens, it is recorded as a "block" of information.

Those exchanges show the development of a resource that can be substantial (anitem) or immaterial (scholarly). The information square can record your preferred data: who, what, when, where, how much and, surprisingly, the condition, such as the temperature of a food shipment.

FIGURE 7.9 Blockchain.

How does a transaction get into the blockchain?

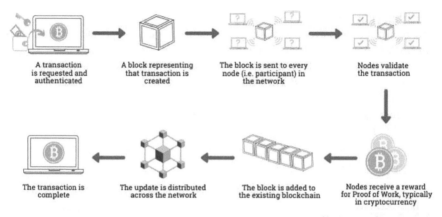

FIGURE 7.10   Blockchain process.

Each block is associated with the ones when these squares structure a chain of information as a resource which moves from one spot to another or proprietorship changes hands. The squares affirm the specific time and grouping of exchanges, and the squares connect safely together to keep any square from being changed or a square being embedded between two existing squares.

Exchanges are constructed together in an irreversible chain: in a blockchain each extra square reinforces the check of the past square and consequently the whole blockchain (see Figure 7.10). This delivers the notion of blockchain conveying the critical strength of changelessness. This eliminates the chance of alteration by a malevolent entertainer–and also constructs a record of exchanges you and other organization individuals can trust.

7.8   BLOCKCHAIN IN HEALTHCARE

Blockchain (see Figure 7.11) has a wide scope of uses, as well as uses in medical care. The record innovation works with protected exchange of patient clinical records, deals with the medication production network and assists medical care specialists with opening hereditary codes.

Securing Patient Data: Keeping significant clinical information free from any danger is the most well-known blockchain medical services application right now, which isn't to be expected. Security is a significant issue in the medical care industry. Somewhere between 2009 and 2017, more than 176 million patient records were uncovered in information breaks. The culprits took charge card and banking data, as well as wellbeing and genomic testing records.

Blockchain's capacity to keep an upright, decentralized and straightforward log of all tolerant information makes it an innovation overflowing with security applications.

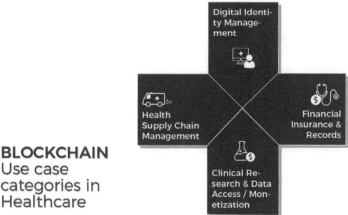

BLOCKCHAIN
Use case
categories in
Healthcare

FIGURE 7.11   Blockchain in healthcare.

Moreover, while blockchain is straightforward it is likewise private, disguising the personality of any person with intricate and secure codes that can safeguard the awareness of clinical information. The decentralized idea of the innovation additionally permits patients, specialists and medical care suppliers to have access to similar data rapidly and securely.

Companies who are applying blockchain in healthcare security:

1) Akiri: Akiri works an organization as-a-administration advanced explicitly for the medical care industry, safeguarding patient wellbeing information while moving it. The Akiri framework doesn't store information of any sort, it works as both an organization and a convention to set strategies and arrange information layers while checking the sources and objects of information continuously.

2) Burst IQ: Burst IQ's platform helps healthcare companies safely and securely manage massive amounts of patient data. Its blockchain technology enables the safekeeping, sale, sharing or license of data while maintaining strict compliance with HIPAA rules.

   The company uses blockchain to improve the way medical data is shared and used.

3) Factom: Factom makes items that help the medical services industry safely store advanced records on the organization's blockchain stage that is open simply to emergency clinics and medical services overseers. Actual papers can be furnished with unique Factom security chips that hold data about a patient and put away private information that is open simply by approved individuals. Factom utilizes blockchain innovation to safely store computerized wellbeing records.

4) Medical Chain: Medical Chain's blockchain keeps up with the uprightness of wellbeing records while laying out a solitary mark of truth. Specialists, medical clinics and research facilities can all demand patient data that has

a record of beginning and safeguards the patient's character from outside sources. Medical Chain's blockchain-based stage keeps a record of beginning and safeguards patient character.

5) Guard Time: Guard Time is helping medical organizations and states carry out blockchain into their online protection strategies. The organization was crucial in helping to execute blockchain in Estonia's medical services frameworks, and it as of late marked an arrangement with a private medical care supplier in the United Arab Emirates to bring blockchain to its information security frameworks. Guard Time utilizes blockchain for network safety applications, including medical services.

Miscommunication between clinical experts costs the medical care industry a faltering $11 billion every year. The tedious course of acquiring admittance to a patient's clinical records depletes staff assets and delays patient consideration. Blockchain-based clinical records offer a solution for these ills.

The decentralized idea of the innovation provides an environment where patient information can be rapidly and proficiently referred to by specialists, clinics, drug specialists and any other individual associated with treatment. Thus, the blockchain can prompt quicker analyses and customized care plans.

How much do we truly have any familiarity with our medication? Would we be able to be certain it hasn't been tampered with? Is it coming from a real provider? These inquiries are the essential worries of the clinical production network, or the connection between the lab and the commercial center.

To answer the above query, we have blockchain (Figure 7.11), it has genuine ramifications for drug store network, the executives, and its decentralization for all intents and purposes ensures full straightforwardness in the delivery interaction. When a record of a medication is made, it will check the starting place (i.e., a research facility). The record will then keep on storing information constantly, including who took care of it and where it has been, until it arrives at the purchaser. The cycle could in fact screen work expenses and waste outflows.

Data Pre-processing:
Now, before heading towards implementation, it's important to understand your data and take out the information from this raw data. There are different methods and libraries like pandas, seaborn, etc., which help us to perform feature engineering, visualization, and data pre-processing.

Data scientists or data analysts usually spend 60–70% of their time in analyzing or cleaning their data, because it improves the performance of the machine learning model and enhances its accuracy.

So here we start by understanding the features that are used in this data:

1. cp-->chest pain type.
2. trestbps-->resting blood pressure (in mm Hg on admission to the hospital).
3. chol-->serum cholesterol in mg/dl.
4. fbs-->(fasting blood sugar >120 mg/dl)(1=true; 0=false).
5. restecg-->resting electrocardiographic results.
6. thalach-->maximum heart rate achieved.

7. exang-->exercise induced angina (1=yes;0=no).
8. oldpeak-->ST depression induced by exercise relative to rest.
9. slope-->the slope of the peak exercise ST segment.
10. ca-->number of major vessels (0–3) colored by fluoroscopy.
11. thal--> 0 = normal; 1 = fixed defect; 2 = reversable defect.
12. target --> have disease or not (1=yes, 0=no).

In this dataset we use these features and we measure them, for example: exang which is exercise induced angina, if it is 1 then it's yes and if it is 0 then it's a no.

Now we use some visualization techniques to know more about the data.

It shows the distribution of output variables, and by looking at the image we can conclude that it follows normal distribution and it's not an imbalanced dataset. An imbalanced dataset means that it contains 70% or more as a "yes" or "no" and it is biased towards one decision. Hence, our dataset is balanced (see Figure 7.12).

Here 1 represents male and 0 represents female, and we can clearly see that there are more men compared to women in our dataset, because men usually have a stressful life that increases the risk of heart disease (see Figure 7.13).

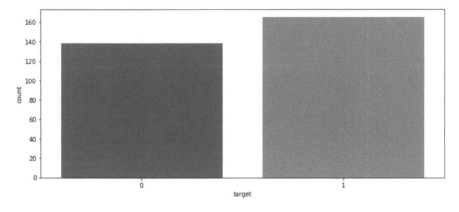

FIGURE 7.12   Dataset target.

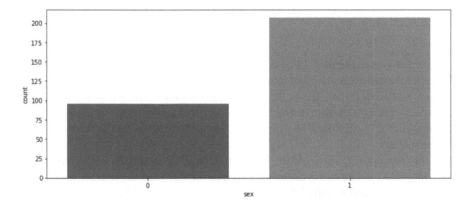

FIGURE 7.13   Gender dataset.

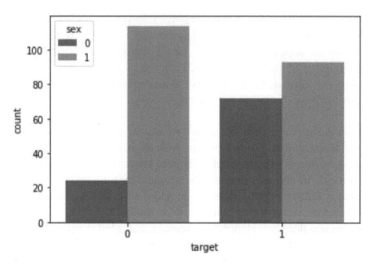

FIGURE 7.14   Output based on gender.

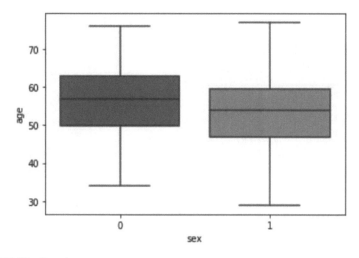

FIGURE 7.15   Boxplot.

In the bar graph (Figure 7.14), we can see the output according to gender. Here, the blue color represents female and orange represents male.

After visualizing the data in the form of a bar graph, we are using box plots. A boxplot represents the data distribution based on five numbers, which are Minimum, First quartile (Q1), Median, Third quartile (Q3) and Maximum. It is also used to identify the outliers.

In this boxplot (Figure 7.15) the box in the middle contains 50% data, the lower line contains 25% data and is called the first quartile (Q1) and the line above contains 75% of the data and is called the third quartile (Q3) the middle one known as the median. This plot is built with respect to age and gender features.

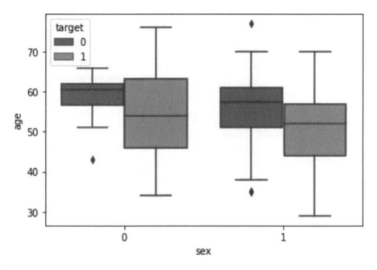

FIGURE 7.16   Boxplot based on gender.

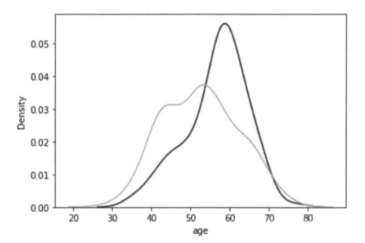

FIGURE 7.17   Age-based plot.

Now this boxplot explains a lot about data. It is created with reference to gender, age and target features. The blue color represents the 0, which means that the person doesn't have heart disease and the orange one indicates that the person has heart disease. The gender 0 represents female and 1 represents male (see Figure 7.16). Black dots are the outliers in the data.

Here we can see that most of the people having heart disease are from theage group of 45 to 60 years.

In Figure 7.17 we use distplot. It is used to visualize the parametric distribution of an individual feature. We use this plot with reference to age and target variable. The

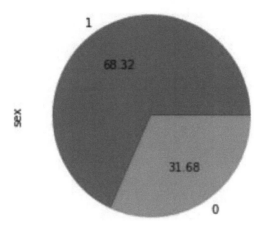

FIGURE 7.18   Pie chart.

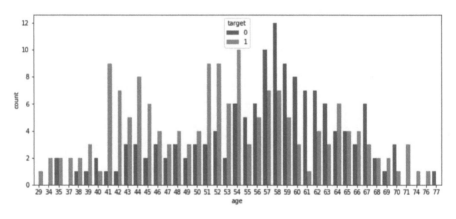

FIGURE 7.19   Count vs Age.

orange line depicts the people who have heart disease and the blue one represents the people who don't have heart disease.

It is a pie chart which we all know (Figure 7.18). This pie chart represents data with respect to gender, we already did this using the bar graph in Figure 7.17, but the difference is that it depicts it in a percentage. There are 68.32% of males in this data and 31.68% of females.

Here we use countplot (Figure 7.19) for every age and the target or output for that age too i.e., the person has heart disease or not. We can clearly see that as the age increases the number of people having heart disease is also increasing. But after the age of 54 the number of people having heart disease is decreasing, this is because most of the people having heart disease will expire at the older age or they are fit and they don't have heart disease at all.

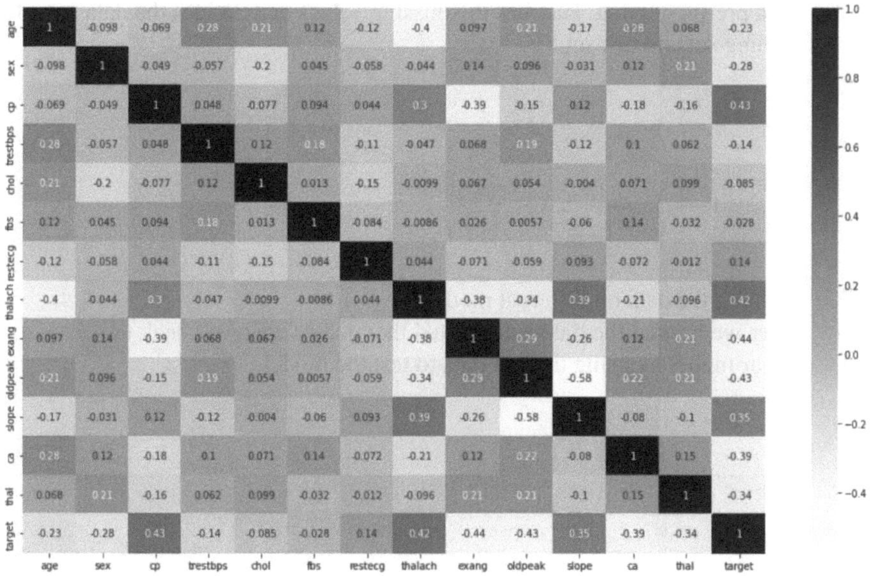

	age	sex	cp	trestbps	chol	fbs	restecg	thalach	exang	oldpeak	slope	ca	thal	target
age	1	-0.098	-0.069	0.28	0.21	0.12	-0.12	-0.4	0.097	0.21	-0.17	0.28	0.068	-0.23
sex	-0.098	1	-0.049	-0.057	-0.2	0.045	-0.058	-0.044	0.14	0.096	-0.031	0.12	0.21	-0.28
cp	-0.069	-0.049	1	0.048	-0.077	0.094	0.044	0.3	-0.39	-0.15	0.12	-0.18	-0.16	0.43
trestbps	0.28	-0.057	0.048	1	0.12	0.18	-0.11	-0.047	0.068	0.19	-0.12	0.1	0.062	-0.14
chol	0.21	-0.2	-0.077	0.12	1	0.013	-0.15	-0.0099	0.067	0.054	-0.004	0.071	0.099	-0.085
fbs	0.12	0.045	0.094	0.18	0.013	1	-0.084	-0.0086	0.026	0.0057	-0.06	0.14	-0.032	-0.028
restecg	-0.12	-0.058	0.044	-0.11	-0.15	-0.084	1	0.044	-0.071	-0.059	0.093	-0.072	-0.012	0.14
thalach	-0.4	-0.044	0.3	-0.047	-0.0099	-0.0086	0.044	1	-0.38	-0.34	0.39	-0.21	-0.096	0.42
exang	0.097	0.14	-0.39	0.068	0.067	0.026	-0.071	-0.38	1	0.29	-0.26	0.12	0.21	-0.44
oldpeak	0.21	0.096	-0.15	0.19	0.054	0.0057	-0.059	-0.34	0.29	1	-0.58	0.22	0.21	-0.43
slope	-0.17	-0.031	0.12	-0.12	-0.004	-0.06	0.093	0.39	-0.26	-0.58	1	-0.08	-0.1	0.35
ca	0.28	0.12	-0.18	0.1	0.071	0.14	-0.072	-0.21	0.12	0.22	-0.08	1	0.15	-0.39
thal	0.068	0.21	-0.16	0.062	0.099	-0.032	-0.012	-0.096	0.21	0.21	-0.1	0.15	1	-0.34
target	-0.23	-0.28	0.43	-0.14	-0.085	-0.028	0.14	0.42	-0.44	-0.43	0.35	-0.39	-0.34	1

FIGURE 7.20   Heat map.

The graph in Figure 7.20 is known as a heatmap. It is the most common and widely used technique in the feature selection process. Heatmap is used to visualize the concentration of values between two features. Sometimes we have thousands of features in the dataset, and we have to reduce the features to increase the performance of the model, and then we eliminate those features which have the same impact on the dataset. To know the impact we use heatmap, it represents how features are correlated to each other, for example if two features have collinearity (1), then it means they are directly proportional i.e., if we increase one feature then the other is also increased.

Import the libraries and read the dataset.

```
In [1]: import pandas as pd
        import numpy as np
        import matplotlib.pyplot as plt
        import seaborn as sns
        %matplotlib inline
```

```
In [3]: df = pd.read_csv('heart.csv')
        df.head()
```

1. Divides the dependent variables and independent variables (output) using pandas.

```
In [9]: x = df.iloc[:,:-1].values
        y = df.iloc[:,-1].values
```

2. Data pre-processing: Handles the missing values and divides the data set into training set and test set.

```
In [10]:  from sklearn.model_selection import train_test_split
          x_train , x_test, y_train, y_test = train_test_split(x,y, test_size = 0.2, random_state=0)
```

```
In [12]:  from sklearn.ensemble import RandomForestClassifier
          classifier = RandomForestClassifier(n_estimators = 5,criterion = 'entropy', random_state=0)
          classifier.fit(x_train, y_train)
```

3. Training the data on different models.
4. After we trained the data and created the model, now we check the accuracy of our model by using the test data to test the model.

```
In [14]:  from sklearn.metrics import confusion_matrix, accuracy_score
          cm = confusion_matrix(y_test, y_predict)
          print(cm)
          accuracy_score(y_test, y_predict)

          [[23  4]
           [ 5 29]]

Out[14]:  0.8524590163934426
```

7.9 RESULTS AND COMPARISON

The most interesting part of this study is after applying different ML algorithms on the dataset, identifying which algorithm outnumbered every other algorithm and was able to obtain the highest accuracy. Let's start with Naïve Bayes.

Naïve Bayes gave us accuracy of 70.49%, sensitivity of 72.22% and specificity of 69.76%. As our first model, it shows some decent results (Figure 7.21).

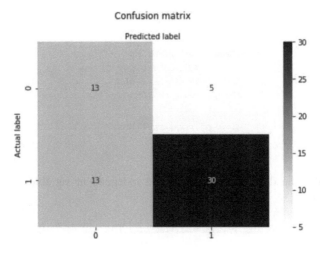

FIGURE 7.21 Confusion matrix.

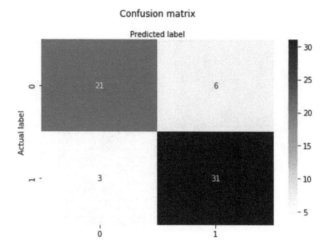

FIGURE 7.22   Confusion matrix (Logistic Regression).

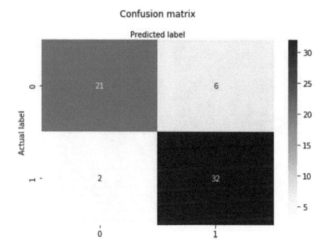

FIGURE 7.23   Confusion matrix (SVM).

Logistic regression:
This model (Figure 7.22) gave an accuracy of 85.24%, sensitivity of 77.77% and specificity of 97.17%. This shows great improvement on Naïve Bayes.

Kernel SVM:
This model (Figure 7.23) worked way better than logistic regression, with an accuracy of 86.88%, sensitivity of 77.77% and specificity of 94.11%. This model also shows some improved results and a considerable amount of satisfaction.

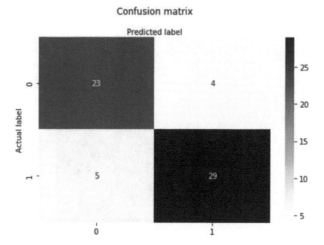

FIGURE 7.24   Confusion matrix (Random Forest).

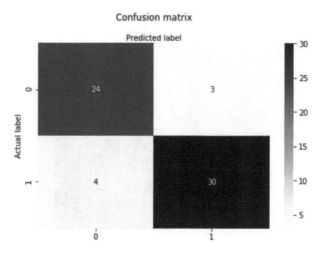

FIGURE 7.25   Confusion matrix (KNN).

Random Forest:
In this model (Figure 7.24) we used five numbers of decision trees with the criterion of entropy and got an accuracy of 85.24%, sensitivity of 85.18% and specificity of 85.29%. This model also worked really well, with great results.

K-Nearest Neighbor (KNN)
In this model, we use ten neighbors with metric of minkowski, and this shows significant results with an accuracy of 88.52%, sensitivity of 88.88% and specificity of 88.23%. So far KNN (Figure 7.25) is the pre-eminent algorithm with these results.

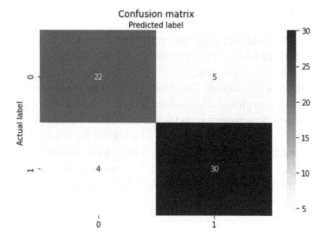

FIGURE 7.26 Confusion matrix (XG Boost).

XG Boost

XG Boost (Figure 7.26) comes up with the accuracy of 85.24%, Sensitivity of 81.48% and Specificity of 88.23%. This result is nearly same as Random Forest and the reason of it is that both are based on ensemble tree.

7.10   CONFUSION MATRIX

This consists of four sections:

True Positive: These are the cases where we predicted true, and it is actually true.
True Negative: These are cases where we predicted true but it is false.
False Positive: Where we predicted false but it's true.
True Negative: Where we predicted false and it is actually False (see Table 7.1).

TABLE 7.1
Accuracy, Sensitivity and Specificity of Dataset

	Accuracy	Sensitivity	Specificity
Naïve Bayes	70.49%	72.22%	69.76%
Logistic	85.24%	77.77%	91.17%
Kernel SVM	86.88%	77.77%	94.11%
Random Forest	85.24%	85.18%	85.29%
KNN	88.52%	88.88%	88.23%
XG Boost	85.24%	81.48%	88.23%

7.11 CONCLUSION

So far, we analyzed our dataset using different visualization tools to get insights into the dataset. We performed feature correlation analysis and a stepwise analysis for choosing an optimum set of features.

Then we looked at blockchain and how it would be beneficial in the field of healthcare. Lastly, we explored the models and their performance on the basis of accuracy, specificity and sensitivity, and without a doubt we can say that K-Nearest Neighbor was better than every other model with a great accuracy of 88.52%, but we can't ignore the fact that Logistic regression, Random Forest and XG Boost gave the same accuracy of 85.24% so we can say that the average accuracy is around 85%. These models are really useful in the field of science, law, medical fields, etc.

8 A Study on the Role of Electroencephalogram in Cyber Physical System and Security

Ahona Ghosh and Sriparna Saha
Maulana Abul Kalam Azad University of Technology,
West Bengal, India

8.1 INTRODUCTION

A Brain Computer Interface is basically the communication system of a human brain with its circumstances. As the most emerging tool of BCI nowadays, the Electroencephalogram (EEG) is useful in monitoring and evaluating ongoing brain activities and the signal impulses generated due to them, using small metal discs called electrodes attached to the scalp. An EEG measures the fluctuation in the voltage resulting from the neuron's ionic current and is able to detect potential problems associated with the activities. Depending on the recording location, the systems may be categorized into invasive, moderately invasive and non-invasive systems. The moderately invasive systems like electrocorticography are implanted inside the skull, and they are responsible for providing greater selectivity and lower noise signals. EEG-based BCI systems are mostly non-invasive [27] and are basically susceptible to signal distortion and noise. The advantages include easy measurability, low risk and low cost. Invasive BCIs are directly attached to the brain during surgeries and measure brain activity with the best results.

Cyber Physical Systems (CPS) refer to a combination of physical and computing devices where the working mechanism is regulated and controlled by computer algorithms. The application of CPS is in diverse fields including healthcare, manufacturing, transport, civil infrastructure, entertainment and several others. EEG has been proved to work efficiently and effectively as a Cyber Physical System in various situations. In this chapter, those different application scenarios will be discussed to analyze the contribution of EEG in security and the areas which have not been explored much, we will attempt to identify those to find out the probable future research direction in this domain. Figure 8.1 demonstrates the general working mechanism of a cyber physical system in different sectors of application.

In Section 8.2, different terminologies related to EEG data acquisition will be described. Section 8.3 will present related background studies. The advantages and drawbacks for cyber physical systems in a real-life scenario will be discussed. In

DOI: 10.1201/9781003190301-8

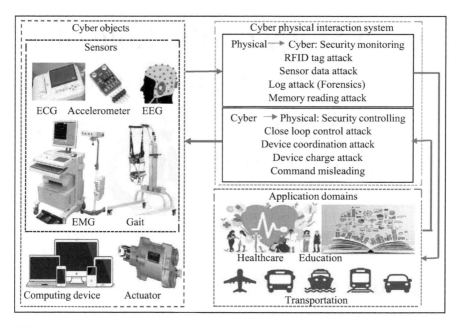

FIGURE 8.1 Pictorial overview of working mechanism of cyber physical system.

Section 8.4, currently available application areas will be highlighted. Section 8.5 will discuss the recent algorithms or techniques used for developing cyber physical systems having EEG as one of the components. Section 8.6 will provide an overall discussion about the scope and limitation of the chapter and probable future direction of the same.

8.2 INTRODUCTION TO ELECTROENCEPHALOGRAPHY

Neurons connect with each other by generating various electrical signals. EEG is a bodily technique of recording the electrical activity which is created by the human brain using electrodes located on the scalp surface [48]. Electrodes are placed with elastic caps like bathing caps for faster results and confirmation of the data collection from similar scalp locations among all respondents. Hans Berger first recorded EEG signals in the human brain in 1929 [49]. By EEG signals, injuries of the brain or disease can be detected. It delivers outstanding time resolution for detecting movement within cortical areas, even at sub-second timescales. After measuring the voltage, the collected data gets digitized and transmitted to some amplifier. This amplified data may be shown as a sequence of voltage values. The overall working mechanism of EEG as a cyber physical system is shown in Figure 8.2. Figure 8.2a shows the International 10–20 system of EEG electrode placement, where the 10 and 20 refer to the distance between adjacent nodes on 10% or 20% of the entire scalp. Every electrode is represented by a letter followed by a digit where the letters F, P, O, C, T stand for the frontal, posterior, occipital, central and temporal region respectively, and the digit is odd representing the left hemisphere and even representing the right one.

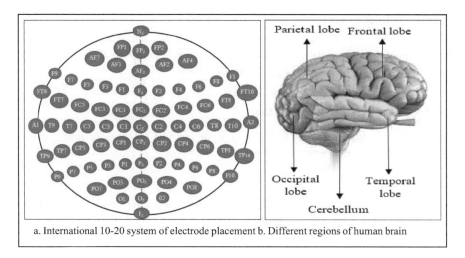

a. International 10-20 system of electrode placement b. Different regions of human brain

FIGURE 8.2   Overview on working mechanism of EEG.

8.2.1   BRAIN REGIONS

The brain consists of three basic parts, namely the brainstem, cerebellum and cerebrum. The cerebrum is the major part and consists of left and right hemispheres. The cerebellum is situated below the cerebrum. The brainstem plays the role of a relay center linking the cerebellum and cerebrum with the spinal cord. The cortex areas in charge of processing information shown in Figure 8.2b are discussed next [50].

8.2.1.1   Occipital Cortex

This is the visual processing center of our brain and is situated in the rearmost portion of the skull. It interprets information from the eyes and turns it into the image as a person sees it. It has different functions like face recognition, movement, object recognition, color determination, depth perception, distance determination, etc.

8.2.1.2   Parietal Cortex

This is one of the cerebral cortex's four main lobes in humans. It is situated close to our parietal bone, near the higher back region of the skull. It is a key interpreter of the sensory environment surrounding the body. The lobe is a primary sensory field since it is the brain's first stop for sensory processing. The parietal lobe is responsible for a variety of sensations, including tension, cold, heat, pain, pressure, touch, etc.

8.2.1.3   Temporal Cortex

This is situated behind the ears and is the second biggest lobe. It is generally linked to the processing of auditory information and memory encoding. Both conscious and long-term memory are mostly created and stored in the temporal lobe.

8.2.1.4 Frontal Cortex

The anterior part of our brain is situated at the front of the skull. Executive activity is the domain of the frontal cortex. It aids us in maintaining power, making plans for the future, and keeping track of our actions and behavior.

8.2.2 BRAINWAVE FREQUENCY RANGE

The brainwave generated from different activities can be categorized into five categories based on its frequency as follows.

8.2.2.1 Delta (1–4 Hz)

Delta brainwaves are slow and loud. These are created during dreamless sleep and during meditation. They are also found during internal work of memory tasks using full concentration.

8.2.2.2 Theta (4–7 Hz)

This is linked to memory encoding. It is also generated during sleep with dreams. When we are assigned a difficult task then theta waves become more important.

8.2.2.3 Alpha (7–12 Hz)

Alpha waves are generated when the brain is resting. Alpha waves take over during eye closing and being in a calm state.

8.2.2.4 Beta (12–30 Hz)

Beta waves take over or get generated when we plan to move any part of the body. This is an activity which is present when we are attentive, alert, involved in focused mental activity, decision making, judgment and problem solving.

8.2.2.5 Gamma (>30 Hz, typically 40 Hz)

These are the fastest among all brain waves. They communicate and exchange data between brain regions.

8.2.3 TYPES OF ELECTRODES

The knowledge of different types of electrodes and their exact application areas is mandatory before developing medical instrumentation systems in a proper way. The various types of body surface recording electrodes that can be used for patient monitoring applications, as well as their important applications, are presented in this subsection.

8.2.3.1 Metal Plate Electrode

This is basically the metallic conductor in contact with skin with the help of an adhesive electrolyte gel and is applied in limb electrodes for electrocardiograph (ECG) systems.

8.2.3.2   Metal Disk Electrode

A metallic disk applied to skin with surgical tape is called a metal disk electrode, it is generally applied in a chest electrode for ECG, surface recording of electromyograph (EMG), EEG, etc.

8.2.3.3   Suction Electrode

A metallic disk electrode placed on the skin using a rubber suction bulb is called a suction electrode and gets applied as a precordial electrode for clinical ECG.

8.2.3.4   Floating Electrode

A floating electrode is basically at the bottom of a cavity filled with electrolyte gel that is mounted on the skin. It helps to reduce the motion artifact between the electrolyte gel and the skin.

8.2.3.5   Flexible Electrode

This type of electrode can easily fix to any topography and gets mostly applied to premature infants.

8.3   LITERATURE SURVEY

Several attempts have been made to review different applications of EEG in cyber physical systems, different implementation perspectives have been analyzed also to have a better insight into their benefits and loopholes for identifying future prospects in the area. An intelligent psycho-physiological method of conceptual design of product to analyze the customer's requirements has been designed by Lou et al. [1] which integrates EEG and Kano model. Non-linear feature extraction has been performed using machine learning algorithms, namely Support Vector Machine classification to detect a customer's mental state. In spite of the classification accuracy being acceptable, factors like stimulus types and experimental model still have an impact on classification which needs to be researched further for better results and data processing. Brain signals from EEG have been used for biometric and password–based authentication purposes by Pham et al. [2], where cryptography has been integrated with the biometric extracted from EEG.

A person authentication scheme has been proposed in Wu et al. [3], where EEG has been used to robustly and accurately analyze an eye blinking signal which easily distinguishes different people. The experimental outcome satisfactorily proves its contribution towards privacy and security, though the performance can be enhanced in future by using other artifacts like electromyogram from teeth biting and electrooculogram from movements of the eye, and practicability can be enhanced by using a commercial portable EEG like the Emotiv EPOC headset. An interdisciplinary approach has been taken up to mitigate the privacy issues linked with EEG during side channel extraction of a user's private information [4].

Different challenges faced by the currently available cyber physical systems include infrastructure of the actuator, monitoring, controlling, computation and communication network [7]. To achieve continuous operation by avoiding these obstacles, and to cope with the ever-changing requirements, dynamic and complicated behavior could be observed in many existing cyber physical systems. Context aware security frameworks have been implemented to address the security challenges which deploy distributed real time software, context coupling and cooperative resource management schemes. To make the systems resilient enough, different techniques have been created involving danger theory based immune systems and artificial intelligence tools which possess self-healing, self-aware and agent-based contexts to have a fault tolerant system. Torngren and Grogan have discussed different complexity factors like complexity awareness, handling rules and impact in future cyber physical systems [10]. For the establishment of new methods, tools and knowledge, efficient collaboration among teams supported by automated computer-aided engineering systems and some systematic treatments to deal with the uncertain and complex circumstances without side effects are required.

Human centric cyber physical system applied in complex manufacturing process needs infrastructures linking physical world entities with the cyber world using immersion sense [15]. Pippos et al. have developed a Linux-based small computing platform brain machine interface which uses EEG data of consumer-grades applying machine learning classifiers to detect a user's command accurately and reliably [16]. Left, Right, Up and Down movements of a pan/tilt servomotor unit have been controlled in the cyber physical system where the classifier performance has been evaluated based on accuracy and execution time. Quadratic Discriminant Analysis and Gaussian Naïve Bayes have shown the best performance, but the system supports only one user at a time which could be further extended for multiple users. Combinations of controllers and classifiers can be tested to achieve a classifier parameter optimization scheme to increase the effectiveness in a real-world scenario. A time series of sensory data has been classified with Fuzzy logic in a cyber physical system [24]. Time series data represented in intervals number induction form has proved its efficiency in classifying the subject as non-alcoholic or alcoholic with C-means and k-Nearest Neighbor, though it can be improved by using optimized parameters for channel selection and time series segmentation for precision farming-based applications in the near future.

8.4 APPLICATION AREAS

Currently available application areas of Cyber Physical System [25] involving EEG include healthcare [51], education, smart transportation system, smart civil infrastructure, etc. This section will discuss the basic working mechanisms of EEG in the above-mentioned sectors.

8.4.1 Healthcare

A novel hybrid BCI prototype embedding two channel small wireless EEG has been proposed [14] to classify tasks for the people suffering from tetraplegia for a series of mental tasks, i.e., mental arithmetic, mental figure rotation, mental word embedding, visual counting, eyes closing, concentrating on LED having flicking frequency 6 Hz, 13 Hz and 16 Hz. The prototype can be applied to avoid obstacles in a real time

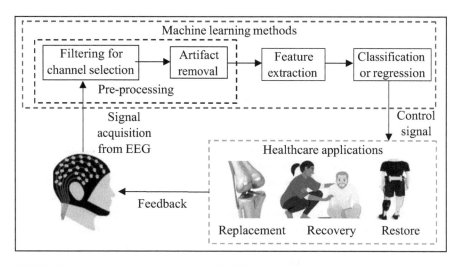

FIGURE 8.3   General block diagram of an EEG based healthcare framework.

brain-controlled wheelchair system. The working mechanism of EEG in a healthcare framework is shown in Figure 8.3. EEG has been widely used in an original ability restoring process called rehabilitation [46],[47] and also in various existing research works. People having motor or cognitive disorders often require alternative techniques of control and communication. Muscle regulation is needed for some of the present augmentative communication techniques. If they use extra ocular muscles to move a speech synthesizer or detour around disruptions in usual pathways (e.g., using shoulder muscles to regulate activation of hand and forearm muscles), they need a degree of voluntary motor function. As a result, they may be ineffective for people who are completely paralyzed (for example, due to amyotrophic lateral sclerosis or a brainstem stroke) or have other serious motor disabilities. They require substitute techniques for expressing their wishes not depending on the brain's usual output trails of peripheral nerves and muscles. Thus, for communicating in an effective way EEG signals have been used.

Neurophysiological CPS applying transcranial magnetic stimulation have been reviewed using a fractional order model predictive control-based case study [19]. Fall risk assessment has been performed during gait monitoring [20]. Four factors have been considered, i.e., subject's health condition, circumstance scenario, co-contraction analysis of electromyograph and movement related and μ-rhythm event related potential desynchronized occurrence of electroencephalogram where the cyber physical system was created by integrating electroencephalogram and electromyogram on a field programmable gate arrays semiconductor board for real time index extraction from subjects suffering from chronic pain, cerebellar ataxia, stroke, Huntington disease, Parkinson's disease, elderly disease and so on. When the fall risk identified is too high, then the subject is instructed to correct the movement by electrical feedback. The cyber physical system designed by De Venuto et al. [26] aimed at fall prevention by identifying cortico-muscular coupling and also introduced a match making algorithm that allows fast classification taking less than 12 milliseconds of nonvoluntary movement and introduces a fall-prevention feedback action. In less than 168 milliseconds, the entire chain action is completed. The sensing nodes can be easily integrated, and the gateway may be a smartphone, making the device wearable and unobtrusive in daily life. The system's components have been put through their paces in real-world scenarios, but complete integration is still ongoing.

The nature of stroke detection and early reaction by an intelligent clinical system to it can save someone's life. Laghari et al. [9] have attempted to identify probable stroke occurrence among persons having a high risk of stroke or having experienced stroke earlier; the cyber physical system designed by them consists of a wearable MUSE headband-based EEG, mobile device and cloud. Since the user datagram protocol is prone to packet loss and the stroke detection system is a critical one where packet loss can be fatal to the user, a transmission control protocol has been used in the system for feasible communication. Relative Delta power, relative alpha to delta ratio and local brain symmetry index have been the three features considered, and the performance of four classifiers, namely, kNN, SVM, multilayer perceptron and hidden markov model have been evaluated on these three [28]. Gait analysis for quantitative drug impact testing in Parkinson's disease has been performed [21] by a cyber physical system consisting of eight EMG and eight EEG wireless nodes implemented on an Altera Cyclone V field programmable gate array. The EEG and EMG response before and after Levodopa treatment have been compared and showed the time of agonist antagonist co-contraction typically reduced 17%, the maximum co-contraction time reduced up to 23% and the number of critical co-contractions decreased 33%.The experimental results indicate a situation of Levodopa-related benefits, like essential muscular activity decrease and brain motor ideation modulation, which are consistent with the drug's expectations. As a result, conditions like motor fluctuations caused by incorrect drug dosages are extremely sensitive to the system. This function, based on precision medicine dictates, qualifies it as a beneficial tool to evaluate any treatment procedure.

A Wireless Body Area Network based cyber physical system to detect cognitive impairment and falling risk by automatic gait analysis in De Venuto et al. [22] is created using synchronized EEG and EMG collection nodes that communicate wirelessly with a gateway using a Bluetooth Low Energy protocol. μ-Rhythm event dependent desynchronizations, EMG co–contraction, EMG trigger generation with dynamic threshold and movement related potential detection have all been developed for gait analysis. The automated EMG trigger creation is used to get a univocal muscle activation flag, greatly decreasing data while keeping the target information intact. Due to the existence of EMGs, a single fixed threshold comparator cannot produce satisfactory outcomes; instead, a dynamic threshold gets measured online for the rectified EMG's instantaneous strength. The co-contraction time is calculated by multiplying and normalizing antagonist–antagonist EMG trigger signals: long co-contraction times (>500–600milliseconds) indicate imbalance or instability during gait. HiLCPSs (human-in-the–loop cyber-physical systems) are a daunting and exciting class of applications with enormous potential to affect many people's everyday lives. Design and implementation of a HiLCPS is a huge undertaking that takes a lot of time. Traditional virtual reality interfaces, like joystick, mouse and keyboard are less suited to augmenting human interaction in the real world. Transparent interfaces that use existing electrophysiological signals like EEG, ECG and EMG are needed in this setting. Intelligent sensor fusion will compensate for inconsistencies in individual sensor measurements and create a complete, coherent picture from multimodal sensor data. Despite recent developments in robotics technology, designing and controlling autonomous robotic systems remains a difficult task. Additional concerns occur in the HiLCPS sense, for example, robots work in close proximity to humans, requiring strict safety criteria [23]. The broad range of monitoring applications available necessitates transmitting periodic scalar data or continuous pulses, which must take precedence over all other types of periodic monitoring, ranging from cardiovascular condition monitoring to one-shot emergency alerts, such as signaling the occurrence of an epileptic seizure [29].

8.4.2 EDUCATION SYSTEM

Brain function mainly regulates learning activities, hence there is a growing need to study how the brain works in education. The EEG measurement should provide a more objective indication of how the brain functions during learning activities over time in comparison to the think-aloud type of self-reporting [30]. Universal primary education is important for individual academic growth, as well as a country's overall adult productivity. Early grade failure is one of the factors in the dropout of 25% of 59 million primary-aged out-of-school students, according to estimates. In order to design effective strategies, an objective and feasible screening measure to identify at-risk children in the early grades is required. Rasheed et al. have used a machine learning approach to assess the predictive power of EEG data collected at the age of four in predicting academic achievement at the age of eight in Pakistani rural children [31]. The algorithm was developed using demographic and EEG data of 96 children in a unit, as well as their academic achievement in grades 1–2 assessed based on academic tests of language and mathematics at 7–8 years of age. On various model combinations of EEG, sociodemographic and home environment variables that were tested, the K–Nearest Neighbor classifier was applied using five Stratified Folds according to specificity and sensitivity. For EEG to be used as a screening test with appropriate specificity and sensitivity to classify preschool-aged children having a high probability of failing at initial standards, the model needs to be validated further (see Figure 8.4).

Concentration power and impulsivity while reading have been analyzed [32] and attention deficit hyperactivity disorder has been attempted to be identified. Figure 8.4 shows an outline of an EEG-based academic performance assessment system. Cognitive load during learning multimedia and hypertext has been analyzed [33]. Since brain wave activity differs with age, brain volume and individual differences, it was suggested that rather than finding the absolute power of a pre-decided frequency band, researchers examine the EEG signal modifications caused by a specific task or event. Event-related (de-)synchronization, which was originally designed for the study of oscillatory EEG dynamics, is a well-established rate-of-change test for oscillatory

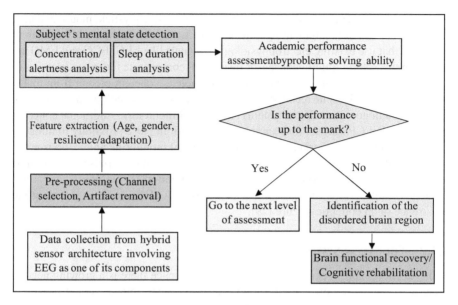

FIGURE 8.4   Overview of the role of EEG in the education sector.

EEG dynamics. Understanding the cognitive mechanisms of different learning environments may be aided by studying educational psychology. However, there are few empirical studies in educational research that use physiological methods, and much more conceptual and trial work is required to enhance the physiological research result conversion to educational research and to deliver the corresponding researchers more resources. E-learning ability has been tried to be enhanced using educational games [34] by implementing an EEG-based fog-assisted virtual reality paradigm. A Software Defined Network has also been used to minimize latency, which increases the quality of the experience. IFogSim has been used to incorporate both optical-fog and cloud-based implementation setups to play games in order to simulate the experiment. Following that, an optical-fog-based module placement strategy has been suggested. The architecture has achieved different benefits such as relatively low energy consumption, cost-effective services, optimum bandwidth capacity and high scalability where educational technologies, optical networks and large-scale 5G have not yet been considered for integration with the existing system to ensure robust and resilient e-learning through educational games.

8.4.3   TRANSPORTATION

Driving behavior has been focused on in different transportation-based literature, particularly for transportation safety, intelligent transportation systems and behavior modelling. Being a non-invasive tool, electroencephalography (EEG) has been effective in different states of the art to identify the driver's cognitive states and to analyze real-world driving. Figure 8.5 shows an outline of an EEG-based driver performance assessment system for improving the transportation sector. An excessive

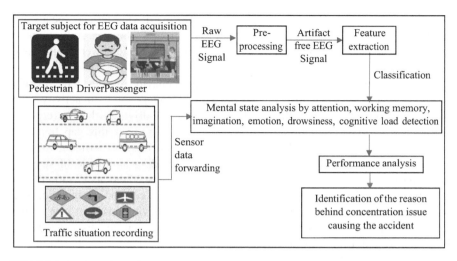

FIGURE 8.5 Overview of the role of EEG in transportation.

cognitive load on the operator can lead to perceptual ability deterioration [35] and can decrease reaction time, which in turn causes incorrect decisions leading to dangerous situations in traffic. A driver's mental state has been attempted to be detected [36] where attention, imagination, emotion and working memory have been considered as the parameters to detect the cognitive load in different situations. Our cities are rapidly expanding, as are the industries that support them and the roads that connect them. The growth of cities has resulted in a slew of issues, the most serious of which is traffic congestion, which has a negative impact on social, environmental and economic sustainability.

An EEG Enobio CAP with eight electrodes has been used [37] to monitor a driver's mental activities, including fear, in a real-time driving session. Continuous monitoring has shown that when the driver is exposed to some unexpected external acoustic or visual event, the reaction and the behavior change cause significant fear, which in turn leads to the possibility of a near miss accident. In two experimental sessions, data related to brain functions correlated with alpha waves showing a strong association in the time and frequency domain. The next step in this research could be to determine how different brain regions are involved in a test drive testing driver performance on curved highways using a driving simulator. Moreover, accident prediction and prevention techniques can also be formed with the application of an artificial neural network in the architecture.

Identification of fatigue in driving has been attempted by Jing et al. [38] in a low-voltage and hypoxia plateau atmosphere. Both linear and non-linear techniques were applied to analyze the EEG recording at three stages, i.e., fatigue, awake and critical. A MATLAB-based EEGLAB toolbox was used for nonlinear processing by power spectral density mapping of alpha, beta and gamma waves, and eigen values were used for the linear one. Whenever driving fatigue occurred, the overall EEG signal amplitude was smooth or did not show any discernible change. During driving fatigue, the wave amplitude and energy of alpha and beta waves decreased noticeably, and the beta wave migrated to the temporal lobe region. During driving fatigue, theta wave energy can increase, and there may be a shift to the frontal lobe area. An upsurge in driving fatigue degree is followed by a reduction in the average power of alpha and beta waves, and a theta wave upsurge in the environment.

Electroencephalography (EEG)-based driving behavior studies have mainly looked at the link between different risky driving behaviors and brain activity, with only a few studies looking at the link between ordinary driving behavior (drivers' behavior in everyday situations) and brain activity. To cover this gap found in existing literature, Yang et al. performed a data collection experiment using a driving simulator on ordinary driving behavior, including amplitude of steering wheel movements, lane deviation, time and space headway and acceleration [39]. Statistical analysis was carried out using the Pearson correlation method. The experimental findings showed that normal driving behavior involves each of the four human brain areas, particularly the temporal, occipital and frontal regions. Beta Log Transformed Power was found to be the most relevant. Furthermore, acceleration, speed and space headway may have potential correlation with EEG features like beta Log Transformed Power. Practical driving trials in future should be carried out to eradicate the possible differences between simulated and real-world driving scenarios.

The detection of a driver's intention to use emergency braking in brain controlled cyber physical devices has been investigated by Teng et al. [40] Some spatial-frequency features have been chosen from the powers of frequency points across 16 channels by conducting a sequential forward floating search. The accuracy of the system at 94%, with a response time of 420 milliseconds is not satisfactory enough, since when any emergency braking detection is missed it may cause unexpected consequences, the false alarm may annoy drivers and eventually it may reduce driver's confidence to use the entire system. Other nonlinear models or integrating EEG with other bio-medical signals and outside data determined by laser or radar techniques can be used to overcome this constraint. The performance of the model has been tested in a two-dimensional simulator which may vary widely from the actual scenario where several factors like vehicle vibration and road congestion can contaminate the EEG signal with noise and artifacts. Moreover, only the unexpected pedestrian crossing has been considered here as the emergency scenario at 108 kilometers per hour speed, but many other emergency situations may occur, like sudden braking of leading traffic and sudden cutting in of a vehicle from the next lane. Thus, the system needs to be tested in a real-time scenario considering other parameters such as road condition, weather and so on.

8.4.4 SECURITY AND AUTHENTICATION

Authentication plays a major role in information security, with rapid growth in technological advancements. The ability to reliably verify whether someone actually is who they say they are is critical for maintaining confidentiality, integrity and availability. EEG acts as a biometric, token and password-based authentication device in various secured applications. Figure 8.6 shows an outline of an EEG based authentication system to achieve privacy and security of cyber physical systems.

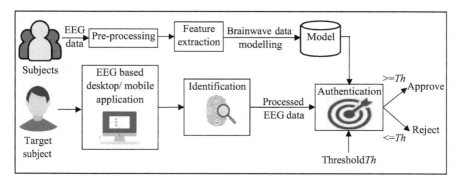

FIGURE 8.6 Overview of the role of EEG in authentication systems for security.

Azizi et al. have introduced EEG as an alternative to conventional fingerprint-based or facial biometric systems since the EEG signal is much harder to replicate or steal [5]. However, the challenges faced by neuroimaging devices processing and performance used to record EEG signals have not been addressed in this study but may be considered in the near future. Alhayajnehet al. [6] have conducted extensive research on the most projecting biometric authentication methods based on implementation feasibility, cost and accuracy. The growing use of remote systems, as well as the constant reduction in the size of electrical devices, has prompted the development of remote body wireless systems. The sensors in these systems are attached to clothing or the human body. The creation of a full machine learning-driven biometric authentication suite is encouraged as part of future research in this area. The system will use a variety of biometric readings as inputs to an algorithm that would assess the patient's authenticity and create a detailed profile for potential use.

To ensure data protection, cryptographic frameworks depend on key sharing. Although keys in cryptographic architectures should be properly reproducible and not unambiguously linked to a user's identity, this is not the case in biometric frameworks. These problems can be solved by combining cryptography and biometrics. A discrete logarithmic problem and Bose–Chaudhuri Hocquenghem (BCH) codes based biometric cryptosystem has been designed by Damaševiliuset al. [8] to carry out a security audit, and show off its security features. Using their own EEG dataset obtained from 42 subjects, the results of the experiments showed that the biometric user authentication method was successful, having an equal error rate of 0.024. Holler and Uhl [11] have evaluated whether the EEG based biometric templates comprise sensitive information about the enrolled users, and whether some personal parameters like age, cognitive disorder information and sex can be revealed by these templates or not. Biometric-based cryptographic key generation is a data mining technique that extracts biometric information using knowledge discovery techniques in order to encrypt data which is widely applied in security systems to reduce weak password-based constraints. A repeatable binary string has been generated from an EEG signal [12] using error-correction data that can be modified to produce different keys. The scheme generated keys long enough and was able to generate separate keys for separate applications, ensuring that an attack on one does not result in an attack on everyone; the security is based on detailed application-specific research and a statistical lower-bound statement.

An individual identification framework to provide mobile security in ubiquitous environments has been implemented [13]. Real-time EEG signals were recorded by a single monopolar channel from a mobile EEG where three types of experiments, namely accuracy test, time dimension test and capacity dimension test, were carried out for assisted living and e-learning applications. Seven possible attacks towards the brain computer interface, namely noise addition, altered stimuli, artificial input, modified input, data leakage via secondary channel, privacy violation and misleading stimuli have been presented [17] using attack flow diagrams that comprehensively define the roles and player communications within the BCI system and help to mitigate them, enhancing security in cyber space. The most vulnerable vectors acting behind the ecosystem were also identified to increase the functionality, accuracy and simplicity of the system.

Lie detectors based on BCI are another example of event related potential-based BCI systems. The polygraph is the most popular lie detector today, a system that measures a person's blood pressure, heart rate and sweat levels as they answer a question set to see if they're lying. The findings of a polygraph test, on the other hand, normally give only a partial image of deception [52] and an interpreter is also required. Furthermore, it is understood that certain people can train their bodies and monitor the inspected vitals when answering questions, allowing them to avoid polygraph lie detection [53]. A BCI framework is used to detect ERPs in a newer approach to lie detection. The basic premise of lie detectors, like BCI-based detectors, is that the average person is unable to regulate their physiological response while lying. The brain's behavior when shown a stimulus is one example of such a reaction. Since ERPs are concerned with memory and emotion which cannot be controlled by the subject undergoing a lie detection test, out of some stress, guilt or other emotions generated from lying can be identified from ERPs recorded by EEG; the most commonly used ERP in this case is P300. A two-phase authentication system using an EEG augmented password has been developed [18]. A subject's concentration and relaxation measurements were applied as additional parameters for enhancing the password. A significant increase in the search space reduced the number of characters in the password parallelly and helped to enhance the shared secret key-based security. A one time password generation mechanism has also been added to prevent replay attack in the said system which can be extended further to eliminate the requirement of entering the password. Further research may also consider music as a tool for stimulating brain function and determining the characteristic vector of each individual person, all while adhering to the general constraints of using low-cost, readily available equipment.

8.5 DESIGN METHODOLOGIES

The recent algorithms or techniques used for developing cyber physical systems having EEG as one of the components will be discussed in this section [41–45].

8.5.1 Physical Process System

The electronic, chemical and mechanical components of a device that are interconnected to perform a specific function are referred to as the physical entity. Energy systems, power systems, nuclear power plants and other systems are examples of this kind. In this case, device resilience is accomplished by enhancing features like reliability and robustness.

8.5.2 Cyber Feedback Loop Control Scheme

The physical processes of the device are tracked and managed by various components in the cyber world. With applications ranging from healthcare to smart grid, a level-based approach has been presented to differentiate the elements based on their functionality; each application uses its own sensing types and network.

8.5.2.1 Actuation and Monitoring Infrastructure Level

The status of physical entities are monitored and it serves as a link between the physical and cyber worlds. It is accomplished by the use of a networked system of sensors and actuators. Since we all remember the cyber physical system having electro encephalogram, electrocardiogram, electro myogram, oxygen saturation level, accelerometer and tilt sensors, photo plethysmography, smart door lock with video camera, audio, radio-frequency identification and video camera sensors for light, smoke and temperature, heat flux, and gas (oxygen, carbon monoxide and carbon dioxide), global positioning system, compass, Camera Wi-Fi, magnetometer and accelerometer are the different sensors applied in different game, smart grids, transport, electronics and clinical applications.

8.5.2.2 Network Communication Infrastructure Level

The status information is forwarded to the Distributed Control and Computation Unit infrastructure by this layer. Network connectivity infrastructure employs a variety of technologies such as switches, routers and gateways, each with its own set of protocols, depending on the type of use. Body Sensor Network, Global System for Mobile Communication, General Packet Radio Service, Internet, Wi-Fi Cellular, Bluetooth, 3G and Wireless Sensor Network are the categories of communication network applied between the controlling, computing, monitoring and actuation unit for diverse applications.

8.5.2.3 Distributed Control and Computation Unit Infrastructure Layer

This level, also known as the supervisory level, provides human–machine interactions, as well as the ability to make centralized decisions. Doctors and nurses, a data acquisition and storage component, an agent-based command-control component, a query manager agent and a collection of C3I user-interface agents to communicate with users, as well as an intelligent traffic signal control procedure to improve car-crossing at intersections and apply smart phone as a control and computing device in a variety of applications.

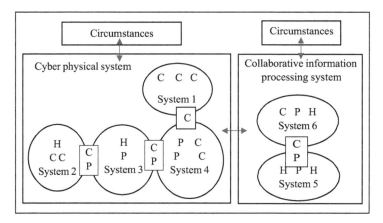

FIGURE 8.7 Conceptual view of a Cyber (C) Physical (P) System (S) with human (H) components organized in multiple systems and a Collaborative Information Processing System.

8.5.2.4 Human in Loop

This level was surrounded by a distributed computation and control layer, and it was here that higher-level policies and decisions were made on which question to use. In certain cases, human involvement is needed in addition to an information decision support system or a knowledge database. If a human CPS is considered where humans are integral parts along with technical components, the system gets developed, used and maintained by human teams surrounded by different supporting tools like computer aided engineering software and simulation of hardware in the loop (C and P). The collaboration between the human team and tools is called the collaborative information processing system and they operate in their specific environments. Figure 8.7 demonstrates the conceptual view of CPS having cyber, physical and human components and a Collaborative Information Processing System responsible for maintenance, production, and design.

8.6 CONCLUSION

In this chapter, different contributions of EEG in designing cyber physical systems for healthcare, security and privacy maintenance, the education sector and different other purposes have been discussed. The target demographic must be included in BCI assessment due to the many variations in body functions and application scenarios between people with disabilities and people who are able-bodied. In order to prevent learned helplessness in children with disabilities, it is critical to establish a consistent communication pathway during the early stages of development. In terms of assessment, it was suggested that conventional metrics of device output be supplemented with those relating to contextual variables in order to achieve user-centric architectures suitable for real-world integration. Future cyber physical system research involving people with disabilities can take into account measures of the consumer state and build more successful training paradigms.

REFERENCES

1. Lou, S., Feng, Y., Tian, G., Lv, Z., Li, Z. and Tan, J., 2017. A cyber-physical system for product conceptual design based on an intelligent psycho-physiological approach. *IEEE Access*, *5*, pp.5378–5387.
2. Pham, T., Ma, W., Tran, D., Nguyen, P. and Phung, D., 2013, November. A study on the feasibility of using EEG signals for authentication purpose. In *International Conference on Neural Information Processing* (pp. 562–569). Springer, Berlin, Heidelberg.
3. Wu, Q., Zeng, Y., Zhang, C., Tong, L. and Yan, B., 2018. An EEG-based person authentication system with open-set capability combining eye blinking signals. *Sensors*, *18*(2), p.335.
4. Bonaci, T., Calo, R. and Chizeck, H.J., 2014, May. App stores for the brain: Privacy & security in Brain–Computer Interfaces. In *2014 IEEE International Symposium on Ethics in Science, Technology and Engineering* (pp. 1–7). IEEE.
5. Azizi, M.M., Puwakpitiyage, C.H., Rao, V.P., Tee, W.J., Murugesan, R.K. and Hamzah, M.D., 2018, October. Authentication with brainwaves: a review on the application of EEG as an authentication method. In *2018 Fourth International Conference on Advances in Computing, Communication & Automation (ICACCA)* (pp. 1–6). IEEE.
6. Alhayajneh, A., Baccarini, A.N., Weiss, G.M., Hayajneh, T. and Farajidavar, A., 2018. Biometric authentication and verification for medical cyber physical systems. *Electronics*, *7*(12), p.436.
7. Lokesh, M., R.,Kumaraswamy, Y.S. andTejaswiniK.N., (2016) Challenges and Current Solutions of Cyber Physical Systems, *IOSR Journal of Computer Engineering,* 18(2), pp. 104–110.
8. Damaševičius, R., Maskeliūnas, R., Kazanavičius, E. and Woźniak, M., 2018. Combining cryptography with EEG biometrics. *Computational Intelligence and Neuroscience, 2018*.
9. Laghari, A., Memon, Z.A., Ullah, S. and Hussain, I., 2018. Cyber physical system for stroke detection. *IEEE Access*, *6*, pp.37444–37453.
10. Törngren, M. and Grogan, P.T., 2018. How to deal with the complexity of future cyber-physical systems? *Designs*, *2*(4), p.40.
11. Höller, Y. and Uhl, A., 2018, June. Do EEG-biometric templates threaten user privacy? In *Proceedings of the 6th ACM Workshop on Information Hiding and Multimedia Security* (pp. 31–42).
12. Nguyen, D., Tran, D., Sharma, D. and Ma, W., 2017. On the study of EEG-based cryptographic key generation. *Procedia Computer Science, 112*, pp.936–945.
13. Hu, B., Liu, Q., Zhao, Q., Qi, Y. and Peng, H., 2011, December. A real-time electro-encephalogram (EEG) based individual identification interface for mobile security in ubiquitous environment. In *2011 IEEE Asia–Pacific Services Computing Conference* (pp.436–441). IEEE.
14. Chai, R., Naik, G.R., Ling, S.H. and Nguyen, H.T., 2017. Hybrid brain–computer interface for biomedical cyber-physical system application using wireless embedded EEG systems. *BioMedical Engineering OnLine*, *16*(1), p.5.
15. Govindarajan, U.H., Trappey, A.J. and Trappey, C.V., 2018. Immersive technology for human-centric cyber-physical systems in complex manufacturing processes: a comprehensive overview of the global patent profile using collective intelligence. *Complexity, 2018*.

16. Pippos, G., Maurer, R., D'Souza, M. and Ros, M., 2018. Investigating Machine Learning Classifiers on a Brain Machine Interface, for Cyber Physical Systems Applications. In *Proceedings of the International Conference on Embedded Systems, Cyber-physical Systems, and Applications (ESCS)* (pp. 65–70). The Steering Committee of The World Congress in Computer Science, Computer Engineering and Applied Computing (WorldComp).

17. Landau, O., Puzis, R. and Nissim, N., 2020. Mind Your Mind: EEG-Based Brain-Computer Interfaces and Their Security in Cyber Space. *ACM Computing Surveys (CSUR), 53*(1), pp.1–38.

18. Švogor, I. and Kišasondi, T., 2012, June. Two factor authentication using EEG augmented passwords. In *Proceedings of the ITI 2012 34th International Conference on Information Technology Interfaces* (pp. 373–378). IEEE.

19. Romero, O., Chatterjee, S. and Pequito, S., 2020, July. Fractional-Order Model Predictive Control for Neurophysiological Cyber-Physical Systems: A Case Study using Transcranial Magnetic Stimulation. In *2020 American Control Conference (ACC)* (pp. 4996–5001). IEEE.

20. Annese, V.F. and De Venuto, D., 2015, June. FPGA based architecture for fall-risk assessment during gait monitoring by synchronous EEG/EMG. In *2015 6th International Workshop on Advances in Sensors and Interfaces (IWASI)* (pp. 116–121). IEEE.

21. De Venuto, D., Annese, V.F., Defazio, G., Gallo, V.L. and Mezzina, G., 2017, April. Gait analysis and quantitative drug effect evaluation in Parkinson's disease by jointly EEG-EMG monitoring. In *2017 12th International Conference on Design & Technology of Integrated Systems in Nanoscale Era (DTIS)* (pp. 1–6). IEEE.

22. De Venuto, D., Annese, V.F. and Sangiovanni-Vincentelli, A.L., 2016, May. The ultimate IoT application: A cyber-physical system for ambient assisted living. In *2016 IEEE International Symposium on Circuits and Systems (ISCAS)* (pp. 2042–2045). IEEE.

23. de Tommaso, M., Vecchio, E., Ricci, K., Montemurno, A., De Venuto, D. and Annese, V.F., 2015, June. Combined EEG/EMG evaluation during a novel dual task paradigm for gait analysis. In *2015 6th International Workshop on Advances in Sensors and Interfaces (IWASI)* (pp. 181–186). IEEE.

24. Kaburlasos, V.G., Vrochidou, E., Panagiotopoulos, F., Aitsidis, C. and Jaki, A., 2019, June. Time Series Classification in Cyber-Physical System Applications by Intervals' Numbers Techniques. In *2019 IEEE International Conference on Fuzzy Systems (FUZZ-IEEE)* (pp. 1–6). IEEE.

25. Bhrugubanda, M., 2015. A review on applications of cyber physical systems. *International Journal of Innovative Science, Engineering and Technology, 2*(6), pp.728–730.

26. De Venuto, D., Annese, V.F., Ruta, M., Di Sciascio, E. and Vincentelli, A.L.S., 2015. Designing a cyber–physical system for fall prevention by cortico–muscular coupling detection. *IEEE Design & Test, 33*(3), pp.66–76.

27. Gupta, G., Pequito, S. and Bogdan, P., 2018, April. Re-thinking EEG-based non-invasive brain interfaces: modeling and analysis. In *2018 ACM/IEEE 9th International Conference on Cyber-Physical Systems (ICCPS)* (pp. 275–286). IEEE.

28. Sun, S., Zheng, X., Gong, B., Garcia Paredes, J. and Ordieres-Meré, J., 2020. Healthy operator 4.0: A human cyber–physical system architecture for smart workplaces. *Sensors, 20*(7), p.2011.

29. Moghimi, S., Kushki, A., Marie Guerguerian, A. and Chau, T., 2013. A review of EEG-based brain–computer interfaces as access pathways for individuals with severe disabilities. *Assistive Technology*, *25*(2), pp.99–110.
30. Kim, S., Paik, W., 2019. Use of Electroencephalography (EEG) In Academic Achievement Assessment. *International Journal of Scientific & Technology Research*, 8(11), pp. 2185–2189.
31. Rasheed, M.A., Chand, P., Ahmed, S., Sharif, H., Hoodbhoy, Z., Siddiqui, A. and Hasan, B.S., 2021. Use of artificial intelligence on Electroencephalogram (EEG) waveforms to predict failure in early school grades in children from a rural cohort in Pakistan. *Plos one*, *16*(2), p.e0246236.
32. Monastra, V.J., Lubar, J.F., Linden, M., VanDeusen, P., Green, G., Wing, W., Phillips, A. and Fenger, T.N., 1999. Assessing attention deficit hyperactivity disorder via quantitative electroencephalography: an initial validation study. *Neuropsychology*, *13*(3), p.424.
33. Antonenko, P., Paas, F., Grabner, R. and Van Gog, T., 2010. Using electroencephalography to measure cognitive load. *Educational Psychology Review*, *22*(4), pp.425–438.
34. Sood, S.K. and Singh, K.D., 2018. An Optical-Fog assisted EEG-based virtual reality framework for enhancing E-learning through educational games. *Computer Applications in Engineering Education*, *26*(5), pp.1565–1576.
35. Galant, M. and Merkisz, J., 2017. Analysis of the possibilities of using EEG in assessing pilots' psychophysical condition. *ZeszytyNaukowe. Transport/PolitechnikaŚląska.*
36. Zeng, H., Yang, C., Dai, G., Qin, F., Zhang, J. and Kong, W., 2018. EEG classification of driver mental states by deep learning. *Cognitive Neurodynamics*, *12*(6), pp.597–606.
37. Zero, E., Bersani, C., Zero, L. and Sacile, R., 2019. Towards real-time monitoring of fear in driving sessions. *IFAC-PapersOnLine*, *52*(19), pp.299–304.
38. Jing, D., Liu, D., Zhang, S. and Guo, Z., 2020. Fatigue driving detection method based on EEG analysis in low-voltage and hypoxia plateau environment. *International Journal of Transportation Science and Technology*, *9*(4), pp.366–376.
39. Yang, L., He, Z., Guan, W. and Jiang, S., 2018. Exploring the relationship between electroencephalography (EEG) and ordinary driving behavior: a simulated driving study. *Transportation Research Record*, *2672*(37), pp.172–180.
40. Teng, T., Bi, L. and Liu, Y., 2017. EEG-based detection of driver emergency braking intention for brain–controlled vehicles. *IEEE Transactions on Intelligent Transportation Systems*, *19*(6), pp.1766–1773.
41. Hu, F., Lu, Y., Vasilakos, A.V., Hao, Q., Ma, R., Patil, Y., Zhang, T., Lu, J., Li, X. and Xiong, N.N., 2016. Robust cyber–physical systems: Concept, models, and implementation. *Future Generation Computer Systems*, *56*, pp.449–475.
42. Bai, Z.Y. and Huang, X.Y., 2012. Design and implementation of a cyber physical system for building smart living spaces. *International Journal of Distributed Sensor Networks*, *8*(5), p.764186.
43. Hossain, M.S., 2015. Cloud-supported cyber–physical localization framework for patients monitoring. *IEEE Systems Journal*, *11*(1), pp.118–127.
44. Sokolov, S., Zhilenkov, A., Chernyi, S., Nyrkov, A. and Glebov, N., 2020. Hybrid neural networks in cyber physical system interface control systems. *Bulletin of Electrical Engineering and Informatics*, *9*(3), pp.1268–1275.
45. De Venuto, D., Annese, V.F., Mezzina, G. and Defazio, G., 2018. FPGA-based embedded cyber-physical platform to assess gait and postural stability in Parkinson's

disease. *IEEE Transactions on Components, Packaging and Manufacturing Technology, 8*(7), pp.1167–1179.

46.   Saha, S. and Ghosh, A., 2019, December. Rehabilitation Using Neighbor-Cluster Based Matching Inducing Artificial Bee Colony Optimization. In *2019 IEEE 16th India Council International Conference (INDICON)* (pp. 1–4). IEEE.

47.   Ghosh, A. and Saha, S., 2020. Interactive Game-Based Motor Rehabilitation Using Hybrid Sensor Architecture. In *Handbook of Research on Emerging Trends and Applications of Machine Learning* (pp. 312–337). IGI Global.

48.   Elsayed, N., Zaghloul, Z.S. and Bayoumi, M., 2017. Brain computer interface: EEG signal preprocessing issues and solutions. *Int. J. Comput. Appl, 169*(3), pp.975–8887.

49.   Millett, D., 2001. Hans Berger: From psychic energy to the EEG. *Perspectives in Biology and Medicine, 44*(4), pp.522–542.

50.   Sanei, S. and Chambers, J.A., 2013. *EEG signal processing.* John Wiley & Sons.

51.   Tong, S. and Thakor, N.V., 2009. *Quantitative EEG analysis methods and clinical applications.* Artech House.

52.   Bablani, A. and Tripathi, D., 2018. A review on methods applied on P300-based lie detectors. In *Advances in Machine Learning and Data Science*(pp. 251–257). Springer, Singapore.

53.   Cook, L.G. and Mitschow, L.C., 2019. Beyond the polygraph: deception detection and the autonomic nervous system. *Federal Practitioner, 36*(7), p.316.

9 Sentimental Analysis of Social Context Using Integration of PSO-Cuckoo Optimization and SVM Classifier

Ajesh F[1], Praveetha Gobinathan[2], Shermin Shamsudden[2] and Muhammad Arif[3]
[1]Sree Buddha College of Engineering, Alappuzha, Kerala, India, [2]Jazan University, Saudi Arabia, [3]Superior University Lahore, Pakistan

9.1 INTRODUCTION

As the internet becomes instantly and easily available, social networking sites such as Facebook, Twitter and YouTube have become the perfect forum for individuals around the world to express their views on different issues and problems. Sentiment analysis is one of the handling procedures of common language that assists with grouping emotions that empower business people to gather data on their customer sets through different online channels, for example, web-based media, studies, e-commerce site surveys and so on [1]. This knowledge will allow us to understand the causes and variables that cause product degradation. This shows that analyzing such a large amount of multimedia data is necessary. One situation in which people have begun to air their views is the e-commerce sector. Consumers have useful inputs on the goods bought to help other prospective purchasers make the right decision. It also gives businesses the ability to use social media not only as a forum for interaction, but also through customer reviews to gain valuable insight into their products[2].

Blogs, web forums, discussion pages on media sites and social networking sites like Facebook and Twitter can be categorized as social media. These social media can capture the views or word-of-mouth of millions of people. There is a revolution in communication studies on computer linguistics and social networks and the availability of these real-time insights from people around the world. Social networking for an organization is becoming an increasingly useful source of data. On the other hand, through social media, individuals are more willing and readier than ever to share the truth about their lives, insights, perspectives and views with the entire world. They participate in activities by voicing their views and communicating their

DOI: 10.1201/9781003190301-9

comments to society. This way of sharing their awareness and feelings with society and social media allows companies to gather more information about their markets and products, and to realize how trustworthy they are among individuals, and therefore make choices to continue with their businesses efficiently. It is also evident that sentiment analysis is a central element for leading companies that concentrate on innovative management of customer service and marketing of customer relationships. Furthermore, companies want to market their products, find new markets and manage their image[3]. They recognize the interactions, acknowledge the relevant material and take appropriate action on it as organizations aim to automate the noise filtering process. Some are now looking into the field of sentiment research. Sometimes referred to as the information age, or knowledge society, access to large quantities of information in the time we live in today means it is no longer a challenge to look at the tons of new information generated every day on the web. Data has become the primary trading object in this era for many businesses. If we are able to build and use methods for searching and extracting appropriate data and knowledge, and mine them with precision and timeliness to move them on to expertise, that is where the exact use of this vast volume of information available to us is. However, in many situations, this essential knowledge and data is not found in organized sources, such as tables or databases, but in unstructured documents written in human language. Human languages are ambiguous, and two different meanings can be conveyed using the same emotion in two different ways. Furthermore, some people use different jargon, slang communication and shortened words[4] for their convenience. In terms of their polarity, such as positive, negative or neutral, and the subjectivity of thoughts, it is often hard to accurately quantify and calculate emotions. In order to communicate feelings about a letter, tweet, Facebook wall post, etc., most of today's business solutions rely on simple Boolean words. But this is not sufficient to address the above-mentioned sentiment analysis issues and it will not generate accurate and timely knowledge of aggregate feelings. In order to obtain correct information after analyzing a thought, it should be mandatory to solve the above problems. Many other systems are still at the research level trying to solve these issues, some systems are still trying to analyze multi-language emotions, and few systems are still commercially able to correct some of the above-mentioned disadvantages (Figure 9.1).

Sentiment assessment is consistently used in realities mining, wherein one needs to separate simple current realities and concentrate records from current realities. There are varieties of natural language records: one is dependable records, the alternative is records that are subjective. The predefined and simple to-decipher genuine record is reality, while emotion is emotional records that differ from character to character. The word "Sentiment" might be perceived as feeling, consideration and disposition. The view is a time span portrayed as a judgment or view on a chosen angle in the considerations of an assessment holder. Both assessment mining and feeling appraisal are compatible terms. Sentiment analysis is a natural language dealing with locale[5] that avoids the trouble of eliminating the assessment of printed content. The conclusion in classification is fixated on surveying whether online media assessment is favorable or unfavorable. Deeper insights that take a look at opinion can be very beneficial in regions including politics, economics, business and marketing. Previous studies have

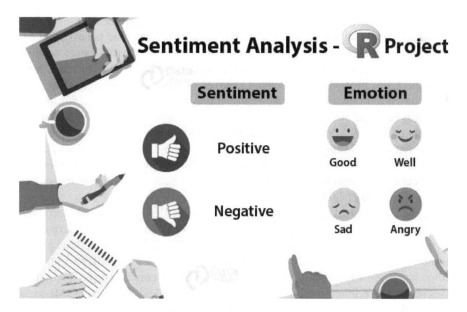

FIGURE 9.1   Sentimental Analysis [93].

proven how notion and public opinion can have an effect on economic markets, retail prices, polls and public health. Sentiment evaluation is used as an automation of the given textual content evaluation to decide the expressed sentiments. Aspect stages, textual content and sentence are three main ranges of category. In preceding figures the subject of sentiment evaluation, gadget studying algorithms had been used as a category. In preceding years, the usage of function choice strategies has also been elevated to enhance the classifier's accuracy.

9.2   SENTIMENT ANALYSIS METHODS USED IN SOCIAL MEDIA

All the papers established the usage of both Lexicon-based methodology, system getting to know techniques or an aggregate of each strategy based on the papers studied in the implementation of sentiment analysis. The lexicon-based technique is utilized by seven of the reviewed articles, ten papers used machine getting to know and seven papers illustrated the aggregate of each method in undertaking sentiment analysis.

A lexicon-based framework is called unsupervised learning. The dictionary method requires no data from training and only depends on the dictionary. In conducting sentiment analysis, most research has modified the SentiwardNet and TF-IDR framework. This strategy is determined depending on the recurrence of words in the content information, alongside other positive or negative words in pre-created polarity word references, for example, SentiwardNet. This converts words into numbers relative to the TF-IDR framework, and the frequency of the document is measured using the inverse frequency method[8].

Techniques rely on professional resources, and the effectiveness of the whole approach depends on the accuracy of professional resources. The polarity that can be derived from the polarity of words that make up a piece of text depends on it[9]. Given the complexity of natural languages, especially when it comes to slang, irony and neglect, this method is not intended to cover all aspects of language. There is no compelling reason to utilize sensory expression. A few issues remain, for instance a few words have various implications relying upon the application, a few expressions with emotional words may not communicate any feeling and a few expressions without emotional words may likewise establish a connection[10]. In any case, the vocabulary-based methodology has its own favorable circumstances, as it empowers fast calculation of positive and negative words, adaptability to change for various dialects and speed of analysis.

The ML framework goes under the direction of learning and the technique requires processing the training information. The SVM and Naïve Bayes model is the most generally utilized tool for ML strategies. Be that as it may, these are the most broadly utilized ML models. Gullible Bayes prevails with regards to supporting vector machines when applied to a very much shaped content corpus[11], which gives sensible execution to a low-design informational index. However, the ML algorithm works inadequately on Facebook with individuals posting irregular lengths and spelling errors and requires a lot of process to change the framework, as the size of the dataset influences the size and quality of the yield[10,12]. Also, ML algorithms require some investment when the perplexing ML model takes hours, particularly if preparation is required[7]. With the small size of the training set, the strategy is quick, yet it brings about less accurate grouping exactness[13].

Interestingly, researchers claim that the two types of analytical methods are very similar in terms of accuracy[13]. In order to predict the speed of emotions using the Naïve Bayes multi-event model, there are options for combining two word-based emotion classification methods by word, with an emotional scoring function, and a machine learning approach. Research has shown that instead of focusing on one approach, combining the two methods[11] increases efficiency. Subsequently, it is proposed to consolidate the two techniques, as they supplement each other to improve the outcome, and the outcome is improved compared with the utilization of just a single methodology, which is valuable for depicting the pattern of a hybrid approach[13]. It can likewise improve the treatment of unstructured information[14],[15].

Here in this chapter, we used both lexicon-based analysis approaches and apply three most useful machine learning methods such as Support Vector Machine (SVM), Naïve Bayes and Maximum Entropy (MP) classifiers as a contrast to our proposed SVM methods along with hybrid optimization.

9.3 MACHINE LEARNING APPROACH FOR SENTIMENTAL ANALYSIS

Behavior towards any sort of event is called sentiment. It also includes many kinds of emotions: happiness, tenderness, sadness or nostalgia, which is self-indulgent. Emotional labels can be defined as polarity or valence or different kinds of emotions (e.g., positive, neutral and negative) or e.g., anger, happiness, sadness, pride. The notion of mood tags affects the outcome of emotion analysis, so we need to carefully define mood tags. Studies have recognized at least three disposition names (e.g., opinion points, emotion sentiments), and a few examinations have included two-dimensional names (e.g., positive and negative). Albeit huge advances have been made in sentiment examination, binary sentiment classification is intricate; for instance, the viability of late analysis (for example exactness) goes from 70% to 90% regarding data qualities.

Support Vector Machine (SVM), Naïve Bayes (NB), Maximum Entropy (ME) and Stochastic Gradient Descent (SGD) can be used to inspect feelings. N-gram is potentially the most consistently used attribute. Read[75] used a component of letter mix to acknowledge equivalent arrangements and achieved 88.94% precision using SVM. Kennedy and Inkpen[76] proposed the ability to see the coordinating strategy of monograms and diagrams, and used SVM to achieve precision of film diagram data[77] at 84.4%. Wan[78] gave the equivalent strategy of letters and two-fold character works and got 86.1% exactness for the decoded Amazon thing study information. Akaichi[79] utilizes a blend of unigram, bigram and trigram quality to achieve 72.78% exactness. Valakunde and Patwardhan[80] focused in on five sorts of hypothetical designs (for example, solid, moderate, positive, sensible, negative and solid negative), and used SVM bigram highlighting to gain 81% precision. In the assessment of Gautam and Yadav[81], they utilized SVM close by a semantic appraisal model to assess the equal outline of Twitter messages, and utilized a monogram to reach a precision of 89.9%. Tripathy et al.[82] have used the SVM with n-gram credits and got 88.94% exactness for thought identical sales. Hasan et al.[83] got unigram characterization for emotion joined portrayal and achieved 79% using the NB for unraveled Urdu tweets data. As a rule, 70–90% accuracy was refined by these evaluations utilizing n-gram order, and SVM was the best.

There has likewise been research for the characterization of sentiment that has recognized hand-created highlights. Yassine and Hajj[84] utilized the full of feeling lexicon, misspelling and emojis as attributes and got 87% exactness for ternary order utilizing SVM. Denecke[85] portrayed three scores as characteristics (e.g., motivation, negativity and objectivity) and got 67%precision and 66% using the combined gathering Logistic Regression (LR) classifier. Jiang et al.[86] utilized SVM to beat the binary classification and accomplished Twitter messages with 67.8% exactness, following two sorts of target-autonomous comfort (e.g., twitter content highlights and opinion word dictionary highlights). Bahraini and Dengel[87] utilized a number of positive and negative words as quality, and utilized Twitter messages for equal classification, with a precision speed of 86.7%. Neethu and Rajasree[88] joined unigram including their own Twitter unequivocal featuring to utilize SVM for organizing and accomplished 90% precision. Karamibekr and Ghorbani[89] describe the number of evaluation things as a noun, and the element is combined with letters. Using SVM, the accuracy of the ternary sequence reaches 65.46%. Antai[90] used SVM to take the normalized frequency of words as the attribute of the parallel order and obtained 84% accuracy. Ghiassi and Lee[92] focused on five types of emotional groupings and recognized the spatial autonomy of Twitter information collections. They got a F1 score of 92.7% utilizing SVM. Mensikova and Mattmann[93] utilized the extraction results of named segments (NS) as the center and got a phony positive rate of 099

(FPR). Rather than simply using n-gram works, these examinations expanded the importance of the limit and gained better results (e.g., 92.7% F1 score). Obviously, since they utilized diverse datasets, contrasting the exhibition between the past examinations isn't reasonable. Notwithstanding, it is self-evident, as appeared in [89],[93], that the mix of hand-created and n-gram qualities should be superior to utilizing just n-gram attributes.

9.4   LITERATURE REVIEW

To convey enlightening data about individuals' considerations, dispositions and sentiments about any item, idea or strategy with interpersonal interaction locales, for example, Twitter, Facebook, Instagram and WhatsApp are overwhelming the universe of correspondence; information found on these online media platforms has become significant. To examine the Twitter content and perform assessment mining on Twitter data, a few studies have been undertaken. A way to deal with assessing the twitter channel utilizing the deep convolution neural network was recommended by Jianqiang, Xiaolin and Xuejun[16]. By examining Twitter information, the list of capabilities was consolidated into profound CNN for preparation and forecasting of sentiments. Text pre-processing has a major task to carry out with regards to Twitter information analysis. In Jianqiang and Xiaolin[17], a few pre-preparing techniques have been tried and thought about. Since conclusion analysis includes dissecting and deciphering different sorts of emotions, Complex and Intelligent Systems are profoundly significant for multi-class emotion examination and are discussed by Bouazizi and Ohtsuki[18]. An apparatus named SENTA has been created,[19] which utilizes an example examination way to perform multi-class emotion analysis. It is critical to consider, as examined in [20], the new changes in assessment mining, the significance and the perplexing occasions that occur during the Twitter conversations.

Further research work was incited by the utilization of Twitter to comprehend emotions using Twitter information. One such research, examined in [21], uses a hybrid model to direct conclusion of analysis utilizing a genetic-based approach. The point of this work was to build up the structure from the viewpoint of adaptability. Tan et al.[22] have utilized a measurable model to distinguish the frontal area subjects and urge great competitor positioning to assess the varieties of general assessment on a given issue. An interesting action significant for thoughtful exploration is the characterization of sentiments dependent on the topic of conversation. Liu, Cheng, Li and Li[23] gave a significant subject classification of versatile sentiments over tweets. The various difficulties raised were tended to by Bouazizi and Ohtsuki[24] during multiclass sentiment analysis, and another model was additionally worked on by the creators utilizing multiclass sentiment analysis over Twitter information. Trilla and Alias[25] recommended a successful content dependent on the expressions given for the transformation of words in the Twitter subtleties. Yu, Xu, Wang and Ni[26] executed another structure for various levelled subjects demonstrating Online Analytical Processing utilizing Twitter information (OLAP). Wide OLAP information bases, for example, Vertica[27], Greenplum[28] and Teradata DB[29], have been proposed to improve the viability of analysis related questions. Vertica utilizes projection to build question proficiency. Rather than building conventional records on sections, it saves the points of interest of min/max levels, prompting less gainful higher latencies from lower pruning. Greenplum and Teradata DB approve savvy store sections and grant clients column indexing. Nonetheless, there are two downsides: at first, it is unnecessary to change section records in the composing way for every segment list; also, for point-query inquiries, it needs more arbitrary input/output. Without much of a stretch it can be perceived from the above works that the substance of twitter information or any media give significant bits of knowledge into any subject being discussed, and frequently express the perspectives of people worried about the particular issue. Removing the pith of the given issue is the key to increase the unique capacity of machine learning algorithms. This gives total information depictions and empowers the engineer to consider choosing the right calculation that can be utilized for the question. Clustering, sorting, regression and rule extraction are a portion of the predominant classes of machine learning algorithms.

As specialists have put forth significant attempts throughout the last20 years in the field of sentiment analysis, numerous methodologies and models have been proposed. There are two options in contrast to the accompanying models: supervised learning[30],[31],[32],[33],[34],[35] and lexicon-based learning[36],[37],[38]. The lexicon is a predefined word assortment where a polarity score[39] is related to each word.

It is the easiest way to deal with emotion classification. To classify an expression, this methodology utilizes the lexicon and performs word coordinating. The proficiency of this characterization strategy depends on the size of the dictionary. The greater the vocabulary, the higher the exactness. Different word dictionaries, for example, SentiWordNet, General Inquirer, MPQA Lexicon and VADER Lexicon, and so forth, are accessible. Preparing ML algorithms, for example, SVM, Naïve Bayes, Neural Network, Random Forest and so on were utilized by oversaw frameworks, close by various highlights, for example, word n-grams, Part-of-Speech (POS) marks and exceptional tweet information, for example, capital verbalization, emojis, hashtags and retweets, and so forth. Exploration on the Sentiment Analysis strategy for online media information is given by Sharma et al.[40], where they said that SVM was broadly used for these purposes. Sentimental Analysis is a multi-step technique including pre-processing, feature extraction, feature selection, gathering of emotions using figuring's for ML calculations and results assessment. The element determination stage in sentiment analysis plays a huge part in achieving the unrivalled success of the estimation classifier model. Different strategies, for example, data pick up, TF-IDF, Chi-square and so on are the customary

element determination methods used. These procedures create an imperfect list of capabilities as sentiment analysis is a NP-Hard issue. Advancement procedures might be utilized over these strategies to accomplish a streamlined list of capabilities that improves the exactness just as the handling season of the characterization model. In sorting the examination, the grouping model likewise assumes a critical job.

Kumar et al.[41] made a study on multitude knowledge for feature improvement in sentimental analysis in which they found that the estimation of exactness is favored by swarm streamlining. They likewise attempted a near analysis of different multitude knowledge. Agarwal et al.[42] did an assessment on Twitter information. Their earlier POS-based extremity includes and utilizes the tree kernel for work designing.

Their research is better than the established methods. Jianqiang et al.[43] suggested an unsupervised learning method for enormous Twitter data for word insertion. In conjunction with word emotion extremity and n-gram, word insertion was used to construct a tweet and included a package used to prepare CNN (convolution neural network). The exhibition of the implemented work and the n-gram technique have been contrasted with respect to F-measure and accuracy.

They in addition utilized specific datasets, yet the most exactness is 87.62%. Xia et al.[44] present a controlled model of how to survey the impressions of beast data. This procedure helps with saving the results for conceivable confirmation. The scope of solicitation in this paper is up to 81% and 81.7% using Naïve Bayes and vital regression. Udochukwu et al.[45] suggest techniques called a standard-based pipeline that helps with the OCC model manual to organize sentiments from the material. Five feeling bunches were used in this test study. In this proposed work, the accuracy goes up to 82.7%. In this paper, Li and Liu et al.[46] further improved their present work by handling and modifying the different instruments of emotions for separating data from the tremendous dataset. In three adjusted and unequal classes, the survey of results is completed. By means of non-opinion content processing, the best results are acquired. The after-effect of accuracy fluctuates between 89.67% and 88.00%. Maximal outcomes are acquired on account of a fair cosine distance estimation strategy. Results for exactness range from 60.17% to 64.13%.

While, for unbalanced gatherings, the answer for the voting framework is utilized for ideal proficiency. The precision result is in the scope of 49% and 53.76%. Luts et al.[47] executed work in which a web-based classification mining system is created using the SVM classifier. The solicitation task precisely portrays the web text without assistance from any other individual learning, strong model social occasion and SVM well-hypothesis. The consequence of their assessment shows that this figuring for classification is more suitable and reasonable. To satisfy the text classification, Wei Zhao et al.[48] used the k-means count and GA estimation for the determination of highlights. The fundamental results indicated that the blend of the k-means and GA calculations is essentially significant in diminishing the confirmation of high-dimensional features, correspondingly improving the abundance and accuracy of text classification. As we noticed, various specialists utilized various systems and on various sorts of the information bases to play out the assumption investigation, however, a couple of works should be finished utilizing sentimental analysis streamlining techniques.

9.5   PROPOSED METHODOLOGY

There are two kinds of arrangement strategies for sentiment, the parallel classification procedure and the grouping strategy for multi-class estimation. Each li record in L is grouped in the double order procedure where L={l1,l2,l3, ln}is characterized into class K where K={Positive, Negative}and the di is arranged into classification in the multi-class estimation characterization: K={Positive, Neutral, Negative}[49].

In the case of forecasting better goods, shops and all across social media, this chapter aims at the machine learning method of sentimental analysis. So, data is

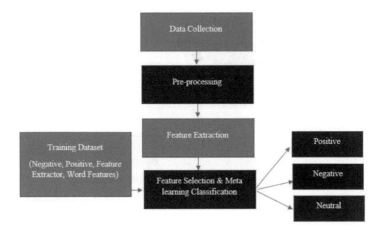

FIGURE 9.2   Workflow of entire process.

initially collected in which social media messages about the goods are pre–processed so that stop-words and noise are eliminated. Then these data will be matched in sentimental lexicons, once matched it will undergo a second matching process in the emoticon dictionary and then feature extraction occurs and the vectorized types of machine learning techniques are implemented in which we use Support Vector Machine (SVM), Naïve Bayes and Maximum Entropy as methods of comparison on the proposed method SVM with Hybrid Optimization. The flow of work is shown in Figure 9.2.

9.5.1   DATA COLLECTION

We need data for sentimental analysis here as we analyze social media comments and thus suggest products and shops, so a web crawler based on an application processing interface is generated to retrieve social media data, and these data are translated for pre-processing into .csv format. In Figure 9.3, the web crawler is shown.

9.5.2   PRE-PROCESSING

This stage is one of the most critical stages in which output quality is improved by data cleaning and the elimination of stop words, etc.[50–55].

(a) Data required for the classification of reviews shall be documented in the combinable vectorization process and the technique of the vector space model shall be used for the same.
(b) POS tagging is part of speech tagging that allows POS, i.e., verb, adverb, noun, pronoun, adjective, etc., to label any data term.
(c) In order to reduce the spatiality between the words, stemming and lemmatization is used. The phrases "light" "brighter" "and" "brightening" are, for example, taken as a single phrase, "bright".

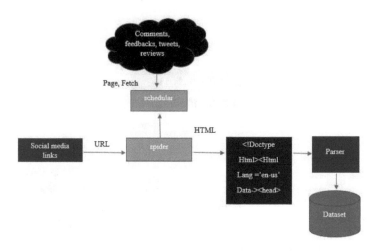

FIGURE 9.3 Web Crawler.

   (d) There should not be any effect on the final meaning of the data sentiment while removing the terms–Stop word deletion.

Each word in each sentence is changed into a vector after the pre-preparing stage. The vectors are then differentiated, in light of their level of cosine closeness and the vectors of the emotion word. To be merged, the emotion word vectors with expanded vicinity scores are picked. By sorting out different wellsprings of semantic data, the recommendation helps increase the "semantic force" of standard semantic space models for feeling analysis. Because of the presence of the emotion vocabulary, the word dictionary-based component extraction strategy is promising. An emotion word dictionary consistently comprises of a movement of language-unequivocal words, including particulars of the emotion network with which it has an area, the repeat of furthest point and so on.

   To make the model and produce the emotion word vectors, a bunch of records and emotional dictionaries is given. A corpus, D, comprises of an assortment of writings, $D = \{d1, d2 \cdots, dn\}$, and a vocabulary, $T = \{t1, t2 \cdots, tm\}$, got from D, which are explicit words. From the Word2Vec model, the word depiction of the term ti is arranged, and thereafter a lot of word depictions of all words in the jargon are separated, i.e., $V = \{v1, v2 \cdots, vm\} = Rmxd$, where m is the vocab size, and d addresses the vector space estimations. The center of this methodology is to develop eager word vectors that impersonate the feeling information for every vocabulary word, however, the greater part of them pass on those feelings that are not customary scientific expression, so the strategy utilizes all feeling terms as the dictionary's feeling $E = [E1, E2,.. ., .Ek]$, $VE = \{VE1, VE2, \cdots, Vek\}$, and get depictions of their terms. There is a low level of incorporation issues due to the scale issue of word introducing the model by setting up the corpus, for instance, there are a couple of terms in the vocabulary of feeling, however, not in the vector spaces through which they are instructed. These expressions may likewise be skipped and erased in the resulting classification.

The meaning of words with very emotional extremity that can be utilized to assess the cosine likeness between the vectors characterized by V and E might be the equivalent, i.e., sim (V, E) = cosine (V, E), known as cosine (V, E)

$$\text{sim (V, E)} = (\Sigma d\ i=1\ Vi * Vei) / (\Sigma d\ i=1\ V2\ I * \Sigma d\ i=1\ V2\ Ei) \quad (9.1)$$

where V and E are the vectors of length d.

For anything in T, the closeness to everything in E is endure, and subsequently the results of resemblance are amassed in the grid Y= Rmxk, where m is the length of the substance glossary, k is the length of the jargon of feelings, and Yi, j shows the proportionality of cosine between the lexical thing I and the emotion j. Taking into account lattice Y, the top n feeling names, Ew = {e1,e2, ···en}, are picked by setting the edge. They are the closest neighbors to the thing in T, as per words in Ew, as directed by isolating their sentimental contrasts. Comparability in Y implies that a thing in E and a thing in T have a comparative setting; the intensity of feeling given in the word reference at that point addresses the thing's feeling information in E and builds up the feeling vector by joining the two sorts of information for everything in T.

For each word, the emotional word vector is figured as a weighted total as opposed to a basic normal activity:

$$\text{EmotionVec}_i = 1/n\ \Sigma\ i=1\ \text{to n weight}_i * V_{ei} \quad (9.2)$$

Equation (9.3) is then used to gauge each word's weight; the higher positioned closest neighbors will get higher loads dependent on this recipe:

$$\text{Weight}_i = Y_{ij} * \text{score}_j \quad (9.3)$$

At that point, by power evaluations, we rate the emotional words in Ew. In Ew, the scorej is characterized as the equal position of ej, which is:

$$\text{Score}_j = 1/\ \text{rank}_i \quad (9.4)$$

Where rank signifies the position of ej made by the way toward positioning dependent on strength. To aggregate to one, the loads should be standardized. With the accompanying relationship, this can be accomplished:

$$\text{weighti} = \text{weighti}\ \Sigma n\ j=1\ \text{weightj} \quad (9.5)$$

The impediments of setting-based word solidification achieve emotions in reverse propensity to the uttermost point having a by and large high cosine resemblance in the vector space during the time spent structuring the inclination word vector of words. In the development of word vectors of emotion using word inserting classification and cosine likeness, there are enormous mixups made, so word references are used to address the orchestrating of word portrayals from the word embedding space. To smooth out existing word vectors, it is a nice strategy to use veritable regarded tendency power scores given by the emotion word references and word vector refinement model. Words are moreover closer to words that are semantically and earnestly equal in the words reference (those which have same strengths), and it is not quite possible for those to be avoided, but instead are semantically equivalent.

9.5.3   Feature Extraction

Regardless of whether a word or an arrangement of words might be an element is identified with the distinguishing proof of raw content attributes. The principal ways to deal with the issue of characteristic portrayal are vocabulary packs, a sack of thoughts, basic lexicons, and dictionary-based modifier information, adjectives, nouns and adverbs. Some extraction strategies are discussed in [56–58].

(a) N-grams Characteristics: N-grams are by and large ideas, syllables, different words (bigrams, trigrams, and the sky is the limit from there) or wonders that happen in the grouping of a given book or articulation.
(b) Parts of Speech (POS) Tagging: Part of discourse labelling is a bit of programming that in certain dialects understands text and assigns POS to each word, for example, things, action word descriptors and so forth
(c) Negation: The refutation clause can change the importance of the word conclusion from negative to positive, from positive to negative, for example, not terrible, bad, etc.
(d) Sentiment Analyzer: The positive and negative feelings of words in the paper are assessed by Sentiment Analyzer, for example lovely expressions of a good inclination direction.

9.5.4   Feature Selection and Meta Learning Classification

Using the voting strategy is the least difficult technique to combine a couple of classifiers and select which engraving gets the most votes. Projecting a voting form is a striking notable measure that wires different viewpoints on residents' classifiers into a bigger part. We utilize three classifiers, Support Vector Machine (SVM), Naïve Bayes (NB) and Maximum Entropy (ME) classifiers, and the proposed strategy, SVM with Hybrid Optimization (i.e., cuckoo search and Swarm algorithm) to frame a differentiation.

(a) **Support Vector Machine (SVM):** SVM is a ML classifier that can be utilized for classification and regression issues. Single-piece SVM is broadly utilized for data handling in different settings (counting on the web media). Contrasted with other execution methodologies for text classification, linear SVM is viewed as uncommon. In this count, we draw every data thing as a point in a n-dimensional space, where every limit gauge is a gauge for every classification, where n is the quantity of highlights.
(b) **Naïve Bayes (NB):** Naïve Bayes is a ML model that can be utilized for classification and regression issues. Single-core SVMs are typically utilized in various settings, including online media, for data checking. In this figuring,

we draw every data thing as a point in an n-dimensional space, where the gauge of every limit is a gauge of every change, where n is the amount of value we have.

$$sP(label|features) = P(label)*P(features|label)/P(features) \qquad (9.6)$$

The past likelihood of the mark happening in the above condition is shown by the P (label), which is the likelihood that the name will have an irregular assortment of features. This depends on the quantity of preparing occasions with the image contrasted and the absolute number of preparing examples. P (features |label) is the past probability of a given list of capabilities being set apart as that mark. In the preparation set with each imprint, this spotlights on which features have happened. The past likelihood of the event of a given list of capabilities is P (features). This is the likelihood that an arbitrary list of capabilities is equivalent to the given list of capabilities and depends on the capabilities contained in the information from the instances. P(label| qualities) advises the probability that the predefined attributes be accessible for that name. On the off chance that this capacity is huge, at that point we can be reasonably certain that the name is ideal for the given features.

(c) **Maximum Entropy**: Maximum entropy is additionally called a confined salient classifier. The most extraordinary entropy classifier utilizes encoding to change the named consideration set to a vector. For each component, this code vector is then used to decide the heap, which would then be able to be joined to decide the engraving that is destined to gather the element.

$$H(Y)= -\Sigma P(Y)log2P(Y) \qquad (9.7)$$

$$H(Y)= \Sigma P(Y)log21/P (Y) \qquad (9.8)$$

$$H(Y)= E[log21/P (Y)] \qquad (9.9)$$

9.5.4.1 SVM with Hybrid Optimization

In this chapter, a combination feature set, which is a blend of Particle Swarm Optimization (PSO) and cuckoo search, is proposed. The standard strategy outmaneuvers the hybrid incorporate decision system inferable from the sentiment thought of online media overviews. Indisputably, the underlying advance is to move different sorts of assessment data that can be either positive or negative to readiness for the sentimental analysis measure. Moreover, the communicated data is pre-handled to locate a weighted gauge of every sentiment data. In the third mode, the element deciding advancement code utilizes hybrid improvement to diminish the capacity of pre-arranged emotion information.

The proposed model is prepared in the following stage, with the help of a vector machine, and a prepared model is made. The test information is then coordinated with the qualified SVM structure, and as assessment, the after-effects of the order will be obtained. Finally, performance parameters such as f-measure, recall, accuracy

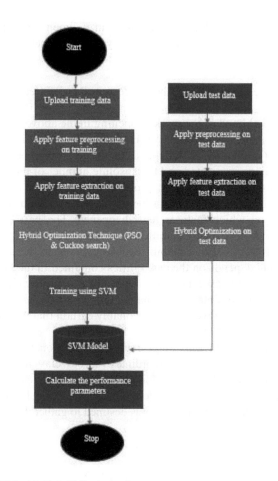

FIGURE 9.4 SVM with Hybrid Optimization.

and precision are calculated and Figure 9.4 shows the SVM approach with hybrid optimization.

Feature selection: Feature selection is the dimensionality decrease component that assists with reducing the weight of processing. Utilizing enhancements, feature selection improves the accuracy of an order and makes orders of emotions simple and effective as advancement strategies help to locate the best subset of highlights. Different strategies for improvement are utilized nowadays. They help by finding the best course of action. In the normal work blend, two primary smoothing out methods are utilized, to be specific cuckoo search and particle swarm (PSO), which have preferred outcomes over cycle work.

(a) **Cuckoo search:** This is one of the most generally utilized advancement strategies. Since, in one moment update, it assists with having better outcomes for each boundary. Thus, nowadays, in numerous zones, this examination is normally used. Yang and Deb recommended CS in the design field in 2010 to solve the problem of improving the design plan. Three ideal principles are the establishment of the cuckoo search. The quest for cuckoos depends on these three ideal principles.

(i)   Every cuckoo lays one egg. In every random nest, the egg laid is discarded.

(ii)   The nest having a high egg content will be taken further for execution for the next generation.

(iii)   There are fixed host nests that are available. The host bird has a chance to find the eggs laid by pa(0,1).

Pseudo Code of Cuckoo Search Algorithm

```
1. Set the initial value of the host nest size n
        and maximum number of iterations Maxgen.
2. Objective function f(x), x= (x1, x2, ..., xd)
3. Generate initial population of
4.        A host nests x(i), (i=1,2,3,..., n)

5. While (t<Maxgen) or (stop criterion)

6.        Get a cuckoo random by Levy Flights
7.        Evaluate its quality/ fitness Fi
8.        Choose a nest among n (say, j) randomly
9.        If (Fi> Fj),
10.                    Replace j by the new solution;
11. End
12.       A function (pa) of worse nests
13.       Are abandoned and new ones are built
14.       Keep the best solutions
                    (or nests with quality solutions);
15.       Rank the solutions and find the current best
16. End while
```

(b) **Particle Swarm Optimization**: One of the populace based stochastic disentanglement methodologies proposed by Dr. Eso and Dr. Kennedy in 1995 is PSO, the improvement of particle swarms, which is brought about by the social conduct of bird or fish training[30]. PSO ought to have shared significantly more highlights that in transformative calculation are equivalent to different methods. In PSO, no administrator evolution, for example, change and hybrid should be done like other genetic algorithms.

Pseudo Code for Particle Swarm Optimization

```
1. Input F: original feature set
2.        N: size of population
3.        D: dimension of feature
```

4.   Output: S optimal feature set
5.   For each particle 1 to N
6.   Initialize particle
7. End for
8. While (Max iteration is not reached
            Or a stop criterion is not satisfied)
9. Do
10.   For each particle 1 to N in D
11.   Calculate fitness value
12.   If the fitness value is better then
                     The best fitness value (pBest) in history
13.   Update current value as the new pBest
14.   End for
15.   Choose the particle with the best fitness value of all the particles
             as gBest
16.   For each particle
17.   Calculate particle velocity
18.   Use gBest and velocity to update particle Data
19.   End for
20. End while
21. **Output** optimal feature subset

In earlier years, in numerous fields of exploration and application, PSO was generally used. Contrasted with other current strategies, it has been noticed that many promising outcomes have appeared in PSO. The essential explanation behind utilizing PSO is that it has few boundaries, so it is easy to change these boundaries. In the quest for a superior outcome, a little change in all would function admirably. PSO has been utilized in the majority of the exploration regions nowadays. In PSO, every molecule goes with its neighbors as indicated by its own insight and experience. Every particle is an answer in D-dimensional space, and has a position p and a speed v. The particles move in D space to locate the best game plan. The best early condition of the atom is called pbest, and the best condition of the whole populace is called gbest.

SVM: SVM is utilized for grouping purposes in the proposed work. To take care of the binary classification issue, SVM[33] is instated, rather surprisingly. The essential assignment of SVM is to attract a hyperplane to build the distance between two classes[34]. SVM is equipped for dealing with confounded errands and linear, quick, characterization undertakings. What's more, it is likewise fit for overseeing divisible and non-distinguishable issues in direct and nonlinear circumstances. The fundamental goal is to plan from an information space the first information focuses to a high-dimensional info vector, for example, X. The planning is done utilizing portion capacities dependent on the measurable learning technique and limiting issues with quadratic programming. Alongside the various elements of the kernel[35], it has heuristic calculations.

FIGURE 9.5 F-Measure, Precision, Recall, Accuracy of SVM with Hybrid Optimization.

9.6 EXPERIMENTAL RESULTS

Figure 9.5 shows the final results on the different boundaries of the F metric, which manages a mixture of accuracy and recall assessments and allows separate expressions. The F measure should be large enough to satisfactorily identify the emotion measuring the accuracy of the test and be the weighted average of the accuracy and recall tests. The review and exactness rate, which is the nearest to the genuine worth and the pace of recuperation, is additionally high. These should be high for high affect ability and exactness, expanding the genuine negative and genuine positive levels. On the off chance that the genuine good rate is high, at that point the exactness rate for distinguishing the programmed grouping of sentiments is likewise high.

9.7 COMPARATIVE ANALYSIS

An examination between the yield of the expected technique and the yield of different original copies is done in this section. Table 9.1 shows that compared to the basic method, the proposed method has higher accuracy, higher recall, higher precision and higher F estimate. It should also be noted that the recommended techniques are suitable for high recognition of sentiment analysis.

9.7.1 PRECISION

The precision of the model is expressed by accuracy. It is the proportion of the anticipated sentence that is effectively certain to the anticipated sentence that is by and large sure. Based on exactness examination between proposed techniques and different strategies, the accuracy estimation of SVM with Hybrid Optimization gives a better outcome in Figure 9.6 and Table 9.2.

$$\text{Precision} = TP/ (TP + FP).$$

TABLE 9.1
Comparing Performance of Different Methods with Proposed Method

Parameters	SVM	Naïve Bayes	Maximum Entropy	SVM with Hybrid Optimization
Precision (%)	92.22	80.00	80.85	98.24
Recall (%)	89.56	84.36	79.56	94.82
F–Measures (%)	89.98	81.77	79.98	96.55
Accuracy (%)	90.01	82.67	80.04	91.91
Sensitivity	94.3	88	84	97
Specificity	93	85.3	83.8	96.2

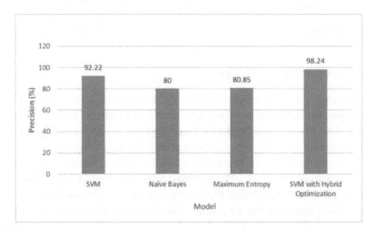

FIGURE 9.6 Comparing models with the parameter "Precision".

TABLE 9.2
Comparison of Methods with Precision as Parameter

Model	Precision (%)
SVM	92.22
Naïve Bayes	80.00
Maximum Entropy	80.85
SVM with Hybrid Optimization	98.24

9.7.2 RECALL

This decides the totality of the classifier. It is the extent of the anticipated sentence that is effectively sure to the all-out number of positive sentences that are valid. Table 9.3

TABLE 9.3
Comparison of Models with the Recall Parameter

Model	Recall (%)
SVM	89.56
Naïve Bayes	84.36
Maximum Entropy	79.56
SVM with Hybrid Optimization	94.82

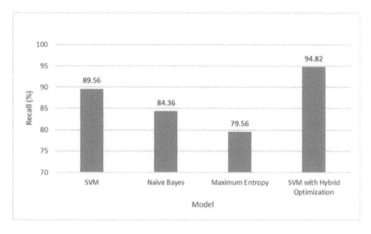

FIGURE 9.7   Comparison of methods with Recall parameter.

and Figure 9.7 will show the correlation of models with the Recall boundary where SVM with Hybrid Optimization beats different techniques.

$$Recall = TP/ (TP + FN).$$

9.7.3   F-Measure

This is the meaning of review and accuracy. The F metric can be determined as

$$F\text{-Measure} = (2 + Precision + Recall)/(Precision + Recall)$$

Table 9.4 and Figure 9.8 show a comparison of methods with F-Measure as the parameter in which SVM with Hybrid Optimization outperforms the other methods.

9.7.4   Accuracy

Accuracy is a normal evaluation yield limit, and it gives irrefutably the quantity of sentences present in the dataset as an extent of adequately foreseen sentences.

TABLE 9.4
Comparison of Models with F-measure Parameter

Model	F-Measure
SVM	89.98
Naïve Bayes	81.77
Maximum Entropy	79.98
SVM with Hybrid Optimization	96.55

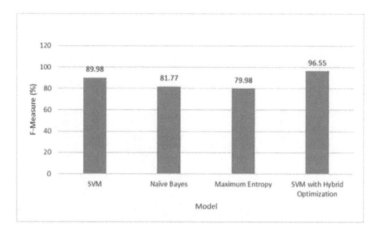

FIGURE 9.8   Comparison of model with F-Measure as parameter.

Figure 9.9 and Table 9.5 show the correlation of models with Accuracy in which SVM with Hybrid Optimization gives preferable exactness over other analyzed techniques.

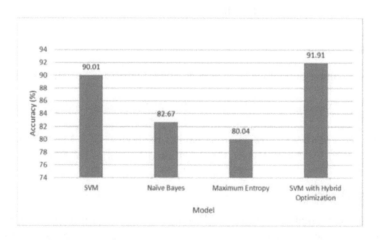

FIGURE 9.9   Comparison of models with Accuracy parameter.

TABLE 9.5

Comparing Models with Accuracy Parameter

Model	Accuracy (%)
SVM	90.01
Naïve Bayes	82.67
Maximum Entropy	80.04
SVM with Hybrid Optimization	91.91

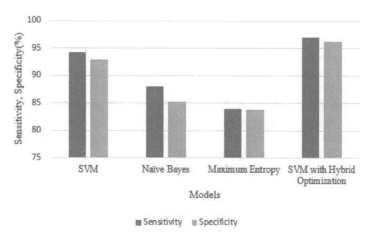

FIGURE 9.10   Models vs sensitivity and specificity.

Figure 9.10 depicts the graphical representation of various models with respect to sensitivity and specificity measures in which the proposed SVM with Hybrid optimization outperforms better with regular SVM, and from that the boosting given by feature selection has more impact on the SVM classifier to perform accurately.

9.8   SENTIMENTAL ANALYSIS: NEW PATHWAY

Verifiably, assumption examination has focused on text analysis utilizing qualities-based strategies for natural language processing and ML. Advances in regions, for example, Big Data and Deep learning (DL), have been influenced by and profited from business improvement. This extraordinary issue is covered in four papers proposing new techniques.In the first paper Ha et al.[59] proposed a method for visualizing emotions in large-scale social media. Therefore, they are making an interlaced emotional network representation system based on emotional terms in the movie survey area. Three perception methods are proposed: the representation of the heat map of the semantic expression of each hub; the two–dimensional guide for the information scaling of semantic words; and the perception of celestial bodies using marked pictures of each group of networks. The proposed representation has been used as a suggestion device to recommend movies that have a sensation compared to the sensation recently viewed. This reliance on more emotional examples suggests that the gradual origin of content can be applied to other informal organizations.

In the second article Kim and Jeong[60] proposed a classification of texts which incorporates an implanting layer of a convolutional neural network (CNN). This model is perceived in three informational collections (film study data, client review data and Stanford estimation tree library data) and is unique in relation to regular ML models and forefront DL models. Their fundamental finding is that the utilization of constant convolutional layers is helpful for messages of medium length.

In the third paper Mao et al.[61], it is proposed to utilize emotion-aware word inserting to improve emotion analysis. The technique sets up a mixture portrayal that joins emotion word implanting that relies upon emotion vocabulary with semantic word installing that relies upon Word2Vec[62]. They utilized the emotion vocabulary of the Chinese cosmology resource DUTIR gathered and named by the Information Retrieval Laboratory of Dalian University of Technology[63].This asset has seven sensory models (joy, trust, anger, bitterness, fear, nausea and shock) for the annotation of the dictionary part. For the evaluation, information from Weibo, a famous person-to-person exchange website in China, was used. This article investigates two techniques (direct mixing and expansion) for developing hybrid portrayals in various data sets. They infer that the trials show that for directed arrangement of feelings, the utilization of crossover word vectors is compelling, drastically improving grouping exactness.

And last, in the fourth article Jabreel and Moreno[64] proposed a multi-class sentiment classification issue dependent on profound learning innovation. The most acclaimed cycle of this issue is to change it into various grouping issues, one for every sensation type. This article proposes another adjustment technique called xy-pair-set, which changes the principal issue to a different binary classification issue. Utilizing the alleged Bnet-based profound learning strategy can tackle the change issue. The structure includes three modules: one using three implanted models and an embedded module that considers the work; one relying on a recurrent neural network (RNN) coding module; and one using two feedforward layers followed by an S-type Unit and a grouping module of an S-type unit.

9.9   APPLICATION

The expansive usage of emotion assessment has progressed its unforeseen development. Sentimental analysis has used a wide range of online media information to recognize more taught choices and to think about social models, thing advertisements or political occasions. The four papers on this extraordinary issue are tied in with utilizing sentiment examination to improve medical services, comprehension and aiding patients, Internet business client profile assessment and acknowledgment of computerized crime.

Van den Broek-Altenburg and Atherly's first article aimed to understand consumers' feelings about health insurance [65]. To this end, a word-based reference method is used to control and check Twitter conversations using NRC Emotion

Lexicon[66], which provides extreme and related feelings for each term (anger, expectation, interruption, fear, joy, trouble, shock and belief).The critical finding of this investigation is that customers are stressed about provider organizations, physician recommended drug points of interest and political feelings. By the by, clients trust clinical professionals, yet fear unforeseen mishaps. These outcomes recommend that more examination is expected understand the origin of customer feelings that drive better protection arrangements for safety net providers.

In the second article Park and Woo[67] put forward an application that can be used in medical areas with the help of sentimental analysis. Specifically, to distinguish gender in health discussions, they apply sentimental analysis dependent on Deep Learning procedures. The creators study messages from a HealthBoard.com AIDS-related release board and survey gender classification systems for both conventional and profound learning.

Liu et al. provide a third method[68]. They explore the prediction and interpretation potential of psychological characteristics in e-commerce consumer preferences. To this end, a vocabulary was established based on the seed terms provided by psycholinguistics, and these vocabulary terms were expanded with WordNet synonyms[69], thus contributing to the Schwartz Meaning Survey (SVS)[70] and Big Five Factor (BFF). Here come a certain vocabulary and negative vocabulary[71] mental model. Utilizing Word2Vec, they at that point make word embeddings and expand the corpus from an Amazon corpus with word embeddings[72]. Then last, they consolidate the vocabularies into a profound neural network-based proposal framework to foresee the web-based buying conduct of clients. BDSCAN clustering based client division is likewise assessed[73], yet this doesn't provide a critical improvement.

Finally, Gutiérrez-Esparza in the fourth paper discussed network attack detection [74]. They manufactured and denoted a corpus of Facebook computerized violent news in Latin America and set up a classification model dependent on ML strategies. The corpus produced will propel assessment in this field, given the lack of lexical resources in lingos specially according to English.

9.10 CONCLUSION

Analyzing how people think about different topics in different ways is a very significant area. When it comes to the business world, this becomes more important because business is based on its clients, and they often want to make goods or services in order to fulfill consumer requirements. So, it is more useful for companies to know what they want, what they think and talk about current products, services and brands to make decisions, such as recognizing rivals and examining trends. It has been possible to do the above-mentioned works by using those data, both because people share their ideas on social media and the data can be accessed. The project, machine learning based customer sentiment analysis for recommending products, shoppers, shops based on social media comments does that. In this chapter, we not only compare basic ML methods for sentiment analysis, but also provide a support vector machine with Hybrid Optimization The performance of the new method is better than other methods in accuracy (98.24%), recall rate (94.82%), F-Measure (96.55%)

and final accuracy (91.91%). With the help of the proposed model, we can easily recommend new products and shops based on the social media comments, reviews, feedbacks and tweets.

REFERENCES

[1] Osimo, D., & Mureddu, F. (2012). Research challenge on opinion mining and sentiment analysis. *Universite de Paris-Sud, Laboratoire LIMSI-CNRS, Bâtiment, 508.*"

[2] Maura Conway, Lisa McInerney, Neil O'Hare, Alan F. Smeaton, Adam Berminghan, (2009) "Combining Social Network Analysis and Sentiment to Explore the Potential for Online Radicalisation," Centre for Sensor Web Technologies and School of Law and Government.

[3] G. Kesavaraj and S. Sukumaran, "A study on classification techniques in data mining," in 2013 Fourth International Conference on Computing, Communications and Networking Technologies (ICCCNT), Tiruchengode, pp. 1–7, 2013

[4] M. S.Akhtar, D. Gupta, A. Ekbal, and P. Bhattacharyya, "Feature selection and ensemble construction: A two-step method for aspect based sentiment analysis,"Knowl.-Based Syst., vol. 125, pp. 116–135, 2017

[5] Sharma, D., & Sabharwal, M. (2019). Sentiment analysis for social media using SVM classifier of machine learning. *Int J Innov Technol Exploring Eng (IJITEE)*, 8(9), 39-47.

[6] Agarwal, Basant, Namita Mittal, Pooja Bansal, and Sonal Garg. (2015) "Sentiment Analysis Using Common-Sense and Context Information." Journal of Computational Intelligence and Neuroscience 9 (2015).

[7] Chekima, Khalifa, and RaynerAlfred. (2018) Sentiment Analysis of Malay Social Media Text. Pp. 205–219.

[8] Das, B., & Chakraborty, S. (2018). An improved text sentiment classification model using TF-IDF and next word negation. *arXiv preprint arXiv:1806.06407..*

[9] Khan, Muhammad Taimoor, Mehr Durrani, Armughan Ali, Irum Inayat, Shehzad Khalid, and Kamran Habib Khan. (2016) "Sentiment Analysis and The Complex Natural Language." Complex Adaptive Systems Modeling 4 (1): 2.

[10] Akter, Sanjida, and Muhammad Tareq Aziz. (2016) "Sentiment Analysis on Facebook Group Using Lexicon Based Approach", in the 2016 3rd International Conference on Electrical Engineering and Information Communication Technology (ICEEICT).

[11] Hassan, Anees Ul, Jamil Hussain, Musarrat Hussain, Muhammad Sadiq, and Sungyoung Lee. (2017) "Sentiment Analysis of Social Networking Sites (SNS) Data Using Machine Learning Approach for the Measurement of Depression", in International Conference on Information and Communication Technology Convergence (ICTC), Jeju, South Korea: IEEE.

[12] Mahtab, S. Arafin, N. Islam, and M. Mahfuzur Rahaman. (2018, 21–22 Sept. 2018). "Sentiment Analysis on Bangladesh Cricket with Support Vector Machine", in the 2018 International Conference on Bangla Speech and Language Processing (ICBSLP).

[13] Dhaoui, Chedia, Cynthia M. Webster, and Lay Peng Tan. (2017) "Social Media Sentiment Analysis: Lexicon Versus Machine Learning." Journal of Consumer Marketing 34 (6): 480–488.

[14] Rahman, S. A. El, F. A. Al Otaibi, and W. A. AlShehri. (2019, 3–4 April 2019). "Sentiment Analysis of Twitter Data", in the 2019 International Conference on Computer and Information Sciences (ICCIS).

[15] Zulfadzli Drus, Haliyana Khalid, Sentiment Analysis in Social Media and Its Application: Systematic Literature Review, vol-161, 2019.

[16] Jianqiang Z, Xiaolin G, Xuejun Z (2018) Deep convolution neural networks for twitter sentiment analysis. IEEE Access 6:23253–23260.

[17] Jianqiang Z, Xiaolin G (2017) Comparison research on text preprocessing methods on twitter sentiment analysis. IEEE Access 5:2870–2879.

[18] Bouazizi M, OhtsukiT (2018) Multi-Class sentiment analysis in twitter: What if reenplumtion is not the answer. IEEE Access6:64486–64502.

[19] Bouazizi M, Ohtsuki T (2017) A pattern-based approach for multiclass sentiment analysis in twitter. IEEE Access 5:20617–20639.

[20] Ebrahimi M, Yazdavar AH, Sheth A (2017) Challenges of sentiment analysis for dynamic events. IEEE Intell Syst 32(5):70–75.

[21] Iqbal F et al. (2019) A hybrid framework for sentiment analysis using genetic algorithm-based feature reduction. IEEE Access7:14637–14652.

[22] TanS et al (2014) Interpreting the public sentiment variations on twitter. IEEE Trans Knowl Data Eng 26(5):1158–1170.

[23] Liu S, Cheng X, Li F, Li F (2015) TASC: topic-adaptive sentiment reenplumtion on dynamic tweets. IEEE Trans Knowl Data Eng 27(6):1696–1709.

[24] Bouazizi M, Ohtsuki T (2019) Multi-class sentiment analysis on twitter: reenplumtion performance and challenges. Big Data Min Anal 2(3):181–194.

[25] Trilla A, Alias F (2013) Sentence-based sentiment analysis for expressive text-to-speech. IEEE Trans Audio Speech Lang Process 21(2):223–233.

[26] Yu D, Xu D, Wang D, NiZ (2019) Hierarchical topic modelling of twitter data for online analytical processing. IEEE Access7:12373–12385.

[27] Lamb, A., Fuller, M., Varadarajan, R., Tran, N., Vandier, B., Doshi, L., & Bear, C. (2012). The vertica analytic database: C-store 7 years later. *arXiv preprint arXiv:1208.4173.*.

[28] Suleykin, A., Bobkova, A., Panfilov, P., & Chumakov, I. (2021). Comparing HDFS–Greenplum Data Loading Options. *Annals of DAAAM & Proceedings*, 10(2).

[29] Solutions TW (2002) Teradata Database technical overview, pp1–7. http://www.teradata.com/brochures/Teradata-Solution-Technical-Overview-eb3025.

[30] H. Saif, Y. He, and H. Alani, "Semantic Sentiment Analysis of Twitter," in The Semantic Web–ISWC 2012, pp. 508–524, 2012.

[31] S. Kiritchenko, X. Zhu, and S. M. Mohammad, "Sentiment Analysis of Short Informal Texts," J. Artif. Intell. Res., vol. 50, pp. 723–762, Aug. 2014.

[32] N. F. F. da Silva, E. R. Hruschka, and E. R. Hruschka, "Tweet sentiment analysis with classifier ensembles," Decis. Support Syst., vol. 66, pp. 170–179, Oct. 2014.

[33] M. Hagen, M. Potthast, M. Büchner, and B. Stein, "Twitter Sentiment Detection via Ensemble Classification Using Averaged Confidence Scores," in ECIR, 2015

[34] Z. Jianqiang and C. Xueliang, "Combining Semantic and Prior Polarity for Boosting Twitter Sentiment Analysis," in 2015 IEEE International Conference on Smart City/SocialCom/SustainCom (SmartCity), pp. 832–837, 2015.

[35] Z. Jianqiang, "Combing Semantic and Prior Polarity Features for Boosting Twitter Sentiment Analysis Using Ensemble Learning," in 2016 IEEE First International Conference on Data Science in Cyberspace (DSC), pp. 709–714, 2016.

[36] Thelwall, M., Buckley, K., & Paltoglou, G. (2012). Sentiment strength detection for the social web. *Journal of the American Society for Information Science and Technology*, 63(1), 163–173.

[37] G. Paltoglou and M. Thelwall, "Twitter, MySpace, Digg: Unsupervised Sentiment Analysis in Social Media," ACM Trans. Intell. Syst. Technol., vol. 3, no. 4, pp. 1–19, Sep. 2012.

[38] A. Montejo-Ráez, E. Martínez?Cámara, M. T. Martín-Valdivia, and L. A. Ureña-López, "A knowledge-based approach for polarity classification in Twitter," J. Assoc. Inf. Sci. Technol., vol. 65, no. 2, pp. 414–425, 2014.

[39] Baccianella, S., Esuli, A., & Sebastiani, F. Sentiwordnet 3.0: an enhanced lexical resource for sentiment analysis and opinion mining. *Lrec,* vol. 10, no. 2010, pp. 2200–2204, May 2010.

[40] D. Sharma, M. Sabharwal, V. Goyal, and M. Vij, "Sentiment Analysis Techniques for Social Media Data: A Review," was presented in First International Conference on Sustainable Technologies for Computational Intelligence, on 30th March 2019 given at Sri Balaji College of Engineering and Technology, Jaipur, Rajasthan, India Jaipur.

[41] A. Kumar, R. Khorwal, and S. Chaudhary, "A Survey on Sentiment Analysis using Swarm Intelligence," Indian J. Sci. Technol., vol. 9, no. 39, Oct. 2016.

[42] Agarwal, B. Xie, I. Vovsha, O. Rambow, and R. Passonneau, "Sentiment Analysis of Twitter Data," in Proceedings of the Workshop on Languages in Social Media, Stroudsburg, PA, USA, pp. 30–38,2011.

[43] Z. Jianqiang, G. Xiaolin, and Z. Xuejun, "Deep Convolution Neural Networks for Twitter Sentiment Analysis," IEEE Access, vol. 6, pp. 23253–23260, 2018.

[44] R. Xia, J. Jiang, and H. He, "Distantly Supervised Lifelong Learning for Large-Scale Social Media Sentiment Analysis," IEEE Trans. Affect. Comput., vol. 8, no. 4, pp. 480–491, Oct. 2017.

[45] O. Udochukwu and Y. He, "A Rule-Based Approach to Implicit Emotion Detection in Text," in Natural Language Processing and Information Systems, vol. 9103, C. Biemann, S. Handschuh, A. Freitas, F. Meziane, and E. Métais, Eds. Cham: Springer International Publishing, pp. 197–203, 2015.

[46] G. Li and F. Liu, "Sentiment analysis based on clustering: a framework in improving accuracy and recognizing neutral opinions," Appl. Intell., vol. 40, no. 3, pp. 441–452, Apr. 2014.

[47] J. Luts, F. Ojeda, R. Van de Plas, B. De Moor, S. Van Huffel, and J. A. K. Suykens, "A tutorial on support vector machine-based methods for classification problems in chemometrics," Anal. Chim. Acta, vol. 665, no. 2, pp. 129–145, Apr. 2010.

[48] W. Zhao, Y. Wang, and D. Li, "A new feature selection algorithm in text categorization," in 2010 International Symposium on Computer, Communication, Control and Automation (3CA), vol. 1, pp. 146–149, 2010.

[49] Tripathy, Abinash, Abhishek Anand, and Santanu Kumar Rath. "Document-level sentiment classification using hybrid machine learning approach." Knowledge and Information Systems (2017): 1–27.

[50] Mao, X., Chang, S., Shi, J., Li, F., and Shi, R.. Sentiment-aware word embedding for emotion classification. *Applied Sciences*, vol. 9, no.7, p. 1334, 2019.

[51] Sánchez-Rada, J. F., and Iglesias, C. A. (2020). CRANK: a hybrid model for user and content sentiment classification using social context and community detection. *Applied Sciences*, vol. 10, no. 5, p. 1662.

[52] . Iglesias, C. A., & Moreno, A. (2019). Sentiment analysis for social media. *Applied Sciences, 9*(23), 5037.

[53] Neha Nandal, Rohit Tanwar, Jyoti Pruthi, Machine learning based aspect level sentiment analysis for Amazon products, 2020.

[54] Mai, L., & Le, B. (2021). Joint sentence and aspect-level sentiment analysis of product comments. *Annals of Operations research, 300*, 493–513.

[55] Sangeetha, K., & Prabha, D. (2021). Sentiment analysis of student feedback using multi-head attention fusion model of word and context embedding for LSTM. *Journal of Ambient Intelligence and Humanized Computing, 12*, 4117–4126.

[56] Naresh, A., & Venkata Krishna, P. (2021). An efficient approach for sentiment analysis using machine learning algorithm. *Evolutionary intelligence, 14*, 725–731.

[57] Agarwal, B., Nayak, R., Mittal, N., & Patnaik, S. (Eds.). (2020). Deep learning-based approaches for sentiment analysis. Singapore: Springer, p. 4.

[58] Yi, S., & Liu, X. (2020). Machine learning based customer sentiment analysis for recommending shoppers, shops based on customers' review. *Complex & Intelligent Systems, 6*(3), 621–634.

[59] Ha, H., Han, H., Mun, S., Bae, S., Lee, J., Lee, K. An Improved Study of Multilevel Semantic Network Visualization for Analyzing Sentiment Word of Movie Review Data. Appl. Sci. 2019, 9, 2419.

[60] Kim, H., Jeong, Y.S. Sentiment Classification Using Convolutional Neural Networks. Appl. Sci. 2019, 9, 2347.

[61] Mao, X., Chang, S., Shi, J., Li, F., Shi, R. Sentiment-Aware Word Embedding for Emotion Classification. Appl. Sci. 2019, 9, 1334.

[62] Mikolov, T., Chen, K., Corrado, G., Dean, J. Efficient estimation of word representations in vector space. arXiv 2013, arXiv:1301.3781.

[63] Chen, J. The Construction and Application of Chinese Emotion Word Ontology. Master's Thesis, Dailian University of Technology, Dalian, China, 2008.

[64] Jabreel, M., Moreno, A. A Deep Learning-Based Approach for Multi-Label Emotion Classification in Tweets. Appl. Sci. 2019, 9, 1123.

[65] Van den Broek-Altenburg, E.M., Atherly, A.J. Using Social Media to Identify Consumers' Sentiments towards Attributes of Health Insurance during Enrollment Season. Appl. Sci. 2019, 9, 2035.

[66] Mohammad, S.M., Kiritchenko, S., Zhu, X. NRC-Canada: Building the state-of-the-art in sentiment analysis of tweets. arXiv2013, arXiv:1308.6242.

[67] Park, S., Woo, J. Gender Classification Using Sentiment Analysis and Deep Learning in a Health Web Forum. Appl. Sci. 2019, 9, 1249.

[68] Liu, H., Huang, Y., Wang, Z., Liu, K., Hu, X., Wang, W. Personality or Value: A Comparative Study of Psychographic Segmentation Based on an Online Review Enhanced Recommender System. Appl. Sci. 2019, 9, 1992.

[69] Miller, G.A. WordNet: A lexical database for English. Commun. ACM 1995, 38, 39–41.

[70] Sagiv, L., Schwartz, S.H. Cultural values in organisations: Insights for Europe. Eur. J. Int. Manag. 2007, 1, 176–190.

[71] McCrae, R.R., Costa, P.T., Jr. The five-factor theory of personality. In Handbook of Personality: Theory and Research; The Guilford Press: New York, NY, USA, 2008; pp. 159–181.

[72] McAuley, J., Targett, C., Shi, Q., Van Den Hengel, A. Image-based recommendations on styles and substitutes. In Proceedings of the 38th International ACM SIGIR Conference on Research and Development in Information Retrieval, Santiago, Chile, 9–13 August 2015; pp. 43–52.

[73] Ester, M., Kriegel, H.P., Sander, J., Xu, X.A density-based algorithm for discovering clusters in large spatial databases with noise. In KDD-96 Proceedings; AAAI Press: Portland, OR, USA, 1996; pp. 226–231.

[74] Gutiérrez-Esparza, G.O.; Vallejo-Allende, M.; Hernández-Torruco, J. Classification of Cyber-Aggression Cases Applying Machine Learning. Appl. Sci. 2019, 9,1828.

[75]   Read, J. Using emoticons to reduce dependency in machine learning techniques for sentiment classification. In Proceedings of the ACL Student Research Workshop, Ann Arbor, Michigan, 27 June 2005; pp. 43–48.

[76]   Kennedy, A.; Inkpen, D. Sentiment classification of movie reviews using contextual valence shifters. Comput. Intell. 2006, 22, 110–125.

[77]   Wan, X. A comparative study of cross-lingual sentiment classification. In Proceedings of the 2012 IEEE/WIC/ACM International Joint Conferences on Web Intelligence and Intelligent Agent Technology, Macau, China, 4–7 December 2012; Volume 1, pp. 24–31.

[78]   Pang, B., Lee, L. A sentimental education: Sentiment analysis using subjectivity summarization based on minimum cuts. In Proceedings of the 42nd Annual Meeting on Association for Computational Linguistics, Barcelona, Spain, 21–26 July 2004; pp. 271–278.

[79]   Akaichi, J. Social networks' Facebook' statutes updates mining for sentiment classification. In Proceedings of the 2013 International Conference on Social Computing, Alexandria, VA, USA, 8–14 September 2013; pp. 886–891.

[80]   Valakunde, N., Patwardhan, M. Multi-aspect and multi-class based document sentiment analysis of educational data catering accreditation process. In Proceedings of the 2013 International Conference on Cloud & Ubiquitous Computing & Emerging Technologies, Pune, India, 15–16 November 2013; pp. 188–192.

[81]   Gautam, G., Yadav, D. Sentiment analysis of twitter data using machine learning approaches and semantic analysis. In Proceedings of the 2014 Seventh International Conference on Contemporary Computing (IC3), Noida, India, 7–9 August 2014; pp. 437–442.

[82]   Tripathy, A., Agrawal, A., Rath, S.K. Classification of sentiment reviews using n-gram machine learning approach. Expert Syst. Appl. 2016, 57, 117–126.

[83]   Hasan, A., Moin, S., Karim, A., Shamshirband, S. Machine learning-based sentiment analysis for twitter accounts. Math. Comput. Appl. 2018, 23, 11.

[84]   Yassine, M., Hajj, H. A framework for emotion mining from text in online social networks. In Proceedings of the 2010 IEEE International Conference on Data Mining Workshops, Sydney, Australia, 13 December 2010; pp. 1136–1142.

[85]   Denecke, K. Using sentiwordnet for multilingual sentiment analysis. In Proceedings of the 2008 IEEE 24th International Conference on Data Engineering Workshop, Cancun, Mexico, 7–12 April 2008; pp. 507–512.

[86]   Jiang, L., Yu, M., Zhou, M., Liu, X., Zhao, T. Target-dependent twitter sentiment classification. In Proceedings of the 49th Annual Meeting of the Association for Computational Linguistics: Human Language Technologies, Portland, Oregon, 19–24 June 2011; Volume 1, pp. 151–160.

[87]   Bahrainian, S.A., Dengel, A. Sentiment analysis using sentiment features. In Proceedings of the 2013 IEEE/WIC/ACM International Joint Conferences on Web Intelligence (WI) and Intelligent Agent Technologies (IAT), Atlanta, GA, USA, 17–20 November 2013; Volume 3; pp. 26–29.

[88]   Neethu, M., Rajasree, R. Sentiment analysis in twitter using machine learning techniques. In Proceedings of the 2013 Fourth International Conference on Computing, Communications and Networking Technologies (ICCCNT), Tiruchengode, India, 4–6 July 2013; pp. 1–5.

[89]   Karamibekr, M., Ghorbani, A.A. A structure for opinion in social domains. In Proceedings of the 2013 International Conference on Social Computing, Alexandria, VA, USA, 8–14 September 2013; pp. 264–271.

[90] Antai, R. Sentiment classification using summaries: A comparative investigation of lexical and statistical approaches. In Proceedings of the 2014 6th Computer Science and Electronic Engineering Conference (CEEC), Colchester, UK, 25–26 September 2014; pp. 154–159.

[91] Ghiassi, M., Lee, S.A domain transferable lexicon set for Twitter sentiment analysis using a supervised machine learning approach. Expert Syst. Appl. 2018, 106,197–216.

[92] Mensikova, A., Mattmann, C.A. Ensemble sentiment analysis to identify human trafficking in web data. Workshop on Graph Techniques for Adversarial Activity Analytics (GTA 2018), Marina Del Rey, CA, USA, 5–9 February 2018.

[93] online   source: https://data-flair.training/blogs/data-science-r-sentiment-analysis-project/.

10 Cyber Security
Analysis for Detection and Removal of Zero-Day Attacks (ZDA)

Khalid Hamid[1], Muhammad Waseem Iqbal[1], Muhammad Aqeel[1], Toqir A. Rana[2] and Muhammad Arif[1]
[1]Superior University Lahore, Pakistan, [2]University of Lahore, Pakistan

10.1 INTRODUCTION

Zero-day attacks are previously unknown flaws and errors in operating systems, networks and general software that leave holes for external users or hackers for illegal operations before patches can be issued. Cyber criminals have found more than 85 vulnerabilities in different software such as Microsoft, Adobe, Oracle and Apple products, but these remain unknown to the public. Software is continuously growing in size and complexity so as a result, unknown flaws allow attackers to gain illegal access and even take full control over systems[1].Some software developers and distribution companies know about the errors but are hidebound due to the unavailability of solutions. Users even have big defense systems but they still face attacks. Patching and updating virus definitions for antivirus software will not stop them. According to the Internet Security Report, larger numbers of vulnerabilities were discovered in 2014 than in 2013 (Symantec).

In 2013 more vulnerabilities were discovered with a 61% increase as compared to 2012. Even multiple layered defense systems are not enough to avoid zero-day attacks. In zero-day attacks the traditional defenses are powerless. These attacks can convert themselves into polymorphic viruses, worms, Trojans and other malware. The most dangerous attacks which are not prevented by most security systems are polymorphic worms that show different behavior every time such as defense avoidance by complex mutation, multiple vulnerability scanners for identifying the prospective target and targeted exploitation. Zero-day attacks are remote shells that open arbitrary ports and drop malware to download malicious code from an outside source to continue its propagation [2].

We can break the process of zero-day attacks into different steps. Firstly, A developer or developers develop software having unknown vulnerabilities. Secondly, A Threat Actor points out one or more vulnerabilities before the developer knows

DOI: 10.1201/9781003190301-10

about them or fixes them. Thirdly, the Attacker writes and applies the exploit code to open the vulnerability. At last, Users recognize it as information theft or the developer is aware of it and fixes it by introducing patches.

When developers write patches and apply them then this exploit is not called a zero-day exploit. In any case, even users with big defense systems are still open to attack. All software has a chance of unknown vulnerabilities, these errors when known by some attackers are used for cyber-attacks. According to the Security Report 2012, no defense system can avoid zero-day attacks. Still the vulnerabilities have remained, and software developers cannot develop a solution to detect and remove these vulnerabilities by using any techniques[3].

10.1.1 MODERN MALWARE

All advanced cyber-attacks are made possible due to modern malware. The modern threats are vibrant, silent and continual, leaving unknown threats for future disruption. These attacks are polymorphic and also customizable. The special characteristics of these modern exploits change for different attackers accordingly. These modern exploits are used for the following attacks:

- Cyber Crimes
- Cyber Warfare Scenarios
- Cyber Espionages

The best example of modern malware is the targeted Trojan. Modern malware in the form of a targeted Trojan is a very dangerous threat to any enterprise. These are carefully shaped attacks by skilled hackers that take advantage of a previously unknown vulnerability in the user's web or email environment and compromise the entire system. Once the attack is engaged, malware gets installed in the system, and depending on the user environment, can install other components to maximize the malware presence. The malware can be customized with additional downloads to spy on user activity, steal information, generate spam and become part of a network of bots that perform activities directed by the attacker.

One of the most public examples of a targeted Trojan is "Operation Aurora," an attack on Google and other companies. Attackers used zero-day exploits for Internet Explorer which installs email-targeted malware for data-stealing on host machines. These attacks spread dangerous links to many email accounts just by user clicks[4].

10.1.2 EMAIL-BORNE THREATS

Email on the web and computers has been a predominant vector to spread malware for a long time. Email-based malware distribution, particularly as a contributing vector to the web, has seen a resurgence in recent years. Email is a mission-critical application for any enterprise, accessible by everyone inside an enterprise but extending also to everyone outside the enterprise who has access. These same characteristics also make it attractive as a distribution platform for modern malware[5].

The traditional email security solutions are designed to protect against spam and viruses. However, current email security finds itself protecting against a new range of threats such as phishing attacks, targeted malware and zero-day threats. The key differences are the sophistication of the attacks and the methods of delivery.

10.1.3 SPEAR PHISHING ATTACKS

Spear phishing is a very specialized combination of phishing attacks and targeted malware. Any employee in any organization can be targeted with a spear-phished message. These messages are laced with custom-created malware, often zero-day, that bypasses all existing security infrastructures. Phishing attacks involve the fraudulent collection of personal information while the attacker masquerades as a known and legitimate entity to the user. In a typical phishing attack, an email purportedly from a familiar entity tricks the user into either opening a malicious attachment or clicking on an email link that directs the user to a malicious website, from which the user is subjected to "drive-by" downloads and is infected with malware[6].

10.1.4 TARGETED MALWARE

With traditional email threats, the victims of malicious attacks were able to see what was happening, because it was an email message, and they could recognize it as spam. But the current attacks use targeted malware that is covert and installs itself without the user's knowledge. Once the victim's computer is infected by malware, the cyber criminals steal information such as passwords, contacts, personal information and other proprietary information. Targeted attacks can go unnoticed for days, long after the malware has secretly stolen information from the user's device and assets[7].

10.1.5 FILE SERVER MALWARE

Documents are transported into the network from often legitimate websites, FTP servers, drop boxes and webmail, and the files are often stored locally or on a server. As a result, many corporate file servers are hosting resting malware; documents waiting to be retrieved from a network share for later and ongoing dissemination by collaborating teams across departments and business units. When the malicious file is downloaded to an individual's device, the malware lifecycle begins anew: the malware is reactivated when the file is opened, and the infected PC is harvested and robbed of data accounts, social security numbers, bank accounts, passwords and corporate intellectual property and financial information. Network capture methods cannot detect malware at rest on corporate file servers. File MD analysis solves the resting malware problem[8],[9].

10.1.6 CONVENTIONAL SECURITY

Modern crime ware has consistently advanced in sophistication, technology and scale, rendering traditional security technologies largely obsolete. While crimeware has been on an exponential growth curve, traditional security has remained architecturally stagnant. Pattern matching signatures and rate-based heuristics are still common core features of most security methodologies. This has created a false sense of security and a significant gap in the ability of enterprises to defend against new cybercriminals. There are few current deterrents to file-based malware; AV-file scanners are available, but their deployment comes with performance and stability impacts on files and shares.

The current email security solutions focus mostly on "email hygiene" to protect the user against the storm of spam and known viruses. They use signature-based anti-virus (AV) detection technologies to detect viruses, as well as reputation-based and content-based technologies to stop spam. However, these technologies are no match for the sophistication of attacks carried out by cyber criminals, who use zero-day threats combined with sophisticated malware and the latest social engineering to stay ahead of the AV signature databases[9]. Solutions should be far away from the old and conventional security parameters and should give distinct solutions to detect and remove today's complex threats. Researchers broadly work and classify the defense techniques for zero-day attacks. The prime goal of every technique is to detect the exploit in a real-time environment and remove or quarantine the attack to avoid damage. The second most important challenge is to make sure that either the victim's machine is not the threshold to delay analysis or quarantine is not exceeded[10].

We use the virtualization-based technique which uses the hybrid-based technique in the virtual environment by using virtual machine-based protection systems like DFA, Email MD, File MD, MMIS and Web MD, etc.

10.2 BACKGROUND

Researchers broadly worked and classified the defense techniques for zero-day attacks. These techniques are Statistical-based techniques, Signature-based techniques, Behavior-based techniques and Hybrid-based techniques.

10.2.1 STATISTICAL-BASED DEFENSE TECHNIQUE

This strategy for the detection of exploits depends on assault profiles from past endeavors that are currently publicly known. From those known adventures this safeguard method changes the verifiable endeavor's profile boundaries to identify new attacks. The nature of the recognition is straightforwardly connected with threshold limits set by the seller or security proficient in utilizing this method. This strategy figures out what typical movement is, and anything beyond typical is impeded or hailed. The framework which is utilized in this methodology ought to be online. Present techniques in this approach complete dynamic analysis or static analysis relying upon the payloads of parcels, and identify just attacks having unchangeable attributes. This strategy endeavors to recognize the adventure before the execution of the genuine code. This method might bring about a high pace of misleading upsides or bogus negatives based on the thresholds picked. This strategy is likewise known for the possibly high handling above restricting its capacity for ongoing identification. A model that utilizes a statistical-based method would be Semantics Aware Statistical (SAS) calculation. This method joins two sorts of analysis, statistical analysis and semantic analysis, in the mark generation process. The primary period of the SAS calculation is the extraction stage for semantic-mindful marks and is trailed by the mark matching stage. The principal stage is broken into the following modules:

- Payload Extraction
- Payload Disassembly
- Clustering
- Signature Generation
- Valuable Instruction Distill.

The subsequent module recognizes worm bundles after fruition of the principal module by coordinating the State Transition Graph signature with input parcels.

Constraints of the SAS calculation incorporate failure to handle a few expanded capabilities called from several different destinations, or some calling modules called vindictive capabilities from different spots of the program[11]. The second limit of this method is that by utilizing refined encryption aggressors can avoid recognition. Statistical-based techniques involve recently known public weaknesses for the recognition of zero-day attacks. This procedure involves old boundaries for the recognition of new attacks with assistance of profile history[12].

10.2.2 SIGNATURE-BASED DEFENSE TECHNIQUE

Antivirus or virus software vendors have libraries of various malware signatures and virus definitions which are compiled for different malware detection using these signature-based techniques. In this technique, all files like files of networks, files of computers, web pages and emails are matched with these virus definitions according to predefined rules by the user. If the signature matches, this means exploit and blocked otherwise continue to work. These virus definitions are updated regularly for new attacks. There is a cost overhead in this approach to update virus definitions[13]. Signature-based techniques are classified into the following:

1. Content-based Signature Techniques
2. Semantic-based Signature Techniques
3. Vulnerabilities-based Signature Techniques

These are also effective against polymorphic worms to some extent. Polygraph is an illustration of a substance signature-based method that will create marks to coordinate and distinguish polymorphic worms. Polygraphs can produce marks based on these invariant substrings. The vital test to all mark-based method safeguards is the way to precisely and naturally create marks continuously that produce low misleading negatives and low bogus up-sides. When this challenge is met, it can then be presented in off-the-rack items which will bring about additional protection against zero-day attacks[14].

10.2.3   BEHAVIOR-BASED DEFENSE TECHNIQUE

This technique does not use payload byte pre-patterns of data packets for detection of worms, but it uses the specific behavior of worms. It is based on the flow of traffic of data. It predicts the behavior of future traffic based on previous data traffic flow and current data traffic flow by interactions with a file server, web server, local server or infected computer. So, analyze these behaviors and act by denying specific traffic if not expecting, and allowing, if expecting, this type of data traffic, and also set constraints for future traffic. The behavior-based technique is a combination of two techniques, one is a signature-based technique and the other is an anomaly-based technique. The first technique detects the polymorphic worms, and the second technique quarantines the worms. In this scenario, STF investigates all network traffic from one edge and traffic passes at the same time towards the Intrusion detection system and honey net[15],[16].

This approach has the following three components or layers:

* STF Filter
* ZAE Zero-Day Attack Evaluation
* SG Signature Generator

The first defense layer of the system to avoid zero-day attacks is the STF filter. The second defense layer which takes input from the STF filter for evaluation and detection of zero-day attacks is ZAE (Zero-Day Attack Evaluation). The third defense layer generates new signatures for STF, and also updates the STF database as SG Signature Generator. So, these three layers work together in coordination to detect and avoid zero-day attacks[17].

10.2.4   HYBRID-BASED DEFENSE TECHNIQUE

Hybrid-based techniques are problem-solving techniques in which we combine various previously discussed techniques like Statistical-based techniques, Signature-based techniques and Behavior-based techniques. This technique overcomes all disadvantages of previously used techniques and adds up all the advantages of these techniques. Some of the benefits of hybrid-based techniques are:

* This technique identifies zero-day attacks from data collected automatically on high interaction honeypots.
* This technique overcomes all disadvantages of previously used techniques and adds up all the advantages of these techniques.
* This technique does not need prior knowledge of zero-day attacks and uses Honeynet as an anomaly detector[19].
* This technique can detect a zero-day attack in its early phase and can contain the attack before a major penalty occurs[18],[19],[20].

Figure 10.1 represents the hybrid model of all previous techniques to detect and remove zero-day attacks in a real-time environment.

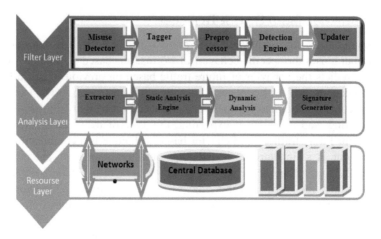

FIGURE 10.1 Hybrid-based layer model.

10.3   LITERATURE REVIEW

The paper illustrates that polymorphic worms are not detectable due to their distinct behaviors. They include complex duplication to avoid detection, identification of potential machines by multi-vulnerability scanning, targeted misuse of a vulnerable host, open arbitrary ports by remote shells and downloaded malicious code for propagation. Researchers give the classification of defending techniques against zero-day attacks as follows: Statistical-based techniques; Signature-based techniques; Behavior-based techniques and Hybrid techniques[21].

The study elaborates that depth strategy is very effective and is critical in stopping and detecting a variety of attacks that organizations face today. It is more important due to multi-layered technology, which ensures that if one security layer is bypassed then the other can protect against zero-day attacks[22].

In 2021, Yaman Romani said that zero-day exploits are those vulnerabilities that are not publicly disclosed. These vulnerabilities are difficult to detect due to their unknown nature because data is not available until the course of attacks has been completed. Governments, cybercriminals and software vendors previously required these types of vulnerabilities for selling and buying purposes, and also for acquiring their interests[23].

The software developing companies leave some flaws in software, sometimes known to the developer but sometimes not. There are more than 5,000 vulnerabilities occurring in networks per day. They proposed a completely novel scenario that counted these vulnerabilities efficiently. They said that zero-day attacks are easily defended against by using the approach of changing configurations. In this paper, they propose a method of counting thousands of vulnerabilities, and then modeled a defense against these attacks. They explain future work by ranking zero-day attacks and developing various technologies for dealing with these attacks. There are also some situations and inputs which are not managed well[24].

The study proposes an unsupervised and effective pipeline-based firewall called ZeroWall for the detection of previously unknown web attacks. This system catches the syntax and semantic patterns of benign requests through the Encoder-Decoder Recurrent Neural Network for training self-translation machines. Most of the benign requests preceding zero-day attacks are not detected by signature-based firewalls, but are detected by self-translation machines in real-time. The study evaluated eight real-world traces of 1.4 billion requests on the web and detected all zero attacks which were not detected by existing firewalls. The request processing involves four steps which are: firstly convert each request into a token sequence; secondly, the neural network reconstructs the token sequence; thirdly compare the score of both with a threshold value and last apply a manual investigation. The results show performance with the best F1scores over 0.98, which is above all baseline approaches. This paper introduces an enhanced system of existing firewalls by endorsing unsupervised and machine learning-based approaches for the detection of zero-day attacks. So, this approach with a neural network-based translation machine is highly recommended to implement in the real-world immediately due to the achievement of a high F1-score over0.98. They said that the proposed approach is also providing new directions for inventing new solutions for detecting known attacks and zero-day attacks on webs[25].

The research paper "A Consensus Framework for Reliability and Mitigation of Zero-Day Attacks in IoT" explains and proposes that the Internet of Things associates the communication fence between computing entities by establishing a network between them. These networks are then free from most of the computing threats using the same type of solution in the context of controlling the IoT devices, and also managing the IoT devices. These types of networks are only threatened by those vulnerabilities which have not been tested before in the testing phase. These types of vulnerabilities or threats are called zero-day attacks. These types of vulnerabilities are detected and handled by present systems, but the performance of the communication system is affected by these types of attacks. In this paper, the study proposed a system by using IoT devices with contextual behavior preceded by an Alert Message Protocol and Critical Data Sharing Protocol for detection and handling of zero-day attacks[26].

In the paper "Efficient hybrid technique for detecting zero-day polymorphic worms" the study showed that Hybrid-based techniques are problem-solving techniques in which various previously discussed techniques like Statistical-based techniques, Signature-based techniques and Behavior-based techniques were combined. This technique overcomes all disadvantages of previously used techniques and adds up all the advantages of these techniques, even though these types of attacks disabled your internet or caused other potential disturbance. This technique is not only effective for zero-day attacks, but is also very effective for polymorphic unknown vulnerabilities. On the other hand, this technique is also effective and valuable for known attacks and viruses over the network and servers[27].

The study proposed a system for the detection of zero-day attacks called auto encoder implementer to minimize the false rate of detecting zero-day attacks. For establishing the best model, they used two well-known datasets to evaluate, NSL-KDD and CICIDS2017, and also compared the results with the Support Vector Machine of Class One to check the performance of their model. Auto Encoder's abilities of encoding and decoding play a vital role to make their model very impressive in the field of detection of complex zero-day attacks. the accuracy of detection of zero-day attacks with two datasets is given as NSL-KDD 89% to 99% and CICIDS2017 75% to 98%. These results show the best system for the detection of complex zero-day attacks. The proposed system avoided all drawbacks of previously used systems for detection of zero-day attacks and provided the best solution according to results, with accuracy ranging from 75% to 99% as an unsupervised technique[28].

In "A Review on Zero-day Attack Safety Using Different Scenarios," Harshpal, Gosavi and Bagade said that software development companies leave some flaws in software, sometimes known to the developer but sometimes not. These flaws are used by some people to attack systems that are using the software. When these flaws are not known to developers then no patch is available and if they are known to developers then no patch is available for a few months. So, zero-day attacks can be carried out, but if the administrator of the system knows about these there are possibilities to do something by changing configurations. There are more than 5,000 vulnerabilities occurring in networks per day. They proposed a completely novel scenario that counted these vulnerabilities efficiently[29].

The study used a combination of two approaches for the detection and investigation of both types of attacks. In the current period, offline intrusion detection is easily possible, but the solution for cyber-attacks on network servers, routers, network applications and other network devices is a big deal. The solution for this scenario is possible by adopting a hybrid approach. The study used two techniques from the field of AI which are Statistical-based Analysis and Machine Learning-based Analysis against complex attacks in the world of cyber-attacks. In Statistical-based analysis, they performed rule-based analysis and outlier detection-based analysis. On the other hand, in Machine Learning based analysis they used Behavioral anomalies detector and Event Sequence tracker. This hybrid approach from the field of Artificial Intelligence protects unauthorized access to data on the network, with integrity constraints and availability of data only to authorized and well-authenticated users[30].

10.3.1 SIGNIFICANCE

This includes awareness about malware and unknown flaws in a wide range of software. It describes how zero-day attacks are different from viruses, worms and Trojan attacks. It also compares traditional and new techniques against zero-day attacks which are very difficult to detect and remove because these are unknown to users and even programmers of the software. This review discovers new and significant solutions for zero-day attacks because no adequate solution has been found till now due to the incremental and unknown nature of these flaws and attacks.

10.3.2 OBJECTIVES

There are six objectives of this review article which are:

1. To investigate zero-day attacks.
2. To find the intensity of seriousness of zero-day attacks in software.

3. To explain the zero-day attacks and their vulnerabilities.
4. To explain and be aware of recent zero-day attacks.
5. To compare and analyze different techniques.
6. To choose the best solution against zero-day attacks.

10.3.3 QUESTIONS ARISE

There are four research questions in this review article which are:

1. Through the literature review do we understand the zero-day attacks and what their effects are on software and computers?
2. We also review the literature for the purpose of finding how these attacks can be detected and these vulnerabilities resolved.
3. How many strategies and intrusion detection systems are used, and we also check their effectiveness.
4. How do we choose the best solution against zero-day attacks?

According to the cyber security report, 2020 vulnerabilities in different years are given in Table 10.1.

Table 10.1 represents the year wise vulnerabilities from 1991 to 2019. It can be seen from the table that zero-day vulnerabilities are much higher in the present as compared to previous years, which is an alarming situation.

The four major vulnerabilities of the year 2019 are shown in Table 10.2 and Figure 10.2. We can see that even the lowest damage caused by vulnerability was 39%, which is very big for an organization. It means the organization is at high risk.

Figure 10.2 shows four major vulnerabilities of the year 2019. Of these, unauthorized cloud access has the highest likelihood to damage systems all over the globe

TABLE 10.1
Year-Wise Vulnerabilities

Year-Wise Vulnerabilities			
SR. NO.	Year	%age	REMARKS
1	2019	2%	Medium
2	2018	14%	High
3	2017	20%	Very High
4	2016	21%	Very High
5	2015	13%	High
6	2014	16%	High
7	2013	4%	Medium
8	2012	3%	Medium
9	2011	1%	Low
10	2010	2%	Medium
11	2009	1%	Low
12	1991–2008	3%	Medium

TABLE 10.2
Major Vulnerabilities

Four Major Vulnerabilities 2019

Sr. No.	Attack On	%age
1	Unauthorized Cloud Access	42%
2	Interface Security Violation	42%
3	Cloud Platform Misconfiguration	40%
4	Hijacking Account	39%

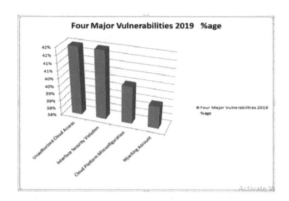

FIGURE 10.2   Four major vulnerabilities 2019.

and at a second level interface security violation vulnerability to damage cyber systems and so on.Figure 10.3 shows major vulnerabilities for zero-day attacks in the year 2020. The remote code execution vulnerability trending highest value could cause damage to the cyber world and it is almost 60%, which is very big for any organization.

Figure 10.4 shows top trends in zero-day attacks in context with several users affected up to 2021. Legitimate users lost billions of dollars due to adopting old-fashioned techniques to avoid and detect zero-day attacks.

MyDoom is a most dangerous virus/worm which has caused damage worth38.5 billion dollars. It opened the backdoor to allow remote access to the computer and was also favorable for DDOS attacks. There are very few chances to detect it. Conventional cyber security techniques fail to detect the zero-day attacks and other related modern attacks to secure networks, operating systems and databases. It required some modern, fast, variable and secure techniques for detection and removal.

Figure 10.5 represents the most used techniques for detection and removal of zero-day attacks. As seen from the figure, signature-based techniques, hybrid-based techniques or behavior-based techniques are used most of the time, which is a common reason for the failure of defense breakage.

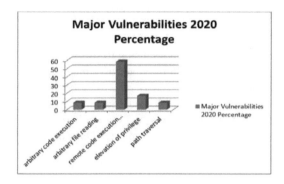

FIGURE 10.3 Major vulnerabilities 2020.

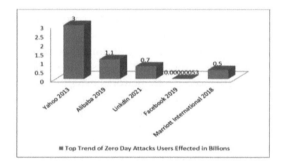

FIGURE 10.4 Top trend of zero-day attacks andusers affected.

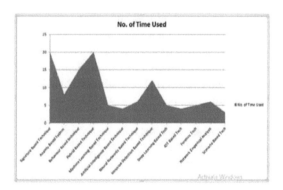

FIGURE 10.5 Number of times techniques used.

10.4   EXPERIMENTATION WITH A VIRTUALIZATION-BASED APPROACH

Virtualization approaches permit high seclusion to software parts, these are coherent parts not physical and give various leveled security plots. In this methodology, we utilize Virtual Machine Monitor as a flimsy layer of software on physical machines introducing the deliberation of Multiple Virtual Machines. A working framework lives and runs in each Virtual Machine as runs on Physical hardware[31]. These physical machines are clueless about the virtualization layer beneath them. Notable instances of virtualization are:

- Microsoft Virtual PC
- Xen
- VM Ware etc.

Various levels of security can be accomplished by separation in which one virtual machine can't be impacted or has some significant awareness of the other virtual machines except if the manager permits them to impart or utilize information from one another in the organization or framework. This is an unmistakable trait of virtualization innovation. Generally, we save frameworks in Virtual Machine for assurance (called Guest Virtual Machine) and one more Virtual Machine is utilized to keep security software in it or security called Secure Virtual Machine which monitors, oversees and controls the Guest Virtual Machine, however, it is not permitted for GVM to control the Secure VM. Thus, on the off chance that aggressors catch GVM then they can't hinder Secure VM. This is an important element of Virtualization Technology utilized in the examination of zero-day attacks[32].

Various peril attacks use different channels and consistent stages to evade ordinary affirmations. An attack could enter the association as an email containing a direct, condensed URL. Right when a client taps the URL, an assortment of drive-by downloads assault the program, searching for vulnerabilities. Every guard framework safeguards against taking advantage of utilizing a solitary security framework, however, virtualization innovation can utilize a mix of numerous clever parts where each has a particular procedure and engineering to distinguish and break down vulnerabilities inside and out which are given here:

- Web-Based Malware Detector (WMD)
- Email Malware Detector (EMD)
- Deep Forensic Analyzer (DFA)
- File Malware Detector (FMD)
- Main Management and Integration Systems (MMIS).

The blend of this multitude of parts isn't required, yet it is suggested involving all these in reconciliation[33].

At the point when Email MD is conveyed related to Web MD, DFA and the MMIS framework, the joined element safeguards the end-client against current malware attacks employing malevolent connections and URLs conveyed in emails, as well as safeguarding against drive-by and social designing attacks executed by aggressors through the web vector.

The File MD is committed to non-problematic file filtering of distant CIFS and additionally SMB-based file shares. Quarantine organizers are alternatively designed with File MD to disconnect distinguished malware in a far-off registry. Also, C&C callback occasions distinguished by examination in the File MD VE motor are shipped off the Web MD for additional criminology. File MD filtering can be planned to run ceaselessly or launched on a specially appointed platform depending on the situation.

DFA can be designed for unattended clump examination of potential malware put away in a network share (a subset of the highlights accessible from the File MD)[34]. The offer is surveyed at ordinary spans to consequently line and test dubious URLs, connections (like PDFs) and executables for inside and out criminology examination and broad malware detailing. All aftereffects of malware examination by the DFA are separated by the MMIS for incorporated circulation to the Web MD, File MD and Email MD identification frameworks. Furthermore, when the DFA is associated with an MMIS, a choice is given that permits you to choose a malware test distinguished by the Email, File or Web MD frameworks and "submit to DFA" for a more profound, as well as redone, criminology examination[35].

10.4.1 WEB-BASED MALWARE DETECTOR

The Web MD framework identifies web-based malware and all known Malware Callback events and attacks that utilize either OS exploits or web diseases as spread vectors. Web-based malware assurance is enacted in two sections: identification and obstruction.

The obstruction of web-based threats expects that Web MD is conveyed inline in the network. With Web MD inline sending, network traffic is caught, and threats are effectively distinguished and hindered on the outbound. A few endeavors don't need their network traffic effectively impeded, so Web MD can be conveyed subtly in non-hindering SPAN/TAP mode. In this mode, traffic is duplicated for examination and threats are distinguished yet never hindered. An undertaking's business prerequisites direct which arrangement strategy is utilized for the Web MD System. While sending the Web MD, place the framework close to the network departure, highlighting the guaranteed ideal permeability of outbound web associations[36]. Figure 10.6 shows the web-based malware detection model for detecting zero-day attacks before reaching the actual user in a real-time environment.

10.4.2 VIRTUAL EXECUTION ENGINE (VEE)

All frameworks like DFA, Web MD, Email MD and File MD completely execute dubious code, connections, files and URLs. Robotization moves dubious malware through a known-rules filter to contrast it and the ongoing arrangement of known-bad rules, after which it is then moved through an instrumented virtual execution engine (VEE)[37].

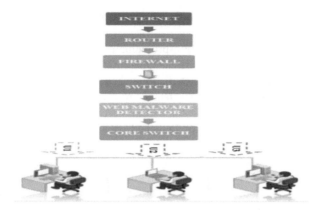

FIGURE 10.6   Proposed model WEB malware detector.

In the VE motor, thought malware is executed in the demonstrating ground and totally reviewed against various working systems, applications, programs and extra things. In the VE environment, certifiable world malware is allowed to set off zero-day attacks, speed increases and another state of art works so that one can check out and assess its full risk potential. Authentic threats to the undertaking are perceived and stopped unexpectedly by malware acknowledgment system VE engines, and testbed VE investigations. The confirmation system accumulates organized information from the VE motor demonstrating grounds. Malware IP addresses:

1. Apply some network protocols.
2. Targets are some specific ports.
3. Attackers wrapping, coordination allocates payloads.

Utilizing this information blocks callbacks and all information trade between the malware and its remote command and control focus. With definite malware examinations and reports, directors can rapidly distinguish which has gone for sterilization.

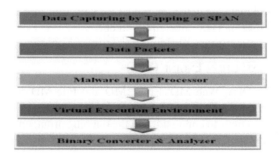

FIGURE 10.7   Architecture for binary analysis.

The inside VE motor of the Web MD framework copies program (client) side of dubious web exchanges between real organization clients and web servers to decide whether the web server is endeavoring to contaminate the program. Dubious code is replayed into and investigated inside the framework's VE, empowering it to discover polymorphic or zero-day malware that might not have been seen before[38].

Figure 10.7 represents the actual working of a virtual execution engine with binaries from input to analyze the data in binary format complete procedure.

10.4.3 STATIC ANALYSIS

The principal static analysis is performed on binaries that are taken care of in the framework. During static analysis, malevolent binaries are distinguished by applying signature matching strategies through custom rules and outsider rules. Custom rules are characterized in YARA and outsider apparatuses are av-suite, ClamAV and Sophos. In the wake of performing static analysis, a weight is relegated and parallel is submitted to VM for behavioral analysis[39].

Different static analysis executions are as follows:

- Blacklist MD5 SUM
- AV-SUITE
- SOPHOS
- YARA

10.4.4 BEHAVIORAL ANALYSIS

Observe OS change events produced by malicious binaries. Examine OS change events and verify their example, values and maliciousness. Replay http-bobax-exe. pcap containing malicious binaries. Check BCA details to verify assuming that the double is acknowledged.

Figure 10.8 represents the detailed statistics of binary analysis during static analysis. One file is acknowledged for paired conversion and analysis. Verify if the pair has been set apart as malicious. Verify if an alarm for binary analysis is produced for the malicious pair [40].

Figure 10.9 represents the verification of binaries' maliciousness with the help event logger which is involved in static analysis and VM.

Figure 10.10 represents the verification of maliciousness of binaries by event logger with alert generation. It displays the name of malware with severness, ip address and time. Figure 10.11 shows the complete detail of malware and analysis procedure used. We use a combination of different techniques in this approach. We are going to use a combination of different signature-based tools on behalf of their priorities at the first level of this approach, because a single tool is not enough to detect all types of malware. At the second level Black List Activity Trackers are used which will track malware callback and C&C communication, mainly using DNS request/response and in the future using TCP communication, detecting dead bots using the static and dynamic list and also block/sinkhole malicious DNS requests in block mode. The third level used a behavioral approach to detect polymorphic worms

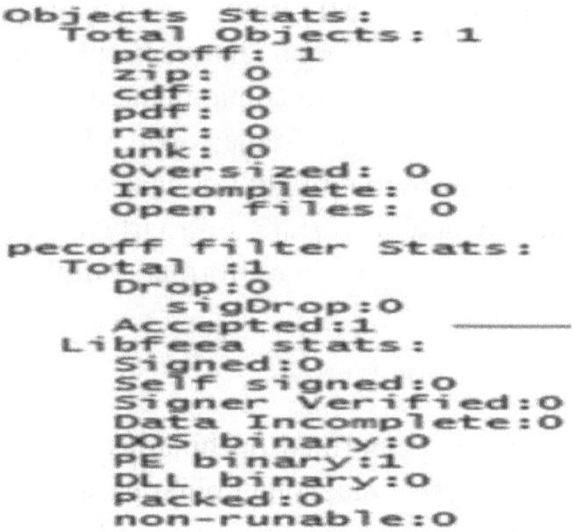

```
Objects  Stats:
   Total  Objects:  1
       pcoff:  1
       zip:  0
       cdf:  0
       pdf:  0
       rar:  0
       unk:  0
   Oversized:  0
   Incomplete:  0
   Open  files:  0

pecoff  filter  Stats:
   Total  :1
       Drop:0
           sigDrop:0
       Accepted:1  ─────
   Libfeea  stats:
       Signed:0
       Self  signed:0
       Signer  Verified:0
       Data  Incomplete:0
       DOS  binary:0
       PE  binary:1
       DLL  binary:0
       Packed:0
       non-runable:0
```

FIGURE 10.8   Binary analysis statistics.

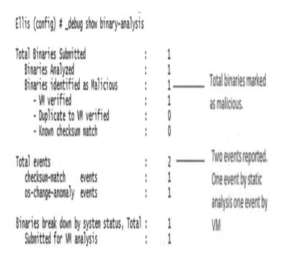

FIGURE 10.9   Verify maliciousness through event logger.

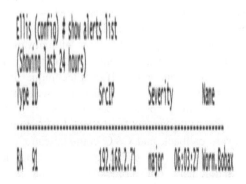

FIGURE 10.10   Verify alert generation through event logger.

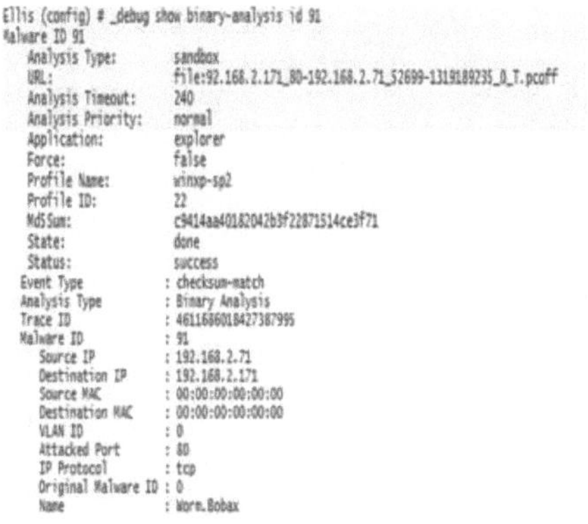

```
Ellis (config) # _debug show binary-analysis id 91
Malware ID 91
    Analysis Type:          sandbox
    URL:                    file:92.168.2.171_80-192.168.2.71_52699-1319189235_0_T.pcoff
    Analysis Timeout:       240
    Analysis Priority:      normal
    Application:            explorer
    Force:                  false
    Profile Name:           winxp-sp2
    Profile ID:             22
    Md5Sum:                 c9414aa40182042b3f22871514ce3f71
    State:                  done
    Status:                 success
    Event Type            : checksum-match
    Analysis Type         : Binary Analysis
    Trace ID              : 4611686018427387995
    Malware ID            : 91
        Source IP         : 192.168.2.71
        Destination IP    : 192.168.2.171
        Source MAC        : 00:00:00:00:00:00
        Destination MAC   : 00:00:00:00:00:00
        VLAN ID           : 0
        Attacked Port     : 80
        IP Protocol       : tcp
        Original Malware ID : 0
        Name              : Worm.Bobax
```

FIGURE 10.11 Malware detail after detection.

and zero-day attacks in a virtual environment dynamically with the help of an event logger[41].

10.4.5 WORKING ANALYSIS

Input packet stream for binary converts it to executable file, performs static analysis and forwards to VM for behavioral analysis. Weight is assigned based on the signature match from YARA, CLAMAV, AV-Suite and Sophos signatures. Weight is assigned and binary is passed to VM for behavioral analysis. The behavior of binary is analyzed and reported through an event logger. The event logger detects OS changes in the VM when the binary is replayed[42]. From the OS correlation file, the events are matched, and the binary is assigned a weight if any malicious activity is found. Both weights of static and behavioral analysis are combined to form total weight, which is used in deciding whether to mark the binary as malicious. If the weight is greater than 100, the binary is reported as malicious.

10.5 RESULTS AND ANALYSIS

The Detection/Protection Summary section reports the total infected hosts and the total number of events that have been observed on the monitored network for the past 24-hour and two-week periods. The different malware types are color-coded with different colors in the bar that is included on the graph. The Monitored Traffic graph displays a 24-hour graph of the traffic that has been seen cumulatively. The different colors in the bar show different traffic types.

10.5.1 SCENARIO I: WEB MALWARE GRAPH FOR 24 HOURS

Displays the following information about current infections.

1. Total Infected Hosts—Total number of unique hosts that are infected in the network.

TABLE 10.3
Detection Summary I

Sr. No	Parameters	Value 1	Value 2
1	Application	Malware Analysis System	Phil2K
2	IP	1.1.1.2	1.1.1.3
3	Last Control UTC		06/06/2022 21:48:07
4	GC	1	1
5	CE	No	Yes
6	Configuration	Disabled	OK
7	Malware Detection Centre	OK	OK
8	Version	6.1.0.66270	6.1.0.66129
9	Application Clock	....	06/06/2022 21:48:07 UTC
10	EULA	OK	OK
11	IP Protocol	....	TCP
12	Attached Port	....	80
13	Traffic Limits	1000 Mbps	1000 Mbps

2. Total Events Count—Total number of infection and callback events observed on the customer network.
3. Total Blocked Events—Total number of events that were blocked according to the currently configured blocking policies.

Table 10.3 represents the malware detection summary with port, IPs, time, infection type and traffic limit, etc.

Figure 10.12 represents the web malware activity graph for 24 hours monitoring which shows different color bars for different malware. Including Malware Exploit Browser, InfoStea*r.Zbot, InfoStea*Ot.DNS, Mal/Generic-L, Malware.*ry.Dlland. Others are represented by colors assigned orange, blue, white, grey, black and brown respectively.

10.5.2 SCENARIO II: WEB MALWARE GRAPH FOR TWO WEEKS

Table 10.4 represents the malware detection summary with source ip, target ip, malware name, its severity, infection type and detail of analysis used.

Figure 10.13 represents the web malware activity graph for two weeks monitoring which shows different color bars for different malware. Malware Bot.Pushdo.B, Bot.Pushdo.C1, InfoStea*r.Bot, Malware.*ry.Pdf, Trojen.G*ic.DNS and others are represented by colors assigned orange, blue, white, grey, black and brown respectively.

10.5.3 ANALYSIS

From Figures 10.9 to 10.13 and conversation we see that signature-based frameworks are incredibly compelling against assault types that have been recognized before, yet they can't identify zero-day attacks. They can be introduced rapidly and take effect

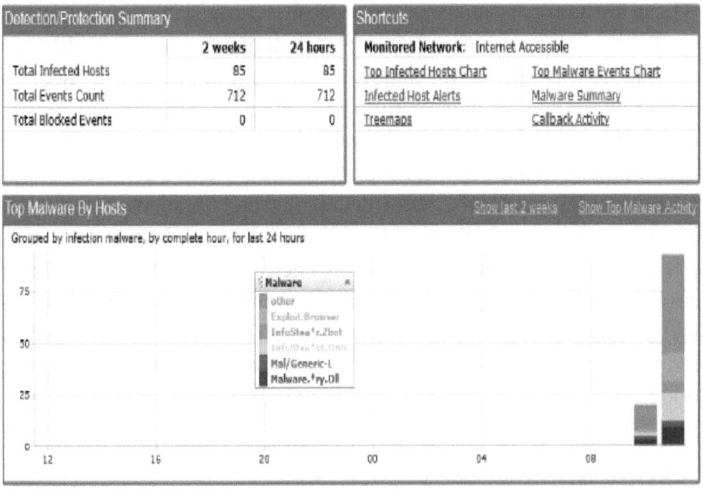

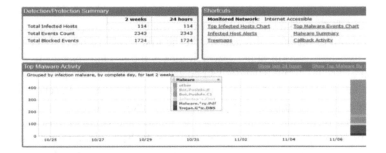

FIGURE 10.12   Web malware for 24 hours.

TABLE 10.4
Detection Summary II

Sr. No	Parameters	Value 1	Value 2
1	Type	Web Infection	Malware Object
2	Id	17130	2164
3	File Type	....	Dll
4	Malware	Exploit.browser	Mal/FakeAV-BW
5	Severity	5/10	4/10
6	Time(PDT)	06/06/2022 15:25:01	06/06/2022 15:18:42
7	Source IP	93.110.111.218	93.110.111.218
8	Target IP	....	51.53.183.63
9	Sophos AV	....	Mal/FakeAV-BW
10	MD5	....	Bca7d492fc25a31032bf043fb3b2a5f8

FIGURE 10.13   Web malware graph for two weeks.

instantly. These frameworks analyze every approaching packet and look at its substance against a rundown of known assault instruments. At the point when we utilized just Whitelisting, it was successful against malware and spam. For most clients, an unadulterated whitelisting arrangement doesn't function admirably for email sifting, since we frequently get mail from individuals we don't realize that is, in any case, authentic and attractive mail. It unquestionably isn't viable for sales reps who get requests from outsiders, essayists who get mail from users, or other finance managers who consistently get mail from likely clients. It might turn out great for the individual email records of people who just need to compare with a set gathering of loved ones. Impediments of these signature engines are that they just distinguish assaults whose signatures are recently put away in the data set; a signature should be made for each assault, and novel assaults can't be identified. This strategy can be handily hoodwinked because they are founded on customary articulations and string coordinating. These systems just search for strings inside packets sent over the wire. Moreover, signatures function admirably against the fixed personal conduct standard; they neglect to manage assaults made by a human or a worm with self-altering social attributes. The productivity of the signature-based frameworks is incredibly diminished, as it needs to make another signature for each variety. As the signatures continue expanding, the framework motor execution diminishes.

The significant disadvantage of anomaly detection is characterizing its standard set. The proficiency of the framework relies upon how well it is carried out and tried on all protocols. A rule characterizing measure is additionally influenced by different protocols utilized by different sellers. Aside from these, custom protocols additionally make rule characterizing troublesome work. For detection to occur correctly, detailed knowledge about the accepted network behavior needs to be developed by the administrators.

The detriment to intrusion detection frameworks and intrusion counteraction frameworks is that they don't have a known standard of legitimate movement on which to reach inferences. They can just draw from a measurable example of what run-of-the-mill network traffic resembles. On a live endeavor network, there might be upwards of 50 million packets of HTTP traffic. These frameworks need to expect to see that if there is an expansion of traffic over some sort of edge that is normal or legitimate, at that point there is an assault in progress. Note that this framework doesn't allude to nectar pots at all and doesn't exploit distinguishing or halting zero-day assaults.

Conventional defense techniques are not appropriate, due to the new worms appearing at a fast pace late in the cyber world. So, these techniques are not covering a wide spectrum of recent worm attacks. At the first level, we used signature-based detection, for known worm attacks, which makes the system operate in real-time. Any deviation from normal behavior can be easily detected by the anomaly detector in the second level. The last level is honeypots which help in detecting zero-day attacks in the machine learning environment. This is the so-called hybrid technique of signature-based technique, anomaly-based technique and behavior-based technique in a machine learning-based environment which is the best solution for detection and removal of zero-day attacks without compromising security and avoiding any delay.

FIGURE 10.14   Proposed model for detecting and removing ZDA's.

10.6   PROPOSED MODEL

In the light of the analysis and conclusion, we proposed a new model which adds up the advantages of the above techniques and overcomes the flaws in the techniques which were previously used. We proposed a model which used hybrid techniques in the machine learning environment.

Figure 10.14 represents the proposed model after discussion and analysis of the study. This model proposed a virtualization-based hybrid technique in a machine learning environment by avoiding the flaws of all techniques and summing up the advantages of all.

10.7   CONCLUSION

The very hot issue in today's world is to secure systems from zero-day attacks. The study also discussed and analyzed problems with existing techniques regarding zero-day attacks, and tried to provide the best, although not perfect, solution to the zero-day, polymorphic and other known malware-related problems. The operating system level safeguards are effective against known attacks, but not against zero-day attacks. Conventional defense techniques are not appropriate, due to the new worms appearing at a fast pace late in the cyber world. So, these techniques are not covering a wide spectrum of recent worm attacks. In this combined approach, a different level has been involved and we used signature-based techniques at the first level. If any anomaly remains then we used anomaly-based techniques at the second level, and if any more anomaly remains we used behavioral-based techniques at the third level. All these were done in a virtual environment which is the next level because operating system level safeguards are effective against known attacks, but not against zero-day attacks. Our analysis of real-time malware samples shows that Web MD successfully detects malware in the virtual environment. Our results also showed that a hybrid of all techniques in the virtual environment is more appropriate in the modern world of the dynamic zero-day vulnerable environment. In the future, it is recommended that research and development should be on machine learning-based malware detection tools for real-time malware detection. Research and development should be on Microvisor/sandbox-based framework for Malware Detection. Malware Detection

Emulators design, and development instrumentation using open-source tools, for example Light Spark and Spider Monkey for Java Script, etc., is required.

REFERENCES

[1] Kaur, R., Singh, M. (2014). Efficient hybrid technique for detecting zero-day poly-morphic worms. In: 2014 IEEE International Advance Computing Conference (IACC). Pp. 95–100.

[2] Kaur, R., Singh, M. (2015). A Hybrid Real-time Zero-day Attack Detection and Analysis System. Int. J. Comput. Netw. Inf. Secur. 7, 19–31https://doi.org/10.5815/ijcnis.2015.09.03.

[3] Bhattacharyya, D. K., & Kalita, J. K. (2013). Network anomaly detection: A machine learning perspective. Crc Press..

[4] Chang, J., Venkatasubramanian, K.K., West, A.G., Lee, I. (2013). Analyzing and defending against web-based malware. ACM Comput. Surv. CSUR. 45, 1–35.

[5] Modeling and Analysis on the Propagation Dynamics of Modern Email Malware, https://ieeexplore.ieee.org/abstract/document/6671578/.

[6] Allodi, L., Chotza, T., Panina, E., Zannone, N. (2020). The Need for New Antiphishing Measures Against Spear-Phishing Attacks. IEEE Secur. Priv. 18, 23–34https://doi.org/10.1109/MSEC.2019.2940952.

[7] Chen, P., Huygens, C., Desmet, L., Joosen, W. (2016). Advanced or Not? A Comparative Study of the Use of Anti-debugging and Anti-VM Techniques in Generic and Targeted Malware. In: Hoepman, J.-H. and Katzenbeisser, S. (eds.) ICT Systems Security and Privacy Protection. Pp. 323–336. Springer International Publishing, Cham.

[8] Xu, Y., Koide, H., Vargas, D.V., Sakurai, K. (2018). Tracing MIRAI Malware in Networked Systems. In: 2018 Sixth International Symposium on Computing and Networking Workshops (CANDARW). Pp. 534–538.

[9] Damshenas, M., Dehghantanha, A., Choo, K.-K.R., Mahmud, R. (2015). M0Droid: An Android Behavioral-Based Malware Detection Model. J. Inf. Priv. Secur.11, 141–157https://doi.org/10.1080/15536548.2015.1073510.

[10] Wu, N. (2001). Audit data analysis and mining. George Mason University (2001).

[11] Shamsolmoali, P., Zareapoor, M. (2014). Statistical-based filtering system against DDOS attacks in cloud computing. In: 2014 International Conference on Advances in Computing, Communications and Informatics (ICACCI). Pp. 1234–1239.

[12] Khalaf, B.A., Mostafa, S.A., Mustapha, A., Mohammed, M.A., Abduallah, W.M. (2019). Comprehensive Review of Artificial Intelligence and Statistical Approaches in Distributed Denial of Service Attack and Defense Methods. IEEE Access. 7, 51691–51713https://doi.org/10.1109/ACCESS.2019.2908998.

[13] Alzahrani, A.J., Ghorbani, A.A. (2015). Real-time signature-based detection approach for SMS botnet. In: 2015 13th Annual Conference on Privacy, Security and Trust (PST). pp. 157–164.

[14] Masdari, M., Khezri, H. (2020). A survey and taxonomy of the fuzzy signature-based Intrusion Detection Systems. Appl. Soft Comput. 92, 106301https://doi.org/10.1016/j.asoc.2020.106301.

[15] Saravanan, R., Shanmuganathan, S., Palanichamy, Y. (2016). Behavior-based detection of application layer distributed denial of service attacks during flash events. Turk. J. Electr. Eng. Comput. Sci. 24, 510–523https://doi.org/10.3906/elk-1308-188.

[16] Han, J., Lin, Z., Porter, D.E. (2020). On the Effectiveness of Behavior-Based Ransomware Detection. In: Park, N., Sun, K., Foresti, S., Butler, K., and Saxena, N.

(eds.) Security and Privacy in Communication Networks. pp. 120–140. Springer International Publishing, Cham.

[17] Emmah, V.T., Ugwu, C., Onyejegbu, L.N. (2021). An Enhanced Classification Model for Likelihood of Zero-Day Attack Detection and Estimation. Eur. J. Electr. Eng. Comput. Sci. 5, 69–75 https://doi.org/10.24018/ejece.2021.5.4.350.

[18] Salahuddin, N.A., EL-Daly, H.A., El Sharkawy, R.G., Nasr, B.T. (2020). Nano-hybrid based on polypyrrole/chitosan/graphene oxide magnetite decoration for dual function in water remediation and its application to form fashionable colored product. Adv. Powder Technol. 31, 1587–1596. https://doi.org/10.1016/j.apt.2020.01.030.

[19] Osanaiye, O., Choo, K.-K.R., Dlodlo, M. (2016). Distributed denial of service (DDoS) resilience in cloud: Review and conceptual cloud DDoS mitigation framework. J. Netw. Comput. Appl. 67, 147–165. https://doi.org/10.1016/j.jnca.2016.01.001.

[20] Lekha, J., Padmavathi, G., Vimal, A.S., Shijumon, S., Lakshanaa, K. (2019). A Comprehensive Study on Machine Learning and Optimization Methods to Mitigate Denial of Service Attacks in Hybrid Intrusion Detection System. In: 2019 International Conference on Intelligent Sustainable Systems (ICISS). pp. 610–615.

[21] Singh, U.K., Joshi, C., Kanellopoulos, D. (2019). A framework for zero-day vulnerabilities detection and prioritization. J. Inf. Secur. Appl. 46, 164–172 https://doi.org/10.1016/j.jisa.2019.03.011.

[22] Wen, S., Rao, Y., Yan, H. (2018). Information Protecting against APT Based on the Study of Cyber Kill Chain with Weighted Bayesian Classification with Correction Factor. In: Proceedings of the 7th International Conference on Informatics, Environment, Energy and Applications. pp. 231–235. Association for Computing Machinery, New York, NY, USA.

[23] Roumani, Y. (2021). Patching zero-day vulnerabilities: an empirical analysis. J. Cybersecurity.7, tyab023 https://doi.org/10.1093/cybsec/tyab023.

[24] Innab, N., Alomairy, E., Alsheddi, L. (2018). Hybrid System Between Anomaly Based Detection System and Honeypot to Detect Zero Day Attack. In: 2018 21st Saudi Computer Society National Computer Conference (NCC). pp. 1–5.

[25] Tang, R., Yang, Z., Li, Z., Meng, W., Wang, H., Li, Q., Sun, Y., Pei, D., Wei, T., Xu, Y. (2020). Zerowall: Detecting zero-day web attacks through encoder-decoder recurrent neural networks. In: IEEE INFOCOM 2020-IEEE Conference on Computer Communications. pp. 2479–2488. IEEE.

[26] Sharma, V., Lee, K., Kwon, S., Kim, J., Park, H., Yim, K., Lee, S.-Y. (2017). A consensus framework for reliability and mitigation of zero-day attacks in IoT. Secur. Commun. Netw.

[27] Kaur, R., Singh, M. (2014). Efficient hybrid technique for detecting zero-day polymorphic worms. In: 2014 IEEE International Advance Computing Conference (IACC). pp. 95–100.

[28] Hindy, H., Atkinson, R., Tachtatzis, C., Colin, J.-N., Bayne, E., Bellekens, X. (2020). Utilising Deep Learning Techniques for Effective Zero-Day Attack Detection. Electronics. 9, 1684 https://doi.org/10.3390/electronics9101684.

[29] Bherde, G.P., Pund, M.A. (2019). Protect System Using Defense Techniques of Zero Day Attacks. *OAIJSE*, 4, 5, 2019

[30] Parrend, P., Navarro, J., Guigou, F., Deruyver, A., Collet, P. (2018). Foundations and applications of artificial Intelligence for zero-day and multi-step attack detection. EURASIP J. Inf. Secur.2018, 4https://doi.org/10.1186/s13635-018-0074-y.

[31] Wang, X., Qi, Y., Wang, Z., Chen, Y. and Zhou, Y. (2019). Design and Implementation of SecPod, A Framework for Virtualization-Based Security Systems. *IEEE Transactions on Dependable and Secure Computing* 1644–57.

[32] Park, S., Kim, C. H., Rhee, J., Won, J.-J., Han, T. and Xu, D. (2020). CAFE: A Virtualization-Based Approach to Protecting Sensitive Cloud Application Logic Confidentiality. *IEEE Transactions on Dependable and Secure Computing* **1 7** 883–97.

[33] Kapil, D. and Mishra, P. (2021). Virtual Machine Introspection in Virtualization: A Security Perspective. In *2021 Thirteenth International Conference on Contemporary Computing (IC3-2021)* pp 117–24. Association for Computing Machinery, New York, NY, USA.

[34] Sharif, M. H., Biswas, S., Hassan, M. M., Bhuiyan, T. and Sohel, M. (2018). SAISAN: An Automated Local File Inclusion Vulnerability Detection Model. *International Journal of Engineering and Technology* **7**.

[35] Spreitzer, R., Moonsamy, V., Korak, T. and Mangard, S. (2018). Systematic Classification of Side-Channel Attacks: A Case Study for Mobile Devices. *IEEE Communications Surveys & Tutorials* **20**465–88.

[36] Hsu, F.-H., Ou, C.-W., Hwang, Y.-L., Chang, Y.-C. and Lin, P.-C. (2017). Detecting Web-Based Botnets Using Bot Communication Traffic Features. *Security and Communication Networks* **2017** e5960307.

[37] deCarvalho Junior, F. H. and Rezende, C. A. (2016). Performance evaluation of virtual execution environments for intensive computing on usual representations of multidimensional arrays. *Science of Computer Programming* **132** 29–49.

[38] Kaur, R. and Singh, M. (2014). A Survey on Zero-Day Polymorphic Worm Detection Techniques. *IEEE Communications Surveys & Tutorials* **16** 1520–49.

[39] Medeiros, I., Neves, N. and Correia, M. (2016). Detecting and Removing Web Application Vulnerabilities with Static Analysis and Data Mining. *IEEE Transactions on Reliability* **65** 54–69.

[40] Ganame, K., Allaire, M. A., Zagdene, G. and Boudar, O. (2017). Network Behavioral Analysis for Zero-Day Malware Detection–A Case Study. In *Intelligent, Secure, and Dependable Systems in Distributed and Cloud Environments* Lecture Notes in Computer Science (I. Traore, I. Woungang and A. Awad, eds) pp.169–81. Springer International Publishing, Cham.

[41] Wei, W., Ke, Q., Nowak, J., Korytkowski, M., Scherer, R. and Woźniak, M. (2020). Accurate and fast URL phishing detector: A convolutional neural network approach. *Computer Networks* **178** 107275.

[42] Anto, A., Rao, R. S. and Pais, A. R. (2017). Kernel Modification APT Attack Detection in Android. In *Security in Computing and Communications in Computer and Information Science* (S. M. Thampi, G. Martínez Pérez, C. B.Westphall, J. Hu, C. I. Fan and F. Gómez Mármol, eds) pp.236–49. Springer, Singapore.

11 Addressing Gestures for One-Handed Mobile Interaction Techniques

Muhammad Waseem Iqbal[1], Syed Khuram Shahzad[2], Muhammad Waseem Aslam[1], Toqir A. Rana[1] and Muhammad Arif[1]
[1]Superior University, Lahore, Pakistan, [2]University of Management and Technology, Lahore, Pakistan

11.1 INTRODUCTION

Old-fashioned input strategies including keyboard and mouse, as well as light pen, remain in use for contributing information. Users interconnect diplomacies to give input and acquire production. Mobile phones have totally transformed interconnection among people[1]. Using the touch screen as an input endeavor dominates the interrelation among users for digital interactions. Cell phone keypads were replaced with touch screens to improve the environment.

Touch screen cell phones involve both hands, one is to handle the set while the other holds the stylus. The stylus appears like a sharp pencil, and benefits objective selection with its tip. Mostly users deploy a finger or thumb for interrelation with their cell phones. It has been observed that most people are using the thumb for usage of their cell phone most of the time[2]. Thus, it makes the choice of mark problematic. It has been observed from the survey that users mostly prefer a single-handed interrelation through the stylus, enabling them to hold as well as operate the cell phone single-handed during walking. Development of the touch screen was targeted to make using the stylus operational. Hence, for assembly usage of the thumb became a thought-provoking undertaking. It is quite difficult to select the right target because the objects are small[3].

To make the thumb functional, the target size is increased, the mobile screen is increased, and subsequently the target becomes challenging to reach. This chapter is marked to launch a model, namely CoGMI, an interrelated model based on a blend of synchronized gestures as well as direct touch. A curved space was applied around the touch screen mobile that remains inside the thumb's reach. This has been divided into three parts in which two sections are used for harmonized signals and one for direct hits[4]. This chapter is separated into different sections. In each section we are going to describe the related work. In the next section we are about to elaborate the planned model, while in some of the sections we are going to include the discussion, as well as our conclusions. The final section describes future work.

DOI: 10.1201/9781003190301-11

11.1.1 One-Handed Mobile Interaction Techniques

A stylus needs both of our hands to operate the touch screen of our mobile phone, but itis not regarded as a favorite input technique by cell phone operators, as found by our research. Cell phone operators maneuver touch screen mobiles single handed; in this way their other hand is free to manage the rest of the tasks in their routine[5]. Additionally, the boundaries of using one finger (or thumb) have also been observed in cell phone users, such that most of them are using only one finger of their hand or their thumb. Diverse techniques are presented to enable easy operation of a mobile single handed.

11.2 TYPES OF ONE-HANDED MOBILE INTERACTION TECHNIQUES

11.2.1 Launch Tile and Applens Techniques

Launch Tile and Applens are both single hand- thumb interactive techniques designed to contact the objects on screen. Launch Tile is a humble drag gesture to move a screen object using the thumb [6]. It makes us able to access 36 apps which are expending meek zooming function. These 36 apps hooked on nine zones, each zone containing four apps surrounded by a blue button. The blue button serves to play four applications and also as an orientation point for panning and zooming tasks. Launch Tile involves three levels of zooming:

1. World level: which indicates the entire 36 apps as nine zones.
2. On screen zooms level: in the designated zone through touching the blue switch once.
3. Zoom level apps.

Users will find back and home, as well as blue buttons. Now I will talk about Applens. Applens employs gestures over the curved space to control the cursor.

Applens uses a flat fisheye concept[7], allowing a user to access nine apps held in reserve, giving the option to the user to select the app of their choice. There are three Applens levels of zooming:

1. Notification level: showing apps in an overlaid form.
2. Context level: dividing the screen area into two sub-areas.
   A screen exhibits the chosen app area which covers roughly three fourths of the space on screen, with the residual app on the screen space to the extent of one fourth.
3. Full level: this provides zoom to the chosen app.

Since Applens employs gestures to perform retrograde functions (getting to the past state) as well as advancing to the next state, and tasks like short key functions on the keyboard. The user finds it a little bit difficult to perform these gestures.

11.2.2   MagStick and Tap-Tap Techniques

MagStick and Tap-Tap are both thumb interactive techniques designed for selecting those targets which are small in size on touch screen mobiles [8]. MagStick makes it easy to select distant targets and avoids the blocking issue. There are four phases used in MagStick.

Within it, the user describes the reference point somewhere upon the screen:

1. On dragging his thumb in relation to the reference point, a stick points to the gesture as if on screen using a single end in order of thumb while the opposite end controls the cursor (both cursor and thumb move together).
2. The user intends to select the target, and for this purpose he moves his thumb so the cursor tends to attract the target like a magnet.
3. When the thumb is lifted, it selects the target. For a cancellation, the thumb can be used at a free space available on screen. Compared with other techniques, MagStick was able to achieve accuracy but less susceptibility with high learnability time.

The Tap-Tap technique enables selection of small targets with ease. Selecting small targets through direct touch remained robust, but with less accuracy. The first tap brings the rectangular area, comprising the chosen object, and zooms in at the desired place on the screen[9]. The second tap enables the right selection. Tap-Tap selects the targets at easy edges. Zooming the target place helps to terminate blank areas on screen, though Tap-Tap provides fast touching itis slow compared to direct touch.

11.2.3   Thumb Space Technique

A most famous usage method has been observed of people using their thumbs to access the targets. Thumb space is the interrelation method for aims which are unapproachable by straight touch. It implemented the idea of "Radar View", which displays the comprehensive screen demonstration in a minor area[10]. By the usage of thumb space the user will be able to specify a rectangular space I on his mobile phone anywhere on the "Presentation Space" (known as the innovative space of the mobile) within thumb reach. For selecting the target, the user keeps a finger on the quadrangular space, changes it and boosts it as the target touches the finger.

11.2.4   Types of Thumb Space

The three types of thumb space are:

1. **Guess phase**
   In this type of thumb space, the user can make a guess about the target on his mobile screen under the thumb space.
2. **Aim phase**
   Aim phase permits the user to change their thumb in the thumb space to choose the anticipated target.

3. **Lift phase**

   This phase ensures the selection of a target by lifting the thumb up. A corresponding selection cursor appears on the display space when the user moves the thumb on the thumb space. If the user wants to abandon the choice they can move their thumb toward the red cross button which is shown on the screen, which appears on the upper right or lower left corner of the thumb space. Thumb space is accommodating in retrieving far targets while the range of near targets is challenging.

11.2.5   Eight Targets Technique

Escape is a selection technique utilizing one hand only and is a one-handed mobile usage technique. It selects the assortment of minor targets to make them easily accessible, and also to make the process fast. Escape uses gestures to select the desired target. When we are going to select a particular target, escape will use a single-level beak icon method in accessing the targets[11]. The beak track specifies the direction of assortment gesticulation. Eight different gestures are performed for selecting eight different goals. Overlying occurs if any goal which can be designated with the same sign is placed near another goal which can also be designated by the same signal.

This problem is well-explained by unfolding a Parhi box. A Parhi box is a squared box in which a total of eight targets are enhanced with different instructions of the beak. When the user is going to select the target, he will touch on that site which is going to trigger that Parhi box[12]. Dragging the user's thumb or finger, whether it is single or not in the direction of a single-leveled beak icon (without lifting thumb or finger) will make the selection easy and convenient. Thus, "escape" will select the targets 30% faster than the shift method[13].

The instructions of the signs used by "escape" for assortment were not totally liked by users. Furthermore, there were boundaries in selection operation, particularly when the goals were at the ends of the display.

11.2.7   Challenges and Issues

Escape selects the targets 30% faster than shift. The directions of the gestures which Escape uses for selection were not absolutely liked by users. Moreover, there were limitations observed in selection operation, especially when the targets were at the edges of the screen.

1. Tap-Tap was much faster than other techniques, but a bit slower than direct touch.
2. MagStick as compared to other techniques was observed to be accurate and less error prone, but its learnability time is higher.
3. In shift technique when a callout pops-up sometimes it is placed at a distant position which distracts user attention. In addition, while lifting the thumb up, a slight movement causes the pointer to move away from the targeted object.

11.2.8 AIMS AND OBJECTIVES

- To make the interface of the touch screen more interactive to the user.
- There were many problems pointed out about the working of the touch screen by one-handed interaction, my thesis work is to highlight those issues so that they can be solved.
- My aim is to develop new interaction techniques and enhanced gestures to provide a rich interface.

11.3 PROBLEM STATEMENT

Touchscreen mobile phones are operationalized using both hands. One hand grabs the device while the second hand is used to hold the stylus or touch the screen. The stylus appears as a sharp pencil, and it enables the selection of targets using its tip to touch the screen. Most users employ a thumb to interact with the mobile device. The target generally remains unmatched with thumb size. Thus, selection of the target isa bit difficult. In my research, I provided an effective and efficient method for touchscreen users, this method can also be used by single-handed people, without feeling any difficulty or complexity.

11.3.1 RESEARCH QUESTIONS

- What are the techniques used to make the mobile touch screen experience rich?
- How many ways are here to interact with the touch screen with one hand?
- Is it a good approach to use a mobile phone with one hand?
- What are the challenges and solutions for one-handed interaction techniques?
- Are there any reforms still to implement to make one-handed interaction better?

11.4 LITERATURE REVIEW

11.4.1 INPUT GESTURES ON MOBILE

Previous work and constructors presented an in-depth variety of enter panels for smartphones of which we supply a precis. We characterized them via their role at the device, and by the estimating participation. Currently the smartphones we have, including the iPhone 7 and Samsung Galaxy S8, use the finger affect sensor and eye detection approach[14]. These capabilities are essentially used for authentication purposes for unlocking the android set, however, we can also perceive guiding swipes of android that act as shortcuts for functions, for example switching or launching applications. Previous work proposed distinct functions that can be enabled using a fingerprint sensor[15].

Small gadgets normally assist the capabilities of the android on the rear; researchers have developed multiple methods to apply built-in sensors for allowing bot interplay, along with the accelerometer.

11.4.2   Touch Inputs on the Whole Touch-Based Device Surface

Previous studies have discussed prototypes of smartphones that are entirely touch based. These smartphones have screens that are completely responsive to touch input. Some newly invented smartphones have taken this concept a step further by incorporating touch functionality into the back and corners of the device. This allows users to interact with their smartphones in new and innovative ways. For example, users can swipe up on the back of the phone to open the notification shade, or they can double-tap on the corner of the phone to take a screenshot [16]. This empowers a complete series of use cases which includes contact-based total authentication at the hindmost facet to keep away from receive browsing.

11.4.3   Convenient Accessibility in a One-Handed Mobile System

In a contact mobile gadget, most people get access to the cell effortlessly and in a convenient manner. Your creation could get confirmation to refining the reachability all through one-passed phone communique [17].

If we're using mobiles in which 3D enhancement is used and we've the 3D technologies and their apps established in the telephones, the consumer will be happy. Plenty of video games and video apps are being developed as 3D structures. Many users in the marketplace are looking for cell phones that are equipped with 3D video games. If this capacity is being enhanced there has to be ease of 3D use, and as a result research and development needs to make entry effortless[18].

11.4.4   User Defined Signs and their Involvement

The success of consumer-described sign participation is likewise vast, because it is the most important component that needs to be implemented. To make your right of entry clean and convenient is vital[19] to get through cellular tasks, as well as recurring life tasks.

Exploring user-defined lower back-of-tool gestures for cell gadgets is discussed in "Court Cases of the 17th Worldwide Conference on Human-Pc Interaction [20]".

11.4.5   Body of Design of a Touch Mobile System Mobile

The layout of the body is going to be the most difficult aspect of design these days. Use is usually looking for a frame which is simple, low weight, easy to get admission to and designed in such a way that each one of the apps are in range and can be effortlessly accessed during use. The device should be designed to allow two iPhones to be attached back-to-back, so that touch input can be used as a modality of input through pressure. This is similar to HTC's Side Sense feature, which was recently announced as a pressure-based input modality for the edges of smartphones [20].

To activate pre-defined features, legacy devices such as the Nexus One and HTC Desire provide physical or optical trackballs for selecting objects. This is because it can be difficult to select objects on small screens with fat finger [21]. As sunshades were receiving extra attention, trackballs were terminated and have been removed.

Likewise, legacy blackberry devices blended a scrolling wheel on the proper facet to empower scrolling.

11.4.6   BUTTONS, ICONS AND QUICK SWITCH SYSTEMS

For many years, smartphones featured a variety of buttons to manage and manipulate the overall advanced functions. Among others, this includes strength and quantity buttons which are usually greater in mobile telephones[22]. There were also a lot of other small capabilities that were included, in addition to hardware buttons, for example the lower back, home and some new buttons on android devices.

Few of the shortcuts currently get closer to functions very quickly, and these are advanced in the iPhone 7 and OnePlus five which feature a hardware tool that can move speedily to the volume manage button, excepting fundamental display contact icons.

Moreover, the Samsung Galaxy S8 provided an extra button at the left of the device as a shortcut to the maneuver assistant at the same time as other gadgets combine a dedicated digicam button within the cell phones. It's understood that having a huge number of buttons on the device clearly messes up the tool, previous paintings castoff the integrated accelerometer to spot taps on the brink of the tool[23].

11.4.7   MODEL DESIGN COMPATIBILITY WITH HAND USAGE

The study of areas on mobile phones that can be easily accessed by the hands is a major foundation for informing the compatibility of on-screen interaction elements and on-device input panels [24]. A maximum of the organizations had been working on the modeling of the thumb's range on smartphones to inform the location of user boundary elements for one-pass collaboration.

In the modeling of mobile phones the major aim is to manipulate a specially sized arm to be well matched with the touch screen and the position of the index finger (adducted).

For the projected kind of thumb, they delivered a time period functional place which is modified from earlier paintings in kinesiology and biomechanics. In these fields, possible postures and movements of the hand are known as useful space[25].

11.4.8   IMPLEMENTED FEATURES IN CONSEQUENTIAL GESTURES

Phones such as S3, S4, Opo and N6 4 that had been used are selected as those mobile phones to get a non-stop boom in tool frame width, as this size has an awesome effect on catching in the hand[26]. Within the relaxation of the work, we've a few abbreviations for the above referred to gadgets: s3, s4, opo and n6. Opo and n6 represent two fashions for the latest leading smartphones (e.g., samsung s8 plus, one plus five or iPhone 7 plus; common on 154% of the s3's location), while the s4 and opo are cell telephones for capable versions (for Instance Samsung S8, OnePlus x and iPhone 7; form 126% of the S3 collection of the Samsung).

The S3 and S4 are those cellular phones which might represent small gadgets, for example the iPhone SE, LG Nexus Five or Sony Xperia compact (carrying 109%

of the s3). Although laser-reduce device replicas might have been an alternative, we used actual campaigns out-of-the-box to maintain the member's hand grip as practically as achievable.

Due to an abandonment distinction in tool width (sd=1:0mm), distinctive tool outlines (e.g., edges and corners) must not disturb the grip and finger activities as the edges are compressed between palms postures and palm postures. To document finger gestures with sub-millimeter accuracy, we cast-off an optitrack motion imprisonment scheme with eight cameras inside the cellular phones (optitrack prime 13w is encapsulating its capabilities at 240fps). The cameras have been resolutely straddled to an aluminum defined shape[27]. Additionally, we connected four indicators at the pinnacle, a part of each smartphone which permits us to avenue the phones in six levels of freedom (dof).

11.5 EXPERIMENTATION

A research-conducted investigation on the application of hand gestures while operating mobile phones found that one-handed operation is the most popular and regular use among users, including the use of index finger, middle finger and little finger while supporting or holding the phone. This research aims to test this theory in the local environment.

The hand-held mobile device has a history that dates back to 1908, when the world watched the launch of the maiden patent in Kentucky relating to a "wireless telephone". Its technical propagation was on the lines of two-way radio instead of phones as they are known today. The Motorola Company made this history and had the privilege of making the first call from its platform through a prototype relating to a model Dyna TAC, the maiden hand-held mobile phone released in the market after a wait of ten years. Consumers received the first, in a real sense, mobile phone developed by Nokia. It required more effort in use due to its weight of 10 KG, and it was not possible for the user to carry it for a whole day. This ground-breaking mobile phone employed '"Nordic Mobile Telephony (NMT) Standard" network, known as the first generation (1G) relating to wireless cellular technology. After one year, the maiden handheld mobile phone was launched, as the Senator Model along with the Dyna TAC 8000X. This phone had a weight of above 1 KG and its battery charging time exceeded ten hours. It took more efforts to improve battery time to 30 minutes for complete charging. The said mobile phone was for the first time deployed in the UK during 1985. The pace of technological advance paused for a period of ten years, however, many similar models in the type of the Dyna TAC 8000X popped up; mostly through Nokia on releasing the City man model under the auspices of the Mobira brand.

The scenario faced a change during 1992 with the launch of the "1011" model that had the facility of free mobility to carry anywhere, as its weight had come down to 500 grams. The mobile phone entered 2G (second generation); credit was taken by the GSM Network as the Global System for Mobile Communication representing wireless-based cellular technology. The handheld handset featured a monochrome based LCD screen with an extendable antenna. The same year marked another historic event when text messaging emerged as a pioneer in the history of the mobile phone, the first message was inscribed as "Merry Christmas". The world saw a paradigm shift in the field of communication when IBM launched for the first time during 1994 and Simon Personal communicator was able to record history with the maiden "smartphone". IBM made an advance into the future when the company presented a touchscreen display, as well as a myriad of pre-installed apps including address book, calendar, calculator, world clock, digital notepad and much more. This revolution in the field of hand-held devices took a great turn in human life and made mobile phones part and parcel of human beings. The growth taken in development to operate the mobile phone further to the level of a smart phone handled with one hand reached the point of ultimate addiction. In a survey conducted at Deloitte among 4,150 British during the year 2017 on their use of mobile habits, 38% admitted to over-use of a smartphone. From the age group of 16 to 24 years, the number exceeded 50%. Habits including checking apps during the hour before going to sleep to the extent of 79% or within a span of 15 minutes after waking up (55%), badly affected mental health. Insomnia and anxiety resulted in great stress on the mind and created psychological issues.

Norway introduced an app with the name of "Hold" to induce users among students to win points by showing a reduction in smartphone habits, and they were given snacks along with cinema tickets. Overuse of a mobile phone occurs due to unawareness about the frequency as well as degree of smartphone use. An expert on hypnotherapy as well as anxiety, Chloe Brotheridge suggested purchasing a time watch for the bedside instead of relying on a built-in-alarm and turning the notification off on the phone. Notifications enable the user to check emails or open the mobile phone. In case of turning the notification off, use of mobile phone will reduce remarkably.

In the disposition of creativity, browsing through Facebook results in loss of precious time employed previously in imagining, instead of looking out the window to let ideas blossom. Powell, a researcher, proposes a discourse that technology is fanciful, but users need to remain conscious about its use.

Some research explores the use of mobile single-handed and for this purpose, offers an insight into the current use of devices (habit), users preference for using devices and the association of device size, as well as thumb freedom (agility). Users in great numbers of mobile phone operations are using a single hand only. There is another reality that users in large numbers prefer to insert personal information to manage tasks single-handed, however, mobile designs currently in vogue resist the interactive mode the majority utilizes. Moreover, with the increase in device size, thumb mobility tends to decrease, but localized movement is open to users, even in the case of large devices.

Throughout the globe, touch-screen mobile phones dominate the mobile industry. Research has found that the market is overwhelmed with mobile phones bigger than 4.0 inches. Research is evident that users in large numbers select to operate a mobile phone with one hand. By study design, this research decided to employ two research methods, one is to conduct a field study observation, the second to carry out a survey to get field study results based on user perceptions with the intent of knowing their preference to deal with mobile tasks with one or two hands, and record an empirical evaluation to comprehend how different locations, device size, as well as movement direction, influences the thumb mobility of users. The thumb has a unique structure that needs to be understood [21], but over the years scientists have underpinned the need to quantify reliably the functional capabilities associated with the thumb. Strength remains the principal parameter utilized to assess mechanical ability, and the influence of movement direction upon thumb strength has been established.

Research found that size of touch screen and single hand operation both significantly affect the operational performance. However, size of the touch screen if it exceeds 5.7 inches, makes reliance on single handed operation difficult. Linked with the previous chapters, the intent of our study is to look for the most commonly used gestures and techniques available to mobile users, particularly in circumstances when a user, either able or disabled, is bound to use a single hand only and out of the existing five techniques of using a mobile phone, there is a need to know which one is the most efficient. Moreover, there is a paucity of systematic study on unearthing the fact of which of the mobile features impede single handed use of mobile phones, furthermore there is a lack of research on supporting technologies as well as interaction techniques.

11.5.1 SCOPE OF THE RESEARCH

- To examine the attitude of youth aged 20–30 years concerning cellular phones.
- To investigate the usage patterns and general style in vogue by gender or age-wise, if there is any.
- To assess noticeable phenomena how young people deal with mobile phones.

11.5.2 FIELD STUDY OBSERVATION METHOD

To get empirical evidence for these questions, this study selected to target an airport location where one has more chances of using a mobile phone with the effort of remaining in coordination walking or standing, besides carrying extra journey items. Moreover, the researcher has the opportunity to have an unobtrusive observation of users with ease of access. During this observational study, an anonymous observation was performed without contacting the observed.

Having a visionary insight into the common and popular pattern of single-handed designs of using mobile devices, this study adopted a field study method. In the first instance, we targeted 150 travelers at an International Airport where the researcher has a six hour stay during peak hours at the time of a rush flight. We set a target to observe the ticketed passengers with access to the passenger lounge where seating options were limited. We observed travelers using cell phones as well as other devices; mostly busy in coordinating transportation, catching work time, and seeking entertainment as well. As a majority of the users use a mobile phone with one hand, so we focused our observation on the users who were using a phone through dialing as well as talking, and those were our targets. It is pertinent to mention here that the observations were made anonymously without involving the observed in which hand gestures operations were examined.

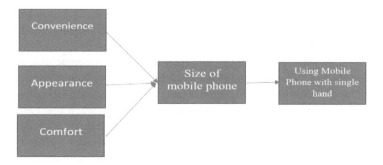

FIGURE 11.1 Theoretical framework.

Furthermore, a literature review helped to identify the responsible variables that are indicative of a users' tendency to use a mobile phone with a single hand, these variables are size of mobile phone with operational convenience, appearance and comfort. The question arises whether the size of a mobile phone has any correlation with convenience, appearance or comfort and what would be the outcome. The following theoretical framework (Figure 11.1) is drawn to show the correlation among variables.

Figure 11.1 takes into consideration convenience, appearance, comfort and size of mobile phone as elements that leave an impact on users, and they start using the mobile phone in a particular style that is common among the public using a mobile phone with a single hand.

11.5.3 SURVEY METHOD: ANOTHER RESEARCH METHOD

This research adopted the technique of employing a structured questionnaire based on the variables selected for the study and was utilized during a survey presented on a single web page which was given access through google from any computer server. The study addressed the potential participants and disseminated survey goals assuring anonymity. The participants were asked to record demographics as well as give their subjective ratings.

The foremost challenge while using mobile phones confronts those users who have restrained physical, as well as impaired attentional, resources and the problem they face is in the form of mobile phone design. To look into future assessment, this study started with an observational study that led us to know that single handed keypad use in mobile phones is extensive, and generally, users in great numbers like to use a single hand while interacting with the device. In addition, research suggested that device size comes up not as the only factor; rather users can also operate a mobile with a single thumb even more effectively. However, in the case of larger devices, it becomes harder to use a single hand to operate. Right-handed users find it difficult to move a thumb in a diagonal direction NW/SE. As a result, portability has become linked with thin/thickness, and that is still in continuous advancement. Unluckily, such divergent trends have made the usability of mobile phones extremely difficult in the wake of a richer flow of content accessing through shrinking input as well as output channels. The problem is compounded when mobile computing has developed unique requirements with certain constraints in usage under unstable environments, avoidance of eyes while interacting, considering resources for competition and changing hand availability. Design is the only element that deals with these constraints and that is our prime interest right now. Devices that can facilitate users to operate mobile phones single handed can be tremendously useful for users when one hand is busy with the rising physical as well as attentional needs common to all. Such devices are available but there is little evidence those are designed with such goals. Small and light phones are available in the markets that are friendly to one hand but difficult with the thumb owing to small buttons as well as crowded keypads.

While it is difficult to manage larger devices with a single hand though they have more features, larger buttons along with a stylus touchscreen rich in absorbing maximum content of information seem more attractive to small thumb interaction. There is a paucity of systematic study on unearthing which of the mobile features impede the single-handed use of mobile phones, furthermore there is a lack of research on supporting technologies as well as interaction techniques.

11.6   RESULTS AND DISCUSSION

Our research is motivated by single handed use of mobile designs that assumes that a multitude of people are persistently using mobile devices. As per current patterns acquired after interaction, such people are bound to do so under the purview of necessity or preference. This predicts the future behavior of users and their intentions to move towards new devices. This necessitates the need to accommodate mobile design that could enable single handed use. To detect the current behavior, we aimed to conduct a study based on user interacting mobile devices. The study directed the environment of an airport to gauge the presence of increased mobile users with ease of access for unhindered observation. Seeing the overwhelming market for bigger touch phones, a smartphone of 5.8 inches size is taken as small, and this size is getting bigger rapidly. This size provably hinders the single hand use of such a sized mobile. As a matter of fact, the latest iPhone 11 Pro Max has weight of 7.97 ounces or ½ a pound. We therefore realize that devices of this massive size make nearly impossible the use of one-handed operation, and it is likely that we may drop these during use. A study conducted research on comparative use of mobile phones with QWERTY and keypads and found user behavior is influenced by device type; users who use keypad-only almost use always one hand, touchscreen users apply two hands, particularly for text-entry (Figure 11.2). But user justifications to make a choice of hand finds a connection with the available hardware/software interface.

Similarly, a survey study conducted on usage patterns in current use with a sample of single- and two-handed users and found no clear winner among the two (Figure 11.3).

As mobile devices as well as applications have extensive landscapes, it would be logical if we took into consideration the fundamental human factors that interact with

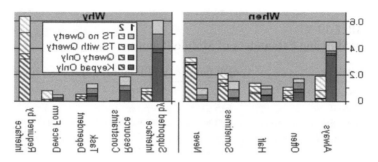

FIGURE 11.2   Hand correlation.

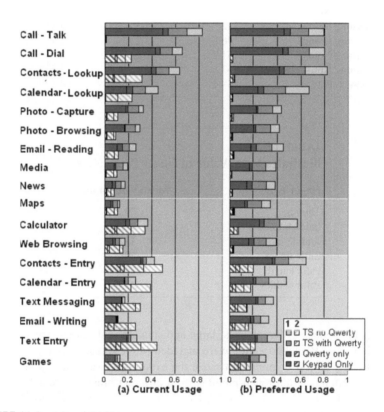

FIGURE 11.3   (a) and (b) Usage.

the device single handed. As per thumb movement while interacting with a mobile device, though the thumb comes up as a versatile attachment to run into an inspiring motion, it quickly adapts itself to grasp tasks and play in reverse of the remaining four fingers.

Following the criteria that only popular phone brands among users should be selected for the study, the study made a choice of 13 best-selling brands that include

TABLE 11.1
List Showing Parameters of Mobile Phones

Models	Length (mm)	Width (mm)	Thickness (mm)
iPhone 11 Pro Max	6.22	3.06	8.3
iPhone 4	115.2	58.6	9.3
iPhone 5S	123.8	58.6	7.6
Samsung Galaxy A30	158.5	74.7	7.7
Blackberry Key one	149.3	72.5	9.4
Samsung S9	147.7	68.7	8.5
iPhone 6	138.1	67	6.9
Samsung Note 9	161.9	76.4	8.8
Samsung S5	142	72.5	8.1
Samsung Grand2	146.8	75.3	8.9
Samsung Note3	151.2	79.2	8.3
Samsung Note4	153.5	78.6	8.5
iPhone 6 Plus	158.1	77.8	7.1

TABLE 11.2
Illustrates Mean Value of Finger Parameters

Finger Type	Mean Value(mm)
Thumb	39.2
Index finger	41.2
Middle finger	43.1
Little finger	29.4
Palm length	37.3
Palm width	35.3

a diversity of models, different sizes, large and small, and different brands such as iPhone, Samsung, Blackberry, etc., were included in the research. Some brands are known for their largest or minimum sizes, the experiment was selected amid these sizes. As an inference, ten touch-mobiles from different brands were selected as a test case. All the sample mobiles had a length starting from 6.61mm to 161.9mm; the thickness covers from 3.06 mm to 79.2 mm. Parameters in detail are described in Table 11.1. Based on this, this research focused on the parameters derived from the three fingers, with palm lengths as well as palm widths of our 150 subjects (Table 11.2).

Table 11.2 illustrates the mean value associated with these parameters. Application of the Kalmagrov Smirnov test using SPSS version 21.0 on six parameters indicate, on the basis of mean values, that all the items fall inside the normal range ($P>0.05$).

11.6.1 RESEARCH METHOD

11.6.1.1 Subject Selection

Selection of 150 test subjects (males are counted as 132 while 18 were females) was made on a random basis in the environment of an educational institute with ages of subjects 20–30 years. Out of the given population, 150 selected students had physically healthy hands, as well as joints, except one who was disabled with missing middle and little fingers.

On investigating the hand gestures reflected by users, single-handed operation gave evidence that utilization of the thumb outnumbered other functions reflected by index, middle and little fingers respectively in supporting or holding the mobile phone; even the disabled person ably operated with the single hand.

As Figure 11.4 demonstrates, six muscular activities are involved in single handed operation. These are named as:

1. Adductor Pollicis
2. Flexor pollicis brevis
3. Abductor pollicis brevis
4. Abductor pollicis longus
5. First dorsal interosseous
6. Extensor digitorum.

According to scientists, these muscles become prey to fatigue quickly during single-handed operation. In these circumstances, most of the users ignore the fatigue factor and continue to operate their phones. In that case, thumb overuse will create health issues for the users.

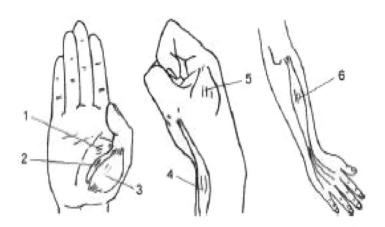

FIGURE 11.4 Usage of mobile using his thumb in all directions.

11.6.1.2   Data analysis

Data analysis presents the mean values of mobile use operation for the purpose of subjective evaluation. Analysis of the data was run with the help of SPSS software and generating output results of the correlation analysis.

11.6.1.3   Performance analysis

Table 11.3 presents the results of correlation analysis among sizes of touch mobiles, and completion rates as well as duration of performance completion. Due to closeness between mobile phone length and width that value indicates their mutual correlation ∧ p=0.00, it reflects that their separate analysis is not possible due to having exceedingly close mutual correlation but recognized as two separate parameters for multiplication and embrace the result as area size as an analytical parameter. Table 11.3 presents correlation analysis using the Spearman Correlation analyzing method.

The analysis of results state that size is positively related with completion rate (0.436** p=0.000) which indicates the significant correlation of size with complete operational rate. Likewise, size is correlated with performance time (0.491** p=0.022). However, the correlation coefficient of thickness with performance time indicates an unclear relationship (0.633*∧P=0.029).

Figure 11.5 presents a curve producing a correlation between convenience and area size using a fitting interpolation method. The curve line visibly indicates that convenience operationally decreases as area size increases, convenience on reaches 3, the area size comes as 9547mm², equaling the 4.7 inch screen.

Table 11.4 demonstrates correlation coefficient results using a sizable mobile phone in the environment of operational convenience, with comfort as well as appearance. The threshold values assigned to convenience, comfort and appearance ranging from 1–5.

The above statistical results reveal that size is positively correlated with operational convenience at 0.471** (p=0.000); similarly positive correlation exists between thickness and operational convenience at 0.524 (p=0.000). This indicates that size influences operational convenience and single-handed use may feel difficult with the increase in size of a cell phone.

TABLE 11.3
Correlations between Size of Mobile Phone and Task Completion Rate and Performance Time

		Completion Rate	Performance Time
Size	Pearson correlation	0.436	0.491
	Significance	0.000	0.022
	N	150	150
Thickness	Pearson correlation	0.696	0.633
	Significance	0.000	0.029
	N	150	150

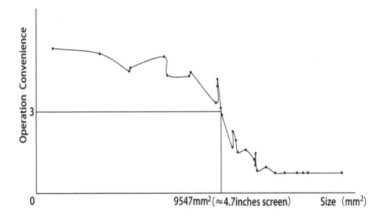

FIGURE 11.5   Curve showing correlation between convenience and size.

TABLE 11.4
Correlation Coefficient between Size of Mobile Phone and Convenience, Comfort and Appearance

		Operational Convenience	Appearance	Comfort
Size	Pearson correlation	0.471	0.601	0.425
	Significance	0.000	0.041	0.000
	N	150	150	150
Thickness	Pearson correlation	0.524	0.640	0.602
	Significance	0.000	0.000	0.001
	N	150	150	150

Particularly, as a touch screen approaches the size 150x80 (5.7 inches), only 20% users are able to operate one single handed. It can be seen that increased thickness leads to more comfortable use. The influence of mobile thickness on performance is significant. To further improve the degree of convenience, screen size must be restricted to 4.7 inches for smooth operation by a single hand by normal and impaired individuals. The correlation between thickness and comfort is significant in that it reflects increasingly comfortable operation.

11.6.2   RETROSPECT AND PROSPECT

There has long been emphasis on analyzing motion in the case of transportation by ergonomics research, as in the case of innovations in cars and planes, analyzing amplitude motion during driving and in fire fighters' work[22]. As our daily life is replete with smart phones having touch screens, their effects on health and human performance cannot be ignored.

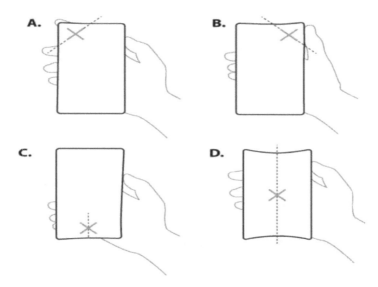

FIGURE 11.6   Four gestures locating in top left, top right, lower bottom and center.

11.6.3 FIELD STUDY RESULTS

Only four users were found using Tab and blackberry besides mobile phones; both of them were sitting and using the mobile with two hands. The remaining 146 phone users (74%) utilized a single hand for dialing. By activity, 65% of users applied a single hand when they had their second hand occupied, 54% were in walking mode, 35% standing while 11% were in sitting mode.

11.7 CONCLUSION AND FUTURE WORK

Literature provides evidence based on results of three studies carried out to comprehend the design needs of mobiles that could facilitate their one-handed use. Firstly, a field study provided observation that use of single hands is a free and natural state. Secondly, we engaged users for interviews directly to transcribe personal accounts based on current as well as preferred patterns of device usage. The results delivered by these studies promoted single handed interface research, and provided a supportive vision about the devices in vogue and tasks that would need new techniques to handle the mobile single handed. Finally, this outcome led us to perform an empirical evaluation on thumb rap speed, unveiling that performance is influenced by device size, movement and target location.

With the view to understand the single hand operational interaction of mobile devices as a popular practice among the public, this study watched the use of mobile sets extensively under use. Our field study indicated that single hand use of mobile devices is commonly popular among the traveler class that is more attached to the use of mobile devices with a single hand, this behavior is reflected in all scenarios, either walking or talking or holding items in an activity during traveling.

Our survey results unveiled that the user's in immense majority stick with the style of using mobile devices with a single hand, but the dilemma is in case of current interfaces, design of touchscreens does not prove supportive to dedicated single handed use of mobile devices. The results demonstrate that out of all parameters, the thumb provides an empirical evaluation of interacting with different sizes of devices. This suggests that the thumb tends to impact performance more than device size, and it is equally vital for able and disabled persons. Finally, right hand users find it difficult to undertake NW/SE movement while having movement distance.

REFERENCES

1. Patrick Bader, Valentin Schwind, Niels Henze, Stefan Schneegass, Nora Broy, and Albrecht Schmidt. 2014. Design and Evaluation of a Layered Handheld 3D Display with Touch-sensitive Front and Back. In Proceedings of the 8th Nordic Conference on Human-Computer Interaction: Fun, Fast, Foundational (Nordi CHI '14). ACM, New York, NY, USA, 315–318. DOI: http://dx.doi.org/10.1145/2639189.2639257

2. Joanna Bergstrom-Lehtovirta and Antti Oulasvirta. 2014. Modeling the Functional Area of the Thumb on Mobile Touchscreen Surfaces. In Proceedings of the 32nd Annual ACM Conference on Human Factors in Computing Systems (CHI '14). ACM, New York, NY, USA, 1991–2000. DOI: http://dx.doi.org/10.1145/2556 288.2557354.

3. Christian Corsten, Bjoern Daehlmann, Simon Voelker, and Jan Borchers. 2017. Back X Press: Using Back-of-Device Finger Pressure to Augment Touchscreen Input on Smartphones. In Proceedings of the 2017 CHI Conference on Human Factors in Computing Systems (CHI '17). ACM, New York, NY, USA, 4654–4666. DOI:http://dx.doi.org/10.1145/3025453.3025565.

4. Shi, L., Yin, Z., Jiang, L., and Li, Y. (2017). Advances in inductively coupled power transfer technology for rail transit. CES Transactions on Electrical Machines and Systems, 1(4), 383–396.

5. Zhu, R., and Li, Z. (2016). An ergonomic study on influence of touch-screen phone size on single-hand operation performance. In MATEC Web of Conferences (Vol. 40, p. 09001). EDP Sciences.

6. Alexander De Luca, Emanuel von Zezschwitz, Ngo Dieu Huong Nguyen, Max-Emanuel Maurer, Elisa Rubegni, Marcello Paolo Scipioni, and Marc Langheinrich. 2013. Back-of-device Authentication on Smartphones. In Proceedings of the SIGCHI Conference on Human Factors in Computing Systems (CHI '13). ACM, New York, NY, USA, 2389–2398. DOI:http://dx.doi.org/10.1145/2470654.2481330.

7. Anna Maria Feit, Daryl Weir, and Antti Oulasvirta. 2016. How We Type: Movement Strategies and Performance in Everyday Typing. In Proceedings of the 2016 CHI Conference on Human Factors in Computing Systems (CHI '16). ACM, New York, NY, USA, 4262–4273. DOI: http://dx.doi.org/10.1145/2858036.2858233.

8. Huy Viet Le, Patrick Bader, Thomas Kosch, and Niels Henze. 2016. Investigating Screen Shifting Techniques to Improve One-Handed Smartphone Usage. In Proceedings of the 9th Nordic Conference on Human-Computer Interaction (Nordi CHI '16). ACM, New York, NY, USA, Article 27, 10 pages. DOI: http://dx.doi.org/10.1145/2971485.2971562.

9. Huy Viet Le, Sven Mayer, Patrick Bader, Frank Bastian, and Niels Henze. 2017b. Interaction Methods and Use Cases for a Full-Touch Sensing Smartphone. In Proceedings of the 2017 CHI Conference Extended Abstracts on Human Factors

in Computing Systems (CHI EA '17). ACM, New York, NY, USA, 2730–2737. DOI: http://dx.doi.org/10.1145/3027063.3053196.

10. Huy Viet Le, Sven Mayer, Patrick Bader, and Niels Henze. 2017. A Smartphone Prototype for Touch Interaction on the Whole Device Surface. In Proceedings of the 19th International Conference on Human-Computer Interaction with Mobile Devices and Services Adjunct (Mobile HCI '17). ACM, New York, NY, USA. DOI: http://dx.doi.org/10.1145/3098279.3122143.

11. Luis A. Leiva and Alejandro Català. 2014. BoD Taps: An Improved Back-of-device Authentication Technique on Smartphones. In Proceedings of the 16th International Conference on Human-computer Interaction with Mobile Devices & Services (Mobile HCI '14). ACM, New York, NY, USA, 63–66. DOI: http://dx.doi.org/10.1145/2628363.2628372.

12. Markus Löchtefeld, Christoph Hirtz, and Sven Gehring. 2013. Evaluation of Hybrid Front–and Back-of-device Interaction on Mobile Devices. In Proceedings of the 12th International Conference on Mobile and Ubiquitous Multimedia (MUM '13).ACM, New York, NY, USA, Article 17, 4 pages. DOI: http://dx.doi.org/10.1145/2541 831.2541865.

13. Andrew Martonik. 2015.How to use the Heart Rate Monitor on the Galaxy S5 (Androidcentral.com). (2015). Galaxy-s5 Last access: 2017-09-09.

14. William McGrath and Yang Li. 2014. Detecting Tapping Motion on the Side of Mobile Devices by Probabilistically Combining Hand Postures. In Proceedings of the 27th Annual ACM Symposium on User Interface Software and Technology (UIST '14). ACM, New York, NY, USA, 215–219. DOI: http://dx.doi.org/10.1145/2642918.2647363.

15. Mohammad Faizuddin, Mohammad Noor, Andrew Ramsay, Stephen Hughes, Simon Rogers, John Williamson, and Roderick Murray-Smith. 2014. 28 Frames Later: Predicting Screen Touches from Back-of-device Grip Changes. In Proceedings of the 32nd Annual ACM Conference on Human Factors in Computing Systems (CHI '14). ACM, New York, NY, USA, 2005–2008. DOI: http://dx.doi.org/10.1145/2556288.2557148.

16. Mohammad Faizuddin, Mohammad Noor, Simon Rogers, and John Williamson. 2016. Detecting Swipe Errors on Touchscreens Using Grip Modulation. In Proceedings of the 2016 CHI Conference on Human Factors in Computing Systems (CHI '16). ACM, New York, NY, USA, 1909–1920. DOI: http://dx.doi.org/10.1145/2858036.2858474.

17. Anna Ostberg, Mohamed Sheik-Nainar, and Nada Matic. 2016. Using a Mobile Device Fingerprint Sensor as a Gestural Input Device. In Proceedings of the 2016 CHI Conference Extended Abstracts on Human Factors in Computing Systems (CHI EA '16). ACM, New York, NY, USA, 2625–2631. DOI: http://dx.doi.org/10.1145/2851581.2892419.

18. Shaikh Shawon are fin Shimon, Sarah Morrison-Smith, Noah John, Ghazal Fahimi, and Jaime Ruiz. 2015. Exploring User-Defined Back-Of-Device Gestures for Mobile Devices. In Proceedings of the 17th International Conference on Human-Computer Interaction with Mobile Devices and Services (Mobile HCI '15). ACM, New York, NY, USA, 227–232. DOI:http://dx.doi.org/10.1145/2785830.2785890.

19. Xiang Xiao, Teng Han, and Jingtao Wang. 2013. Lens Gesture: Augmenting Mobile Interactions with Back-of-device Finger Gestures. In Proceedings of the 15th ACM on International Conference on Multimodal Interaction (ICMI '13). ACM, New York, NY, USA,287–294. DOI: http://dx.doi.org/10.1145/2522848.2522850.

20. Jinghong Xiong and Satoshi Muraki. 2014. An ergonomics study of thumb movements on smartphone touch screen. Ergonomics 576 (2014), 943–955. DOI: http://dx.doi. org/10.1080/00140139.2014.904007.

21. Shen Ye.2015. The science behind Force Touch and the Taptic Engine (iMore. com). (2015). http://www.imore.com/science-behind-taptics-and-force-touch Last access:2017-09-09.

22. Hyunjin Yoo, Jungwon Yoon, and Hyunsoo Ji. 2015. Index Finger Zone: Study on Touchable Area Expandability Using Thumb and Index Finger. In Proceedings of the 17th International Conference on Human-Computer Interaction with Mobile Devices and Services Adjunct (Mobile HCI '15). ACM, New York, NY, USA, 803– 810. DOI: http://dx.doi.org/10.1145/2786567.2793704.

23. Ahmed, S.; Kallu, K.D.; Ahmed, S.; Cho, S.H. Hand Gestures Recognition Using Radar Sensors for Human-Computer-Interaction: A Review. Remote Sens. 2021, 13, 527. https://doi.org/10.3390/rs13030527.

24. K. Hakka, T. Isomoto, and B. Shizuki. One-Handed Interaction Technique for Single-Touch Gesture Input on Large Smartphones. In Symposium on Spatial User Interaction, SUI '19, pp. 21:1–21:2. Association for Computing Machinery, New York, NY, USA, 2019. doi: 10. 1145/3357251.3358750.

25. I. Hwang, E. Rozner, and C. Yoo. Telekinetic thumb summons out-of-reach touch interface beneath your thumbtip (demo). In Proceedings of the 17th Annual International Conference on Mobile Systems, Applications, and Services, MobiSys'19, p. 661–662. Association for Computing Machinery, New York, NY, USA, 2019. doi: 10.1145/ 3307334.3328571.

26. K. Ikematsu, K. Tsubouchi, and S. Yamanaka. Predictaps: Latency reduction technique for single-taps based on recognition for single-tap or double-tap. In Extended Abstracts of the 2020 CHI Conference on Human Factors in Computing Systems, CHI EA '20, p. 1–9. Association for Computing Machinery, New York, NY, USA, 2020. doi: 10. 1145/3334480.3382933.

27. S. Voelker, S. Hueber, C. Corsten, and C. Remy. HeadReach: Using head tracking to increase reachability on mobile touch devices. In Proceedings of the 2020 CHI Conference on Human Factors in Computing Systems, CHI '20, pp. 1–12. Association for Computing Machinery, New York, NY, USA, 2020. doi: 10.1145/ 3313831.3376868.

12 Trust Management in Smart Cities Using Blockchain Technology

Adnan Kalid[1], Nazish Ashfaq[1],
Waqar Ashiq[1], Muhammad Azeem Qureshi[1]
and Muhammad Arif[2]
[1]University of Lahore, Pakistan,[2]Superior University Lahore,
Pakistan

12.1 INTRODUCTION

The internet of things (IoT) is a network of interconnected computing devices, digital and mechanical machines, physical and virtual objects, home appliances, actuators and other devices that allow them to connect, communicate and transmit data through the internet[1]. It allows IP-enabled objects to be monitored and controlled through the network, as well as integrating these devices with current internet infrastructure[2, 68]. IoT is currently the most prevalent topic of conversation[3]. All major players in information technology (IT) are thinking about it due to its great potential. Every day, new IoT implementations are introduced to allow products and applications. Smart cities, smart homes, smart grids, smart farming, smart retail, smart supply chains, wearables, connected cars, connected health, industrial internet, etc., are some of the most well-known IoT applications[4]. The Internet of Things (IoT) based apps revolutionize people's daily lives.

Despite a significant increase in the adoption of IoT-enabled products and applications, IoT still faces numerous security concerns that can be addressed[5]. People continue to assume that security concerns are the primary impediment to the advancement of IoT-based solutions. The biggest problem with IoT is that there are no plans for a generalized security system that could stop all kinds of security attacks. This is because each device in the system has its own security risks, constraints and weaknesses.

A smart city is a place where various types of electronic sensors collect data from gadgets, assets and residents[6,7]. Power plants, trash management, libraries, schools, information systems, transit systems and other community services are monitored and managed by analyzing and processing the acquired data[8–10]. Smart cities are depicted in Figure 12.1. Many security breaches and privacy hazards are feasible at different levels of the smart city infrastructure because the model incorporates the usage of public data. As a result, ensuring data security and privacy is a critical component of such an architecture.

DOI: 10.1201/9781003190301-12

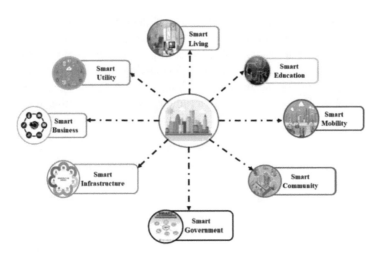

FIGURE 12.1 Smart city's main features.

Blockchain, Bitcoin's underlying technology, was first proposed in 2008–9[11–14]. Because of its adaptability and trustless method of authorization, it is currently being considered as a security alternative by all IT tycoons. Blockchain uses a technology called a distributed ledger (DLT). It provides a validation procedure based on consensus. Furthermore, it offers peer-to-peer networking, which eliminates the need for any centralized security or privacy mechanism [15]. All transactions are recorded in a ledger that is accessible to all nodes, and transactions are carried out in a decentralized way. Applications that use blockchain technology are gaining traction in many areas, such as the Internet of Things, reputation systems, financial services, etc.

As a result, the Blockchain is the most viable solution for IoT security issues. To illustrate this concept, consider CCTV cameras operating in a smart city. Several public places are monitored for security by the government with these cameras. In this case, the government organization is the resource owner, and CCTV cameras are one of the smart city's resources. The people who use this resource are people who work in the security department. The government organization puts a smart contract on the Blockchain so that clients can prove they are who they say they are. The smart contract may need some kind of proof to show that the client is real. This proof is needed to find out if a client is part of a security department or not. This proof is subsequently included in the transaction's data field and transmitted to the smart contract. When the smart contract is executed, a token is issued to the client. The token refers to the client's account address. A token is associated with a certain resource and has a lifetime field. A single resource owner can offer several smart contracts, all of which can be deployed on the same Blockchain resource server. Each contract has its own parameters, and there may be numerous smart contracts for the various smart city resources, each with its own parameters and attributes. In this scenario, the smart contract contains the parameters necessary to identify and verify the validity of the security institution's people. If they have a legitimate request, the smart contract will allocate them tokens; otherwise, the request will be denied.

Recently, blockchain has been applied to IoT devices and related topologies to provide security and privacy[16–22]. IoTChain is an end-to-end (E2E) solution for secure, accredited access to IoT resources that are built on Blockchain[23,24]. It's a hybrid framework of the Internet Engineering Task Force (IETF) Object Security Architecture for the Internet of Things (OSCAR) and the Authentication and Authorization for Constrained Environments (ACE). Preventing illegal access to the smart city's resources is a major challenge. To do this, a robust, tamper-proof authentication system is necessary. Additionally, a user interface is required to operate and track the smart city's resources. The underlying methodology should be all-encompassing. The reader and the end-users must be made aware of all implementation specifics.

Due to resource limits, traditional security and privacy designs are inappropriate for the IoT spectrum[25]. In addition, the majority of IoT devices are not intended to meet fundamental security and privacy requirements, resulting in security, transparency, privacy, verification, data integrity and access control problems. Blockchain is gaining traction in the realm of IoT by improving security and enabling the integration of more devices into the network[26–28].

In this chapter, a Blockchain-based mechanism for secure authorization of smart city resources is shown as a way to make this happen. The ACE framework-based authorization Blockchain and the OSCAR object security model make up the system. The Blockchain provides a secure and scalable method of authorizing transactions. OSCAR, on the other hand, uses a public ledger to create multicast groups for approved clients. Furthermore, a meteor-based application is being built to provide a user-friendly interface for heterogeneous smart city technologies to communicate with and operate the smart city's resources. To assess the efficiency and practicality of the discussed method, the authorization Blockchain is built on top of the Ethereum network. A smart city is emulated using a Raspberry Pi B+ and a security mechanism is implemented in node.js server. Furthermore, the mocha and chai frameworks are utilized to access the performance of different parts of the mechanism. The primary contributions of this study are as follows:

- Designed an efficient authentication and trust management system based on Blockchain for smart cities;
- A real-world application of a security system based on Blockchain for safe authorization of smart city resources;
- Developed a hybrid application that is easy to use for interacting with and managing diverse IoT resources.

It would aid in achieving the following security objectives:

- To mutually authenticate clients and servers and build trust between them so that only authorized users may access the system and clients can validate servers;
- To protect the method for key exchange between clients and servers;
- To restrict access to a resource to only those users who have been granted access to that resource;

- To offer the management or administrator of the system monitoring and control of the smart city's resources.

The remaining part of this chapter is laid out as follows: Section 12.2 contains a history of blockchain. Section 12.3 provides an overview of Blockchain technology. Different techniques are described in Section 12.4. Section 12.5 contains the experimental analysis and commentary. Finally, Section 12.6 draws a conclusion.

12.2 HISTORY OF BLOCKCHAIN AND IOT

Many researchers came up with different architectures for how Blockchain could be used in different areas. Samaniego and Deters[29] demonstrated software-defined IoT devices in conjunction with permissioned Blockchain for connecting edge hosts to IoT services. An intriguing research challenge is how to incorporate software defined IoT devices as smart contracts. Permissioned Blockchain was proposed by Kravitz and Cooper[30] as a speculative technique for creating an ecosystem. Devices and users alike have integrated identity management as part of their operating systems. Although it's a fascinating structure, it's yet to be tested in the field.

Dorri et al.[31] presented a lightweight Blockchain implementation for IoT devices with limited resources and energy. Proof-of-work protocol, which is used in most IoT, uses a lot of energy, so finding a way to replace it is a big research problem. The Ethereum Casper protocol, which was recently released, should allow for the development of more efficient IoT-Blockchain systems. IOTA[32] is a decentralized cryptocurrency of the third generation and its implementation is not available yet. IoTeX[33] is an IoT decentralized network. It boasts rapid consensus and built-in privacy-preserving methods that enable the secure exchange of information and value between real and virtual objects on a global scale. Consequently, it is the impending future technology based on the IoT-Blockchain platform that offers enhanced privacy, security and scalability for the development of new IoT-based applications.

The Watson IoT platform[34] has a built-in mechanism that allows you to contribute selected IoT data to a private Blockchain. It utilizes the IBM cloud, making it ideal for usage in a corporate setting in terms of scalability and quick adaption to changing business requirements. Ambrosus[35] is an IoT network built on the Blockchain. It was developed for use in the food and pharmaceutical industries. It lets Blockchain talk to IoT sensors. It guarantees that product data is correct and improves the quality and tracking of items all along the supply chain. Waltonchain[36] ushers in a new era of value in the internet of things (VIOT). It changes the label, the business, the organization and the network. RFID technology and mobile phones both benefit from it. It employs asymmetric encryption methods and a hybrid of Blockchain and IoT[19].

The origin trail protocol[37] is a Blockchain-based data exchange mechanism for networked devices. It is a decentralized system that runs on a network of public nodes and enables data exchange in the supply chain using Blockchain. Atonomi[38] gives IoT devices a security protocol and makes sure that data for eCommerce apps is safe and reliable. It adds massive IoT devices to the unchangeable ledger of Blockchain[16]. This design applies only to E-commerce devices and is not applicable to smart cities.

OSCAR and ACE systems are used by IoTChain[23]. It is used to provide an end-to-end authorization solution for Internet of Things resources. It renders the resource access procedure secure, scalable, robust and adaptable.

Yup et al.[39] introduced a Blockchain-based intelligent healthcare approach. To protect the user's privacy, they created a data gateway and data access control. Liang et al.[40] employed Blockchain technology to construct a mobile application for sharing healthcare records. With the aid of a channel construction approach, they proposed a user-centric strategy for providing secure access control and privacy. A Blockchain-based medical information exchange system was presented by Jiang et al.[41]. To secure the system storage, they created an on-chain and off-chain verification mechanism. Fan et al.[42] suggested using Blockchain to store medical information about patients and a better consensus protocol to make the system safer and more private overall. Tanwar et al.[43] focused on healthcare 4.0 applications and presented a Blockchain-based electronic health record system. They presented a patient-centric system for symmetric key cryptographic access control across a variety of healthcare providers. They also developed a permission-based electronic health recode sharing system using the concept of chaincode.

Habibzadeh et al.[44] conducted a survey on security and policy concerns related to smart city systems. The authors demonstrated that smart city applications are vulnerable, and that technology and government policies must collaborate to address these vulnerabilities. They envisioned smart cities as a multi-level system with varying levels of protection. This work encapsulates technical and policy concerns, as well as future directions for a secure smart city. Khan et al.[45] presented a Blockchain-based method for verifying data from smart city CCTV cameras. The method aids in the detection of forged video recordings, allowing investigators to locate tampered movies. Blockchain is utilized to circumvent such systems' single point of failure and to assure that video recordings are real and not tampered with. The proposed system is implemented and evaluated using Hyperledger fabric. The results reveal that data is dispersed among several nodes, and the system becomes temper-proof once a transaction is completed. The users are just given view rights.

Malik et al.[46] proposed a methodology for assessing user physical activity patterns in a small city setting. These patterns may aid in passively authenticating a person. Using three separate datasets, many machine learning methods are used to validate user identities. The authors stated that the new system outperformed the existing systems. Meshram et al.[47] proposed an authentication scheme for use in smart cities. The suggested approach uses an extended modulation scheme and is based on smart card and user password-based authentication. Insider attacks detection, erroneous password detection, stolen smart card detection, lost smart card cancellation, mutual authentication and security against client impersonation attacks are some of the important aspects of the proposed protocol. The proposed methodology is robust since it allows for multiple assumptions to be presented and assessed. Esposito et al.[48] employed Blockchain to solve challenges with authentication and permission in smart city applications. The authors addressed the need for decentralized security-related information management. They achieved this by combining FIWARE with Blockchain-based identity management and access control.

When the proposed system is compared against a database-based system, it is clear that the latter is preferable.

Ibba et al.[49] used article co-citation analysis and a keyword co-occurrence network to conduct a bibliometric review. They examined the problems and trends around Blockchain deployment in smart cities. Suciu et al.[50] compared Tangle and Blockchain technologies by presenting their key features. A Blockchain-based system for sensor data storage and administration was presented by Rejeb et al.[51]. Due to its adaptable, flexible and iterative character, they used SCRUM approach to create Blockchain-based software.

In brief, a viable framework that can be deployed to ensure security for smart cities is required. The end-users must be able to see through the implementation's heterogeneity and intricacy. It should be flexible, robust and versatile in addition to providing security.

12.3   OVERVIEW OF BLOCKCHAIN TECHNOLOGY

After the emergence of cryptocurrencies like Ethereum and Bitcoin, Blockchain and smart ledger technologies have emerged as the primary research topics. Data is distributed, immutable and trusted on Blockchain, but it is not editable. Transactions can be examined without the use of intermediaries or centralized reliance [52,53]. The Blockchain's transparency makes retrieving ledger-based transactions over networks a low-complexity method. Hash cryptography, mining, an immutable ledger, a consensus system and distributed peer-to-peer networking are all examples of blockchain services and approaches. These approaches and services are described in more detail.

- For the adding or upgrading transactions to the ledger, a Blockchain uses hash-based encryption methods. The cascading effect, deterministic, one-way cryptography, the need to withstand collisions and speedier processing are all hallmarks of hashing algorithms. The SHA-256 hashing algorithm is used in blockchain.
- The process of securing and confirming transactions is known as mining. To achieve and obtain the prize, it necessitates a high computation speed. It also necessitates the addition of transaction data to the ledger by miners. Blocks are combined in ledgers to form a chain that is safeguarded by Blockchain miners.
- All transactions in a Blockchain network are recorded in an immutable ledger. An immutable ledger means that transactions can't be changed or tampered with after they've been recorded.
- Consensus protocol: This is a technique that allows all Blockchain nodes to agree on the current state of the distributed ledger. It aids in the achievement of reliability and the establishment of trust between unknown nodes in the Blockchain network.
- Distributed P2P Networking: All transactions on the Blockchain network are broadcast over the network to distribute and update the data at the nodes.

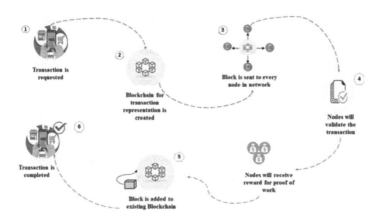

FIGURE 12.2 Blockchain transaction process.

Blockchain technology stores unaltered records on a decentralized network. The addition or modification of transactions is accomplished by generating new hash values. Blockchain technology has various advantages over other existing technologies, including decentralization, security, immutability and transparency. Figure 12.2 depicts the Blockchain transaction procedure.

12.3.1 ETHEREUM BLOCKCHAIN ARCHITECTURE

Blocks, transactions and consensus make up the Ethereum ledger. The Ethereum virtual machine (EVM), transactions, accounts, minor, smart contracts, ethers, consensus and gas make up the architecture. The Ethereum-oriented blockchain architecture is depicted in Figure 12.3.

A Blockchain network is made up of several nodes. Some nodes are miners, whereas the remainder of the nodes do not mine, but rather aid in the execution of smart contracts. EVMs are what they're called. These nodes are linked together to

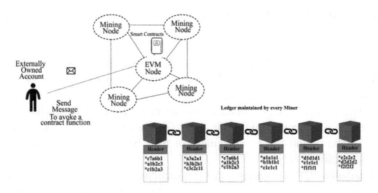

FIGURE 12.3 Ethereum Blockchain architecture.

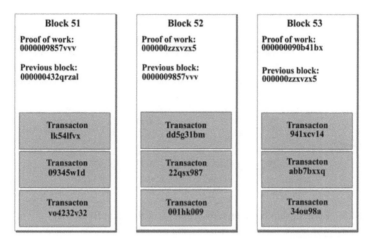

FIGURE 12.4   Parent–child relationship among blocks in Blockchain.

form the network, and they communicate via the peer-to-peer protocol. A ledger instance is present on every miner node. All of the chain's blocks are kept in the ledger. To guarantee uniformity, miners' synchronization is done on a regular basis.

There is a parent–child relationship between blocks in the Ethereum Blockchain. This is a one-on-one relationship. A chain is formed in this manner. The parent–child relationship is depicted in Figure 12.4.

The transactions are recorded in blocks. The top gas limit determines how many transactions a block can contain. Each transaction necessitates the use of a specific amount of gas. As a result, when a block's gas quota is met, a new transaction is added to the next block. Blocks are used to store hashed transactions. A new hash is created by combining the hashes of two transactions. This method continues to operate until all transactions in the block have been combined into a single hash. The Transaction Merkle root hash is the resultant single hash for the block, which is preserved in the block's header. As a result, the chain is immutable. The link between transactions and blocks is depicted in Figure 12.5.

At some point, each miner gets all the transactions from the pool. The miner adds these transactions to a new block if they are not already there. The block header also gets a timestamp and a nonce. The block header and its contents are shown in Figure 12.6.

12.4   BLOCKCHAIN-BASED AUTHENTICATION AND TRUST MANAGEMENT PROCEDURE FOR SMART CITY

Figure 12.7 shows the blockchain-based model for ensuring the security and authorization of entry to smart city assets. It shows the key modules of the model and provides steps leading to approved access to smart city services. To eliminate the confusion surrounding taxonomy and how different entities work, the Internet Engineering Task Force (IETF) has established the following nomenclature:

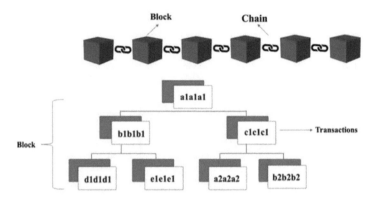

FIGURE 12.5 Relationship between transactions and blocks in Blockchain.

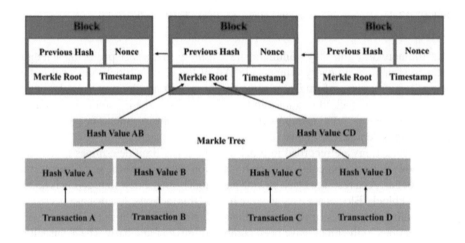

FIGURE 12.6 Block header and its contents.

- Authorization Servers: These are employed to produce entry tokens.
- Resource Servers: These produce/save protected materials.
- Proxy Servers: These save protected materials and act as an entry graphical user interface for customers.
- Resource Publishers/Owners: These are the primary proprietors of asset servers and the materials they contain.
- Key Servers: These are used to create keys for encrypting and decrypting the materials.
- Client/User application: Accessibility to the protective systems resources is requested by a third party.

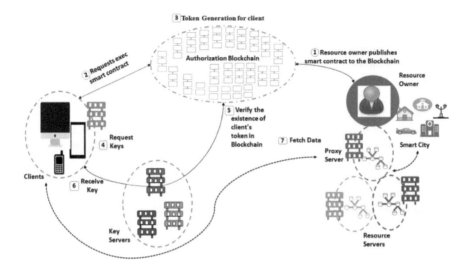

FIGURE 12.7 Block diagram of model.

12.4.1 AUTHORIZATION BLOCKCHAIN

In general, blockchain may be conceptualized as a persistent log in which information is maintained in time-stamped blocks. Blocks are used to keep transactions organized. Every block is identified by its cryptographic hash value, which incorporates the preceding block's hash. The blockchain is managed by a node with (at least) one copy of the last n blocks.

Key servers, authorization servers, and clients are the nodes of the authorization Blockchain. These nodes are not required to hold the whole Blockchain to participate in the consensus mechanism. Some complete nodes exist (e.g., authorization servers and key servers). These maintain the total facts of the Blockchain. Authorization servers are the only servers that act like miners. The key servers are put up by resource owners and are responsible for the resource servers' key-related material. Every other node is recognized by a distinctive Blockchain location, which is made up of two asymmetric keys. The resource owner creates a smart contract to specify access permissions, and it then generates access tokens automatically. Transactions are carried out to engage with smart contracts or between customers and resource owners. The private keys of the various nodes sign these transactions. Then transactions are broadcast to the Blockchain network. The transactions are verified and saved in blocks by the authorization servers (miners). Some consensus procedure seals these blocks, after which they are added to the Blockchain. To verify them, both key servers and resource servers need authentic certificates. A customer demands a key server to transfer a decryption key for their required information. The key server validates the client's permissions by examining the Blockchain smart contract store. If the client is validated, it receives the necessary key that allows it to transfer and decrypt the specified resource.

In this study for smart city resources, the Ethereum[54] Blockchain network is employed as an authorization Blockchain. Customer's and contractors' credentials (data and particulars) are saved in time-stamped blocks on the Ethereum Blockchain. It is a permissionless Blockchain that is open to the public for decentralized applications. The following is the justification for utilizing Ethereum Blockchain:

- One of the most notable characteristics of Ethereum is that it is programmable. All contracts and agreements are included in the code, which allows transactions to be processed automatically. Users may exchange anything of value, including money, property, etc., using its smart contracts. These smart contracts can also trigger multiple contracts and may include a significant list of conditions and compatible formats.
- Ethereum is not limited to cryptocurrency transactions, but to every transaction connected to supply chains, energy grids, real estate, government documents, etc.
- Ethereum has been shown to be resistant to security assaults.
- It's open and adaptable, and it allows both permissionless and permissioned solutions.
- An Ethereum network may accommodate thousands of nodes and millions of viewers, far outnumbering its competitors.
- Ethereum consortia are not limited to a single provider; instead, they are interoperable.

Because of Ethereum's massive ledger size, e.g., 80 GB, each transaction for every activity that is written or validated from the ledger takes too long and consumes too many resources, such as a lot of gas. Due to the vast size of the ledger, it is not possible to construct real-time jobs on a public Blockchain until the system has matured and passed all testing standards.

The Ganache local Ethereum Blockchain is utilized in this chapter to deploy smart contracts and migrations without the need for a large ledger or high gas usage. Users are given ten accounts by Ganache. The users in this case would be either resource owners or customers. The confirmation-of-concept test net is presented in Figure 12.8. One account is assigned to each of the resource servers, proxy servers, key servers and resource owners.

The resource owner associates with a full node to deploy the smart contract on the Blockchain. Figure 12.9 depicts the smart contracts. Clients can begin engaging with smart contracts by calling the contract's public methods. The method addToken() generates an access token for a client. This token is retained in the contract's permanent memory. It comprises the addresses of both the client and the resource server. When a client requests a decryption key from a key server, the key server checks the TTL value of the access token. The deleteToken() method can be utilized to withdraw the client's prior access permissions. Any entity in the Blockchain network can activate the smart contract. More complicated contracts may require various modifiers to regulate access to specific functions or to verify whether a specific condition is reached before method execution by the EVM. For instance, did this customer pay for the entry token?

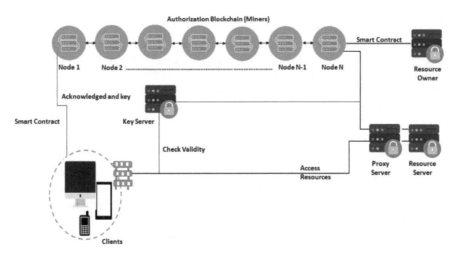

FIGURE 12.8   Blockchain network.

Contract
Struc Client();   *Struc Resource();*   *Struc token();*   *struct Client;*   *struct Resource;*   *struct Token;*   *add Client(name,city) bool;*   *add Resource(name,memory,bool,city)bool;*   *add_Token(id,res_name,c_id,r_Company) bool;*   *get_Token(c_id)constans;*   *delet_Token(id)bool*

FIGURE 12.9   Smart contract deployed on the Blockchain.

12.4.2   Resource Servers

Resource servers store and create the protected resources of smart cities. The resources in smart cities are traffic lights, security surveillance cameras, power plants, water supply network components, etc. In this chapter, the resource server is built using Raspberry Pi B+[56].

12.4.3   Resource Owners/Publishers

The resource owners are the legal owners of the resource servers and the resources they created. A resource owner in the context of smart cities is a government entity or governing authority.

12.4.4   Key Servers

Key servers create the keys required to encrypt and decode the resources. When the user satisfies the contract conditions, a key for a particular period to utilize the resources is produced. In this chapter, the key server is formed on a Core i7 system with 4GB RAM, a Sony Vaio CPU 2.6 GHz and the Ubuntu 16.04.1 operating system. In the Blockchain, the key server has full node status.

12.4.5   Simulation/Creation of Smart City

The smart city employs many types of electronic sensors to collect data, which are then used to operate and maintain resources effectively. In this chapter, the Raspberry Pi B+ is applied to simulate a smart city. Two key smart city functions are simulated: traffic lights and security surveillance cameras. In Figure 12.10, general-purpose input pins (included in the yellow rectangle) are controlled by smart contract tokens, while output pins are linked to real smart city devices. The node.js technology and the git repository are installed on the Raspberry Pi B+ to operate the smart city's physical equipment.

12.4.6   Integration of Smart City with Authorization Blockchain

The truffle framework[55] is used to connect the smart city to the authorization Blockchain. It simplifies smart contract implementation, binary resource management, contract migrations and deployment.

12.4.6.1   Integration of Smart City with Authorization Blockchain

The Ethereum Blockchain includes smart agreements. Ethereum applies these whenever a user is confirmed to have enough transaction cost. The stacking holder is given resources when they have been validated. These are the apps that are executed by Ethereum's virtual machines. The Ethereum virtual machine (EVM) converts the data to byte-code or a string of 0s and 1s that the network can understand. Solidity[57] is an object-oriented high-level programming language that is adopted to create Ethereum contracts. Figure 12.11 elaborates the contract sample.

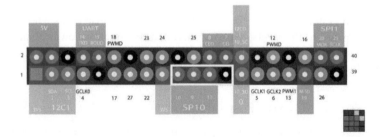

FIGURE 12.10   Raspberry P$_i$ utilized GPIO pins.

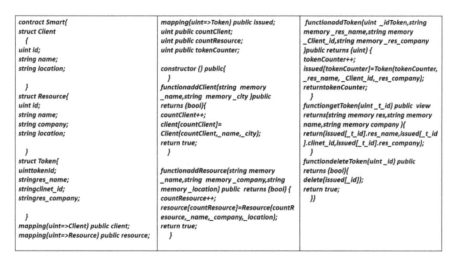

FIGURE 12.11 Smart contracts sample.

12.4.6.2 Migrations

The migration procedure starts after contract writing and module development. All modules, such as Raspberry Pi connection with node.js[58] and smart contract integration at the js level, are completed throughout the migration process. The migration procedure runs first whenever the program is activated.

12.4.6.3 Access Control for Blockchain at Application/Browser Level (metamask)

Remote Procedural Calls (RPC) are utilized to access the Ganache Blockchain. RPC is time-consuming, hence metamask[59] is utilized to speed up the development procedure by providing Ethereum Blockchain access at the browser level. The primary benefit of metamask is that developers do not need to make any RPC calls over the internet to accomplish any test operation. To deploy recommended solutions in smart cities/homes, a clear move from Ganache metamask testing Blockchain to the geth Ethereum ledger is necessary.

12.4.6.4 Data Fetching from Smart Contract

Data retrieving is conducted at the application level to deliver contract data (name, location, resource name, resource pricing, resource supplier, etc.) for publication of resources, the addition of resources and users. In this chapter, Web3.js[60] is employed for data retrieving and addition. Web3.js is a set of libraries that allow users to communicate with Ethereum both locally and remotely over HTTP RPC.

12.4.7 User Application

An application is needed to communicate with and manage IoTchain-based secured smart city assets. The goal of this chapter is to develop a hybrid application that can

FIGURE 12.12   User application.

be used on devices including mobiles (Android, iOS, Windows, and Blackberry) and PCs. The Meteor.js[61] framework was used to develop this application. The user must complete the following steps in order to use the application:

- Make an Ethereum Blockchain wallet and obtain the public and private keys required for wallet authentication.
- Connect your wallet to metamask by entering public and private keys. The metamask includes a 14-word memic that can be used to recover the wallet if the keys are lost.
- As illustrated in Figure 12.12, launching the application prompts the user to provide the required information. The information supplied at the time of starting is utilized to deliver contracts and resources.

12.4.8   Overall Workflow

The system's processing flow is discussed here, and is depicted in Figure 12.7.

- The resource owner/provider (government institutions) prepares a smart contract that is then published on the Blockchain.
- The client wishing to obtain the protected resources submits a transaction to the specific smart contract address. The transaction is broadcast to all nodes in the Blockchain network. The verification process will begin, and miners will participate.
- If the client satisfies specific contract conditions, an access token will be created. The access token specifies the particular access privileges for the protected resources (start time, expiration time, location, resource name).

- When the transaction is confirmed, smart contracts will be implemented following the consensus.
- The contract transaction will be put to the contract, and a token will be produced that will serve as the primary key for subsequent processing.
- The client then requests the appropriate decryption keys from the key server in order to decode the resources.
- The token is replicated on the key server. The key server searches the internal storage of the relevant smart contract for the access token.
- To authenticate the client's validity, the key server generates a challenge response based on the client address contained in the token. Only the authentic client who initiated the smart contract may solve this challenge.
- After finishing the challenge, the client obtains a personal key and participates in the self-healing group key distribution procedure.
- Finally, the encrypted resources can be accessed via a client proxy or a resource server. Both of these servers have a RESTful CoAP API that allows you to GET, POST and PUT resources using the Uniform Resource Identifier (URI).

It can be observed that there is no need for authentication at this stage, because only an authenticated client may acquire decryption cryptographic keys. A symmetric key would be used to secure the protected resources if they were obtained directly from the resource servers. When the proxy server is leveraged to get the resources, however, an asymmetric signature is employed to protect the sanctity of the resources. The key servers provide the appropriate keys in both circumstances.

12.5   EXPERIMENTAL ANALYSIS AND DISCUSSION

This section describes the performance assessment of the fundamental aspects of the discussed architecture, analyzes security issues and technological challenges, and emphasizes the limitations.

12.5.1   EVALUATION OF KEY SERVER AND RESOURCE SERVER

Different types of tools such as the mocha framework and chai assertion library are used to measure the working of distinct elements of the Blockchain-based security measure. For testing each component and measuring its performance Mocha is used, mocha is a JS-based framework. Mocha uses an assertion library named chai to GET, POST and PUT data over the servers. The GET method is used to request data from a specific source. The PUT method is used to submit data to a server to create/update a resource. The GET method is used to request data from a specific site. The PUT method is used to submit data to a server in terms of creating or updating a resource.

Ubuntu 16.4 LTS is used to run the key server. Figure 12.13 depicts the average time taken to complete a handshake process. With an increase in the number of clients, the average hand shaking time appears to rise. The average handshake time for 60 clients is 200 ms, which doubles for 120 customers. The client system has an Intel Core i7-4600M CPU running at 2.60 GHz (4 virtual cores) and 4 GB of RAM.

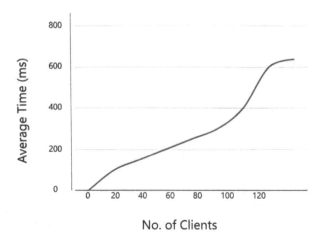

FIGURE 12.13   Average time to achieve the DTLS handshake.

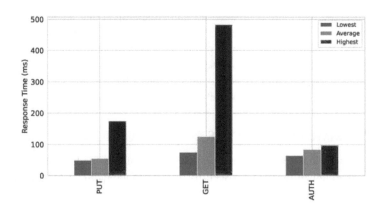

FIGURE 12.14   Performance of the resource server.

In this research, Raspberry Pi B+ is used to develop resource sever and it is developed in C language. Figure 12.14 depicts the response time in milliseconds (ms) for a client's PUT and GET requests to a resource server. Moreover, it also represents the time required to implement the DTLS handshake between a resource server and the key server, as demonstrated by the AUTH. For each request, it shows the fastest, slowest and average response times. It's worth noting that the lowest, average and maximum reaction times are all within a few seconds of each other. It can be seen that the minimum, average and maximum response times for the PUT approach are 50, 55 and 175 ms, respectively. Similarly, the minimum, average and maximum response times for the GET method are 75, 125 and 483 ms. For AUTH, the minimum, average and maximum response times are 65, 84 and 99 ms.

Several experiments were conducted to further assess the usefulness of the system by adjusting various parameters, such as transaction rate, block size and so on. To

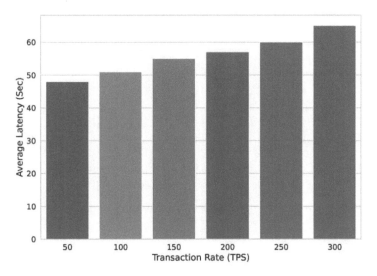

FIGURE 12.15 Average latency with varying transaction rate.

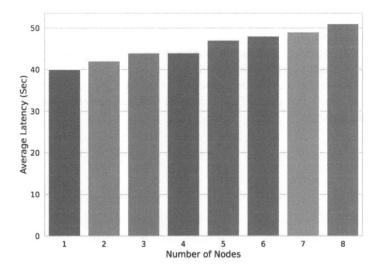

FIGURE 12.16 Transaction average latencies with varying number of nodes.

begin with, the transaction rate is varied. T_R represents the transaction rate. The value of T_R varies from 50 to 300 transactions per second, and the average latency LT_{AVG} is calculated for each T_R value. This experiment's transaction commits time is presented in Figure 12.15. It is clear that when the transaction rate rises, LT_{AVG} also rises.

The second experiment maintains the T_R constant, i.e., 150, but the number of nodes completing these transactions increases from one to eight. Figure 12.16 represents the transaction average. The results show that when the number of nodes participating in transactions rises, LT_{AVG} also rises. It is the minimum when an individual node

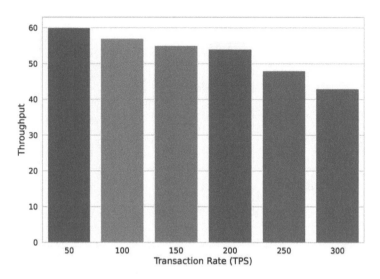

FIGURE 12.17   Transaction throughput with varying transaction rate.

processes 150 transactions per second and the maximum when eight nodes share these 150 transactions.

Figure 12.17 indicates that as the number of nodes participating in transactions increases, the transaction throughput decreases.

When TR is altered, another observation about CPU utilization is made. Figure 12.18 shows that as the T_R is increased, CPU use increases while the block size remains constant.

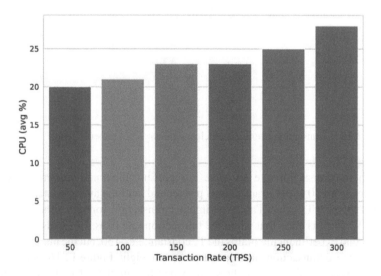

FIGURE 12.18   CPU usage with varying transaction rate.

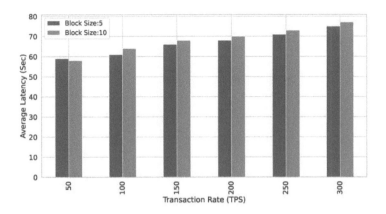

FIGURE 12.19 Average latency with varying transaction rate for different block sizes.

In all the preceding experiments, the transaction and block sizes are kept constant, i.e., two transactions per block. All transactions are carried out in reading mode. By varying the block sizes and determining the LT_{AVG} for varying T_R, a new set of observations is recorded. Figure 12.19 depicts the outcomes of this configuration. To begin, the block size is held constant at five, and LT_{AVG} values are calculated by varying T_R. The block size is then increased to ten and LT_{AVG} values are recorded. The latency of block size ten is slightly lower than that of block size five. In all these studies, the transaction mode is analyzed.

In a nutshell, low T_R on small block sizes has been observed to improve the performance of a Blockchain system. Similarly, higher T_R on larger block sizes improves system performance.

12.5.2 SMART CITY RESOURCE PUBLISHING AND CONTROLLING THROUGH USER APPLICATION

12.5.2.1 Publishing Resources

Through a user application, the resource provider can add or publish smart city resource (CCTV camera, traffic lights, electricity meter, etc.) contracts to the Blockchain. Consider the following scenario: a smart city management organization has installed smart CCTV cameras and street lighting. In order to authorize the clients, the authority publishes a smart contract on the Blockchain. The smart contracts may require some form of proof, such as proof that the client lives at a specific address. This proof is included in the data field of the transaction, which is then sent to the smart contract. On execution, the contract generates a token for the client. The token refers to the client's address (i.e., a public key). The access token also includes a lifetime field that specifies which resources are available. A resource owner can deploy multiple smart contracts on the Blockchain for the same resource server. Every contract is unique in that it takes dissimilar input parameters and generates tokens with varying privileges. Figure 12.20 depicts the page used to publish the resource. There are three fields: resource name, resource cost and company.

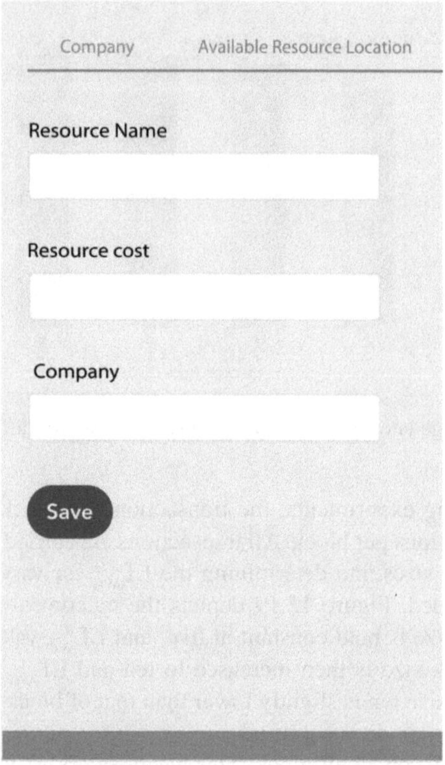

FIGURE 12.20 Resource publishing.

12.5.2.2 Accessing and Controlling Resources

The client will be able to see and manage the resources in their area that have been authenticated. Figure 12.21 depicts the client dashboard, which includes available resources and their status.

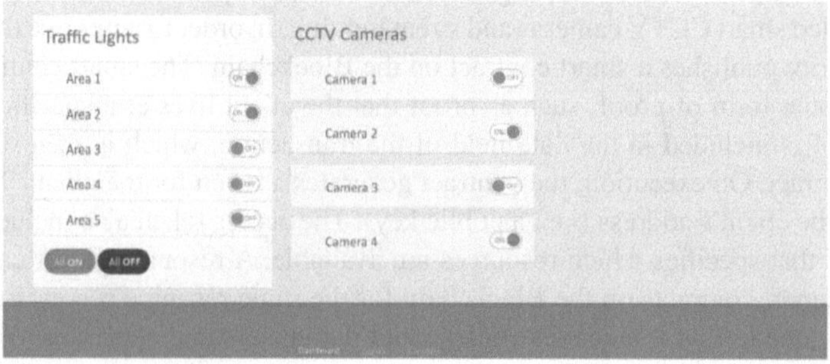

FIGURE 12.21 Client dashboard.

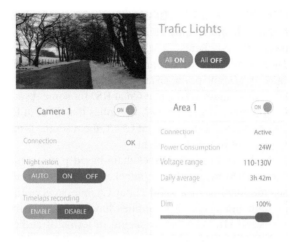

FIGURE 12.22 Resource description.

Users can visualize and access information about the resource after making their choice. Figure 12.22 depicts the features of the traffic signals in Area 1 as well as information on camera 1. These resources are within the control of the user.

12.5.3 COMPARATIVE ANALYSIS OF TECHNIQUES

A comparative analysis of discussed and existing techniques on the basis of a targeted domain, design, implementation and the user interface has been performed in this work. It demonstrates that the majority of existing solutions lack all essential features. Yue et al.[39] used Blockchain technology to improve healthcare. Their work includes design, implementation and user application. This chapter presents a Blockchain-based mechanism for securing smart city resource authorization. It consists of the design and implementation of an authorization blockchain based on the ACE framework and the OSCAR object security model. The Blockchain provides a versatile and trustworthy authorization mechanism. OSCAR, on the other hand, creates multicast groups for authorized clients using a public ledger. Furthermore, a meteor-based application is being developed to provide a user-friendly interface for heterogeneous smart city technologies to interact with and control the smart city's resources.

12.5.4 SECURITY ANALYSIS

The discussed framework relies on secure authorized access to IoT resources. Several security aspects are considered and implemented, as discussed below.

12.5.4.1 Formal Security Analysis

To formally analyze the system's security, the authorization and authentication services provided by the system were evaluated.

Authorization: In the context of a Blockchain-based mechanism, authorization means that an attacker should not be able to acquire or use encrypted resources accessible to some authorized clients C^n at resource server RS^n until more than 50% of authorization Blockchain ABC^n nodes are corrupted. Formally, ABC^n is secure in terms of authorization if, at some point, an attacker can access the encrypted resources that are accessible to some authorized client Cn at RS^n for some resource owner RO^n, then the RS^n is corrupt; otherwise, if C^n 6=?, it implies that C^n or at least one of Cn's trusted RS^n must be corrupted. As we know, if $C^n = 1$, the resource is accessed in client credentials mode and is not related to a client.

Authentication: In the context of a Blockchain-based p mechanism, authentication for resource server RS^n means that an attacker should not be able to obtain an access token under the identity of a valid client C^n unless certain parties involved are corrupt. Being authenticated at RS^n implies having a valid access token from the authorization server (ABC^n). ABC^n is secure in terms of authentication under the following conditions: if an attacker can access the service token provided by a legitimate RS^n for a client Cn, then either the client Cn or one of the valid resource servers RS^n must be compromised. Authentication and authorization are handled by authorization Blockchain ABC^n nodes in the Blockchain-based system. The authorization will never fail unless more than 50% of the ABC^n nodes are corrupted. It is the Blockchain's realistic premise that it will carry more honest nodes H^n than malevolent nodes M^n. Unauthorized access would be impossible in our scenario since $H^n > M^n$.

Session Integrity: From the standpoint of authorization, session integrity means that: (1) a client C^n is only authorized to access the resources of the resource server RS^n if the client C^n has a valid access token; and (2) no other client C^n can generate an access request on behalf of the valid client C^n because each access request is signed by the corresponding valid client C^n. ABC^n is secure in terms of session integrity for authorization if the following conditions are met: (1) the challenge/response flow for a particular client C^n is successful in an iteration for ABC^n; and (2) the resource server RS^n is honest and provides resources only to a client C^n who has already successfully completed the challenge/response flow. The permission is granted if the following conditions are met and the blockchain ABC^n is secure in terms of session integrity for authentication: (1) the transaction request sent by a client C^n is successfully verified by the miners, and a valid access token is granted as a result of the smart contract execution; and (2) the resource server RS^n is honest and provides resources only to a client C^n who has already successfully acquired the access token.

12.5.4.2 Informal Security Analysis

The following scenarios have been discussed informally to assess the system's security.

Scenario 1: Personal keys may be compromised while being shared.

Personal keys are exchanged using TLS-based DTLS channels. As a result, there is no possibility of eavesdropping, tampering or message forgery while exchanging keys. It ensures the safe exchange of personal keys between servers and clients. As a result, only the authorized client/server has access to the key.

Scenario 2: A resource may be requested by an unauthorized client or a fake key server may be present.
Certificates are used to establish trust between key and resource servers. A challenge/response mechanism is used to authenticate clients and key servers. The use of signatures ensures the integrity of transactions.

Scenario 3: The attacker may capture and misuse the access token. The system is based on ACE. In ACE, the client identity is bound to the access token via the concept of proof of possession (PoP). The ACE server binds a key to the token whenever a client requests it. This key is accessible to the resource server, and it is known to the client who made the request. The resource server then generates a challenge/response based on this key to determine whether or not the client is the owner of the token. As a result, the attacker only needs to compromise one authorization server to obtain valid tokens. This issue was addressed in the framework by requiring the client to provide a public key that triggers the smart contract. This client's public key is included in the access token and saved on Blockchain. The key server generates a challenge/response using this key to verify the identity of the client requesting decryption keys. To complete the task, an attacker must now compromise at least 51% of the miners.

Scenario 4: A Denial of Service (DoS) attack can be carried out on any network. A Denial of Service (DoS) attack is always possible on any Blockchain infrastructure. The proposed framework includes several measures to reduce the risk associated with such attacks. A malicious user could, for example, repeatedly activate smart contracts. As all requests must be broadcast and verified by miners, this would result in a massive amount of traffic on the Blockchain network. It is reduced in a Blockchain-based network by presenting a cryptographic puzzle to the client before each transaction. The attack would be flattened as a result. Furthermore, the proposed framework sets the smart contract execution time limit on the lower side. This aided in identifying bogus requests that did not provide the required gas value in the Ethereum Blockchain. In this case, the smart contract would be halted, and all changes would be rolled back.

12.5.5 Technical Challenges and Limitations

The technical challenges associated with implementing Blockchain technology in a smart city environment are as follows:

- Both smart cities and Blockchain are still in their infancy, so much research is still needed to integrate them.
- Shifting from a traditional centralized IoT system to a decentralized Blockchain network necessitates technical efforts in the right direction.
- Due to resource constraints, traditional security and privacy architectures are inapplicable in the context of smart cities. The majority of IoT devices are not designed to meet basic security and privacy parameters, resulting in security, confidentiality, privacy, authentication, data integrity and access control issues.

- A permissionless Blockchain is difficult to implement and deploy in some institutions because it lacks trust and is uncontrollable in nature.
- To implement and assess the efficacy of any given solution, there are only a limited number of accounts available (i.e., ten in the case of Ganache).

Despite the fact that Blockchain provides a decentralized security mechanism that aids in the authentication process, it has numerous limitations. Because of its trustless and uncontrollable nature, the public Blockchain is difficult to implement and deploy in government institutions. Because all nodes in the ledger download and repeat the same data in mining at the same time, it is more expensive in terms of time and transactions. Because each node participates in the mining process, it is slower than other centralized approaches. Any transaction that is broadcast increases the size of the ledger at every node.

It has been observed that the use of public Blockchain in the proposed solution makes this framework less deployable due to issues with speed, cost, complexity and the large amount of data. However, it is applicable to any pure private Blockchain, such as multichain[62], hyperledger[63], chain core[64] and so on. When the proposed architecture is built on private Blockchain, cost complexity, all node mining issues and ledger size increment in transactions can all be controlled. Furthermore, with a private Blockchain, the speed issue can be reduced and solved. There are numerous constraints that could be applied to private Blockchain that could help to control unnecessary user attachment by blocking and controlling. Nodes can also be added and removed for mining, affecting resolution speed. Private blockchains, such as multichain, do not charge a fee for anything that reduces the cost of execution, such as satoshi in bitcoin[65], Ethereum gas[66] and eos[67]. The cost of public Blockchains[65–67] makes them less deployable, whereas some private Blockchains are open source and free[18]. It is possible to conclude that the proposed solution is more appropriate, fast and secure for private Blockchain rather than public Blockchain. Private Blockchain can also control access by area, making it usable by the government of any territory or state.

12.6 CONCLUSIONS AND FUTURE DIRECTIONS

This chapter has presented a secure and dependable authentication and trust management mechanism for smart cities. The proposed mechanism is built on Blockchain technology. Furthermore, a practical implementation of a Blockchain-based security mechanism for secure authorization of smart city resources is presented. In addition, a hybrid application is being developed to provide a user-friendly interface for heterogeneous smart city technologies. This application would allow users to interact with and control smart city devices such as traffic lights and surveillance. This work could be expanded in the future to include healthcare, hospitality, medication, education and so on.

REFERENCES

1. Toward the Resilient Internet of Things for Cyber-Physical Systems. Access IEEE 2019, 7, 13260–13283.
2. Yang, C.; Li, X.; Yu, Y.; Wang, Z. Basing Diversified Services of Complex IoT Applications on Scalable Block Graph Platform. Access IEEE 2019, 7, 22966–22975.
3. Jindal, F.; Jamar, R.; Churi, P. Future and Challenges of Internet of Things. Int. J. Comput. Sci. Inf. Technol. (IJCSIT) 2018, 10,13–25.
4. Ali, M.S.; Vecchio, M.; P incheira, M.; Dolui, K.; Antonelli, F.; Rehmani, M.H. Applications of Blockchains in the Internet of Things: A Comprehensive Survey. Commun. Surv. Tutor. IEEE 2019, 21, 1676–1717.
5. Hassija, V.; Chamola, V.; Saxena, V.; Jain, D.; Goyal, P.; Sikdar, B. A Survey on IoT Security: Application Areas Security Threats and Solution Architectures. Access IEEE 2019, 7, 82721–82743.
6. Yetis, R.; Sahingoz, O.K. Blockchain Based Secure Communication for IoT Devices in Smart Cities. In Proceedings of the 7th International Istanbul Smart Grids and Cities Congress and Fair (ICSG), Istanbul, Turkey, 25–26 April 2019; pp. 134–138.
7. Jyothi, V.; Krishna, M.G.; Raveendranadh, B.; Rupalin, D. IOT Based Smart Home System Technologies. Int. J. Eng. Res. Dev. 2017, 13, 31–37.
8. Alkandari, A.; Alnasheet, M.; Alshekhly, I.F.T. Smart Cities: Survey. J. Adv. Comput. Sci. Technol. Res. 2012, 2, 79–90.
9. Sun, Y.; Song, H.; Jara, A.J.; Bie, R. Internet of Things and Big Data Analytics for Smart and Connected Communities. IEEE Access 2016, 4, 766–773.
10. Song, H.; Srinivasan, R.; Sookoor, T.; Jeschke, S. Smart Cities: Foundations, Principles and Applications; Wiley: Hoboken, NJ, USA, 2017; pp. 1–906, ISBN 978-1-119-22639-0.
11. Zheng, Z.; Xie, S.; Dai, H.; Chen, X.; Wang, H. An overview of Blockchain technology: Architecture, consensus, and future trends. In Proceedings of the IEEE International Congress on in Big Data (BigData Congress), Honolulu, HI, USA, 25–30 June 2017.
12. Chen, J.; Lv, Z.; Song, H. Design of personnel big data management system based on blockchain. Future Gener. Comput. Syst. 2019, 101, 1122–1129.
13. Kim, S.-K. Enhanced IoV Security Network by Using Blockchain Governance Game. Mathematics. 2021, 9,109.
14. Kim, S.-K. Blockchain Governance Game. Comput. Ind. Eng. 2019, 136,373–380.
15. Crosby, M.; Nachlappan; Pattanayak, P.;Verma,S.;Kalyanarman,V. Blockchain Technology; Sutardja Center for Entrepreneurship and Technology Technical Report; University of California: Berkeley, CA, USA, 2015. Available online: https:// scet.berkeley.edu/ wp-content/uploads/BlockchainPaper.pdf (accessed on 24 March 2022).
16. Sairam, R.; SankarBhunia, S.; Thangavel, V.; Gurusamy, M. NETRA: Enhancing IoT Security Using NFV-Based Edge Traffic Analysis. Sens. J. IEEE 2019, 19, 4660–4671.
17. Sagirlar, G.; Carminati, B.; Ferrari, E.; Sheehan, J.D.; Ragnoli, E. Hybrid-IoT: Hybrid Blockchain Architecture for Internet of Things—PoW Sub-Blockchains. In Proceedings of the Internet of Things (iThings) and IEEE Green Computing and Communications (GreenCom) and IEEE Cyber Physical and Social Computing (CPSCom) and IEEE Smart Data (SmartData) 2018 IEEE International Conference, Halifax, NS, Canada, 30 July–3 August 2018; pp. 1007–1016.

18. Paillisse, J.; Subira, J.; Lopez, A.; Rodriguez-Natal, A.; Ermagan, V.; Maino, F.; Cabellos, A. Distributed Access Control with Blockchain. In Proceedings of the IEEE International Conference on Communications (ICC), Shanghai, China, 20–24 May 2019; pp. 1–6.

19. Siris, V.A.; Dimopoulos, D.; Fotiou, N.; Voulgaris, S.; Polyzos, G.C. OAuth 2.0 meets Blockchain for Authorization in Constrained IoT Environments. In Proceedings of the IEEE 5th World Forum on Internet of Things (WF-IoT), Limerick, Ireland, 15–18 April 2019; pp. 364–367.

20. Riabi, I.; Ayed, H.K.B.; Saidane, L.A. A survey on Blockchain-based access control for Internet of Things. In Proceedings of the 15th International Wireless Communications and Mobile Computing Conference (IWCMC), Tangier, Morocco, 24–28 June 2019; pp. 502–507.

21. Siris, V.A.; Dimopoulos, D.; Fotiou, N.; Voulgaris, S.; Polyzos, G.C. Trusted D2D-Based IoT Resource Access Using Smart Contracts. In Proceedings of the IEEE 20th International Symposium on a World of Wireless Mobile and Multimedia Networks (WoWMoM), Washington, DC, USA, 10–12 June 2019; pp. 1–9.

22. Dawod, A.; Kopoulos, D.G.; Jayaraman, P.P.; Nirmalathas, A. Advancements towards Global IoT Device Discovery and Integration. In Proceedings of the IEEE International Congress on Internet of Things (ICIOT), Milan, Italy, 8–13 July 2019; pp. 147–155.

23. Alphand, O.; Amoretti, M.; Claeys, T.; Asta, S.D.; Duda, A.; Ferrari, G.; Rousseau, F.; Tourancheau, B.; Veltri, L.; Zanichelli, F. IoTChain: A Blockchain security architecture for the Internet of Things. In Proceedings of the IEEE Wireless Communications and Networking Conference (WCNC), Barcelona, Spain, 15–18 April 2018. Sensors 2022, 22, 2604 25 of 26.

24. Rescorla, E.; Modadugu, N. Datagram Transport Layer Security Version 1.2. Internet Requests for Comments, RFC Editor, RFC 6347, January 2012. Available online: http://www.rfc-editor.org/rfc/rfc6347.txt (accessed on 2 February 2022).

25. Dorri, A.; Kanhere, S.S.; Jurdak, R. Blockchain in Internet of Things: Challenges and Solutions. 2016. Available online: https://arxiv.org/ftp/arxiv/papers/1608/1608.05187.pdf (accessed on 2 February 2022).

26. Ferrag, M.A.; Derdour, M.; Mukherjee, M.; Derhab, A.; Maglaras, L.; Janicke, H. Blockchain Technologies for the Internet of Things: Research Issues and Challenges. Internet Things J. IEEE 2019, 6, 2188–2204.

27. Danzi, P.; Kalør, A.E.; Stefanovi´c, C.; Popovski, P. Delay and Communication Tradeoffs for Blockchain Systems with Lightweight ˇ IoT Clients. Internet Things J. IEEE 2019, 6, 2354–2365.

28. Novo, O. Blockchain Meets IoT: An Architecture for Scalable Access Management in IoT. IEEE Internet Things J. 2018, 8, 1184–1195.

29. Samaniego, M.; Deters, R. Using Blockchain to Push Software–Defined IoT Components onto Edge Hosts. In Proceedings of the International Conference on Big Data and Advanced Wireless Technologies, Blagoevgrad, Bulgaria, 10–11 November 2016.

30. Kravitz, D.W.; Cooper, J. Securing User Identity and Transactions Symbiotically: IoT meets Blockchain. In Proceedings of the 2017 Global Internet of Things Summit (GIoTS), Geneva, Switzerland, 6–9 June 2017; pp. 1–6.

31. Dorri, A.; Kanhere, S.S.; Jurdak, R. Towards an Optimized Blockchain for IoT. In Proceedings of the Second International Conference on Internet-of-Things Design and Implementation, Pittsburgh, PA, USA, 18–21 April 2017; pp. 173–178.

32. IOTA. Available online: https://www.iota.org/ (accessed on 2 February 2022).

33. Internet of Trusted Things (IoTeX). Available online: https://www.iotex.io/ (accessed on 2 February 2022).
34. Securely Connect, Manage and Analyze IoT Data with Watson IoT Platform. Available online: https://www.ibm.com/internetof-things/solutions/iot-platform/watson-iot-platform (accessed on 2 February 2022).
35. Ambrosus–Decentralized IoT Networks. Available online: https://ambrosus.com/ (accessed on 2 February 2022).
36. Waltonchain-The Global Leader in Blockchain+IoT. Available online: https://www.waltonchain.org/en/ (accessed on 2 February 2022).
37. Origintrail. Available online: https://origintrail.io/ (accessed on 2 February 2022).
38. Atonomi-Bringing Trust and Security to IoT. Available online: https://atonomi.io/ (accessed on 2 February 2022).
39. Yue, X.; Wang, H.; Jin, D.; Li, M.; Jiang, W. Healthcare data gateways: Found healthcare intelligence on blockchain with novel privacy risk control. J. Med. Syst. 2016, 40, 218.
40. Liang, X.; Zhao, J.; Shetty, S.; Liu, J.; Li, D. Integrating blockchain for data sharing and collaboration in mobile healthcare applications. In Proceedings of the IEEE 28th Annual International Symposium on Personal, Indoor, and Mobile Radio Communications (PIMRC), Montreal, QC, Canada, 8–13 October 2017; pp. 1–5.
41. Jiang, S.; Cao, J.; Wu, H.; Yang, Y.; Ma, M.; He, J. Blochie: A blockchain-based platform for healthcare information exchange. In Proceedings of the IEEE International Conference on Smart Computing (SMARTCOMP), Taormina, Italy, 18–20 June 2018; pp. 49–56.
42. Fan, K.; Wang, S.; Ren, Y.; Li, H.; Yang, Y. Medblock: Efficient and secure medical data sharing via blockchain. J. Med. Syst. 2018, 42, 136.
43. Tanwar, S.; Parekh, K.; Evans, R. Blockchain-based electronic healthcare record system for healthcare 4.0 applications. J. Inf. Secur. Appl. 2020, 50, 102407.
44. Habibzadeh, H.; Nussbaum, B.H.; Anjomshoa, F.; Kantarci, B.; Soyata, T. A survey on cybersecurity, data privacy, and policy issues in cyber-physical system deployments in smart cities. Sustain. Cities Soc. 2019, 50, 101660.
45. Khan, P.W.; Byun, Y.-C.; Park, N. A Data Verification System for CCTV Surveillance Cameras Using Blockchain Technology in Smart Cities. Electronics 2020, 9, 484.
46. Malik, M.N.; Azam, M.A.; Ehatisham-Ul-Haq, M.; Ejaz, W.; Khalid, A. ADLAuth: Passive Authentication Based on Activity of Daily Living Using Heterogeneous Sensing in Smart Cities. Sensors 2019, 19, 2466.
47. Meshram, C.; Ibrahim, R.W.; Deng, L.; Shende, S.W.; Meshram, S.G.; Barve, S.K. A robust smart card and remote user password-based authentication protocol using extended chaotic maps under smart cities environment. Soft Comput. 2021, 25, 10037–10051.
48. Espositoa, C.; Ficco, M.; Gupta, B.B. Blockchain-based authentication and authorization for smart city applications. Inf. Process. Manag. 2021, 58, 102468.
49. Ibba, S.; Pinna, A.; Seu, M.; Pani, F.E. CitySense: Blockchain-oriented Smart Cities. In Proceedings of the XP2017 Scientific Workshops, Cologne, Germany, 22–26 May 2017; pp. 1–5.
50. Suciu, G.; Nˇadrag, C.; Istrate, C.; Vulpe, A.; Ditu, M.; Subea, O. Comparative Analysis of Distributed Ledger Technologies. In Proceedings of the IEEE Global Wireless Summit (GWS), Chiang Rai, Thailand, 25–28 November 2018.
51. Rejeb, A.; Rejeb, K.; Simske, S.J.; Keogh, J.G. Blockchain technology in the smart city: A bibliometric review. Qual. Quant. 2021, 1–32. doi: 10.1007/s11135-021-01251-2.

52. Mistry, I.; Tanwar, S.; Tyagi, S.; Kumar, N. Blockchain for 5g-enabled IoT for industrial automation: A systematic review, solutions, and challenges. Mech. Syst. Signal Process. 2019, 135, 1–19.

53. Kabra, N.; Bhattacharya, P.; Tanwar, S.; Tyagi, S. Mudrachain: Blockchain-based framework for automated cheque clearance in financial institutions. Future Gener. Comput. Syst. 2020, 102, 574–587.

54. Ethereum. Available online: https://www.ethereum.org/ (accessed on 2 February 2022). Sensors 2022, 22, 2604 26 of 26.

55. Ganache-One Click Blockchain. Available online: https://www.trufflesuite.com/ganache (accessed on 2 February 2022).

56. Rasberry. Available online: https://www.raspberrypi.org/ (accessed on 2 February 2022).

57. Solidity. Available online: https://en.wikipedia.org/wiki/Solidity (accessed on 2 February 2022).

58. Node.js. Available online: https://nodejs.org/ (accessed on 2 February 2022).

59. Metamask. Available online: https://metamask.io/ (accessed on 2 February 2022).

60. Web3.js—Ethereum JavaScript API. Available online: https://web3js.readthedocs.io/en/v1.2.1/ (accessed on 2 February 2022).

61. Meteor: Build Apps with JavaScript. Available online: https://www.meteor.com/ (accessed on 2 February 2022).

62. MutiChain. Available online: https://www.multichain.com/ (accessed on 2 February 2022).

63. Hyperledger. Available online: https://www.hyperledger.org/ (accessed on 2 February 2022).

64. Chain Core. Available online: http://fedchains.com/core/ (accessed on 2 February 2022).

65. Bitcoin. Available online: https://bitcoin.org/en/ (accessed on 2 February 2022).

66. Gas (Ethereum). Available online: https://www.investopedia.com/terms/g/gas-ethereum.asp (accessed on 2 February 2022).

67. EosWallet. Available online: https://www.ledger.com/eos-wallet/ (accessed on 2 February 2022)

68. Asif, M., Aziz, Z., Bin Ahmad, M., Khalid, A., Waris, H. A., &Gilani, A. (2022). Blockchain-Based Authentication and Trust Management Mechanism for Smart Cities. *Sensors*, *22*(7), 2604.